Memoirs of a Masseuse

By Mingcheng Li

Copyright © 2023 Mingcheng Li

ISBN: 978-0-6483896-3-7

All rights reserved. No part of this book may be reproduced, translated, excerpted, reprinted, or adapted in any form or by any means without the written permission of the copyright owner.

This is a work of fiction. Names, characters, places, and incidents are the product of the author's imagination. The science fiction elements and concepts portrayed in this book, although possibly diverging from current scientific understanding, are the result of the author's creative imagination.

Published in September 2023 in Adelaide, South Australia, Australia

Distributed in the United Stated of America

For information on reprints, adaptations, or other licensing inquiries, please contact the Author: 65663968@163.com

Cover Design & Published by Asian Culture Press

247 South Rd. Mile End, Adelaide, South Australia 5031, Australia

A catalogue record for this work is available from the National Library of Australia

Summary of the Novel

Her name is Xiao Jing, an exceptional masseuse. This is the authentic story of her and her sisters, representing a social phenomenon. Initially an innocent girl from Chongqing, China, she ventured into the dazzling world outside and became a massage therapist who showcased her skills while occasionally finding herself in compromising situations. She once fell victim to a man's persuasive words, resulting in an unexpected pregnancy. Despite realizing men's true nature and society's harshness, she still yearns for a better life.

With a specific aspiration, an individual embarked on a journey across Zhejiang and Suzhou in China. Over the course of three years working as a masseuse, this person underwent significant personal growth and development, ultimately becoming highly respected within their profession. Their achievements garnered genuine empathy, admiration, and introspection from others. It is important to recognize that even seemingly insignificant individuals are part of our community. By embracing and supporting them, we promote social cohesion and compassion, which has greater advantages than excluding or disregarding them.

About the Author

Li Mingcheng, also known as Li Jianrong, hails from Suzhou, China and is a distinguished member of the Chinese Writers Association. He is characterized by his wisdom, integrity, composure and diligence. With over one million words published, his works include "Becoming a Village Official After Graduation", "The Director of an Environmental Protection Bureau", "Masseuse", "Family Education", "Who But You" and "I Am a Teacher", among others. Several of his pieces have been selected for use in Australian college entrance examination materials.

Preface

"Memoirs of a Masseuse" is the first novel in mainland China that vividly depicts the life of a masseuse. It revolves around a girl named Xiao Jing, who ventures alone to the town of Jiangnan. Introduced by Sister Wu, she starts working at a Sea Paradise Sauna City, embarking on a journey into the world of massage, filled with all its temptations. From being a pure and innocent girl to an apprentice without knowledge of massage, she gradually grows into an exceptional masseuse loved by all. Each step of her growth, whether pure or confused, humiliated or proud, kind or beautiful, is meticulously recorded in the more than 200,000-word journal.

Living in a beautiful town but enduring a humiliating life, these women reside at the bottom of society, selling their labor, bodies, and souls. Most people view them with disdain, considering them vulgar and even on par with prostitutes due to their ambiguous relationships with men. However, our heroine still garners our understanding, sympathy, and respect. Although she may have lost her sense of direction, she never loses her conscience. Her arduous and commendable growth journey unfolds with her efforts and intelligence. Her motto is to "fall and get back up."

Like any of us pursuing material comforts, Xiao Jing is not exempt from vulgarity. To survive, she used to provide massages with her body, and at one point, she sold her virginity for a substantial sum. To earn more money, she attended social parties to earn additional income. The life of a masseuse is shrouded in darkness and obscurity. Through this diary novel, we gain insight into their world. However, it's not just a voyeuristic desire; as we delve into their stories, we understand their inner worlds, thoughts, and the burdens of their pasts that they can't bear to remember. They are living, thinking, and feeling individuals, just like us.

This novel, "Memoirs of a Masseuse" gives us a genuine impression, bringing to light the realities of those around us. Many of us might have experienced their services and the comfort they provide through their skilled touch, while others only know them through hearsay, remaining curious and uninformed. Through this diary, we finally glimpse a hidden world within the current massager community, which is so near yet obscure. How much do we truly know about them?

In the eyes of many, men have their merits too. Xiao Jing harbors feelings for men, including her guests, Mr. Zhang, and Mr. Gao. Despite being her guest and boss, they treat each other with basic respect. People may differ in their roles and living environments but are equal in personality, and there is no inherent hierarchy. Respect and tolerance towards others often lead to sincere reciprocation. This is why giving roses to others lets the fragrance linger in our hands.

This work profoundly moves many readers. The part of the diary that touched my friends the most was when Ah Lan fell ill, and Xiao Jing's affection for her sisters and precious friendship brought them to tears. This heartfelt connection represents the most brilliant aspect of the first half of the diary. Xiao Jing's willingness to offer herself to raise money for Ah Lan's treatment deeply touched the guests, and she received a substantial donation of 100,000 yuan. Although Ah Lan eventually passed away, she received friendship and love, which profoundly affected us. Whether dignitaries or humble massage women, they evoke genuine emotions and move us deeply. We may become numb to certain aspects of our daily lives, but experiencing such honest and sincere emotions reawakens our dormant capacity to love.

Sometimes, a person's fate is intertwined with the presence of others. In Xiao Jing's case, her encounters with various individuals have shaped her life's path. Initially, Sister Wu inspired her with the ideas of seizing opportunities and living youthfully, leading her directly into massage. Later, she met Mr. Sun, prompting her to leave the sea paradise and seek a life in Suzhou. Her connection with the shrewd high boss led to misunderstandings and, eventually, her departure from the Oriental Bathhouse. In Suzhou, he was the only man she had contact with, secretly impregnating and leaving her to raise their daughter alone.

Today, massage parlors are ubiquitous, and the industry is chaotic. If not for erotic massages or the allure of pornography, would the massage business thrive as it does? Lustful thoughts blend with warmth, and as long as the massage industry exists, busy figures of massage women will persist. They offer both legitimate massage services and provide special ones to guests. If we don't provide them with proper guidance and support, there will be more cases of women like Xiao Jing and Wang Astray, and our society will be burdened with even more tragic stories. We desperately want to avoid this, primarily as we aim to build a harmonious community where everyone desires a healthy, happy, and peaceful life. With the mounting mental pressures faced by modern people, if they seek therapeutic massages, we should gladly accept them and invite Xiao Jing and her sisters to provide us with soothing massages, allowing us to indulge in relaxation, bliss, and beauty.

"Memoirs of a Masseuse" is a beautiful tale that not only offers a realistic portrayal of massage work but also delves into the hearts of the massage girls while shedding light on the hidden aspects of the massage industry. The saying goes, "There are three hundred and sixty professions, each with its champion." Liu Li used the money she earned from pedicures to support the education of underprivileged students in her hometown. She gained recognition and became a National People's Congress member, where General Secretary Xi Jinping warmly received her. Similarly, Xiao Jing possesses the same kind heart and willingness to help, endearing her to everyone she meets. Another impressive character, Lu Qin, a foot bath girl from Yangzhou, has provided pedicures to Hong Kong stars like Tung Chee-Hwa and Andy Lau, earning recognition and appreciation. Like Liu Li and Lu Qin, Xiao Jing also possesses intelligence and unique skill, unwaveringly pursuing love despite several twists and turns.

"Memoirs of a Masseuse" is a vivid account of Xiao Jing's authentic experiences as a masseuse in the beautiful regions of Zhejiang and Suzhou, China. For a more in-depth understanding, read this book now!

Life treats everyone fairly and becomes glorious and honorable through diligence and wisdom. Every individual has the right to pursue happiness. Let us extend our understanding and care, offering more respect and blessings to those around us.

Table of Content

Chapter 1: I'm a Migrant Woman 1

Chapter 2: Lost in the Red-Light District 9

Chapter 3: An Accident at Work 17

Chapter 4: The Woman's Capital 24

Chapter 5: Massage For the First Time 31

Chapter 6: It Feels Dirty 38

Chapter 7: Apprenticeship in Wisdom 44

Chapter 8: Forget Shame 51

Chapter 9: Unforgettable First Time 57

Chapter 10: Gentleness in Middle Age 64

Chapter 11: Helpless Descent 69

Chapter 12: The Rogue Wu Fang 74

Chapter 13: Smiling Against the Illness 80

Chapter 14: Sistership in Times of Trouble 86

Chapter 15: Desperate Doctoring 92

Chapter 16: Journey through Huzhou 99

Chapter 17: Love Saving a Buddy 105

Chapter 18: The Lady-killer in the Rainy Night 112

Chapter 19: Night of No Return 119

Chapter 20: Massage for Relaxation 127

Chapter 21: Take Me Home 134

Chapter 22: Enchanting Spring Night 140

Chapter 23: Tinder and Blaze 146

Chapter 24: The Taste of Love 153

Chapter 25: Love in Suzhou City 158

Chapter 26: The Best Masseuse 166

Chapter 27: Brief Romance 174

Chapter 28: White lies 182

Chapter 29: Sisters Rival for Boyfriend 190

Chapter 30: Beautiful Beginning 197

Chapter 31: Temptation of Summer 204

Chapter 32: Fragrant Night of Spring 211

Chapter 33: In the Men's River 220

Chapter 34: Money Corrupts 230

Chapter 35: A succession of Accidents 238

Chapter 36: An Anesthesia Robbery 246

Chapter 37: The Desire of Boss Gao 254

Chapter 38: Misunderstanding Ends Future 261

Chapter 39: The Conspiracy of Lover 270

Chapter 40: Rashly Pregnancy 277

Chapter 41: A Date with a Bad Guy 286

Chapter 42: Fatal Love Turns Heartless 294

Chapter 43: Boundless Love 302

Chapter 44: Doing Good is Hard 310

Chapter 45: Seeking Pleasure Alone 319

Chapter 46: Sisters' Reunion of Love 326

Chapter 47: Rekindled Love 334

Chapter 48: Intoxicated Night of Passion 345

Chapter 49: Youthful Stirrings 352

Chapter 50: A Bewildering Enigmatic Fire 359

Chapter 51: No Part-Time Jobs for Me 366

Chapter 52: Injured Body 374

Chapter 53: Fragrance of the Soul 381

Chapter 54: Life Continues 388

Chapter 55: Silent Conclusion (Epilogue) 394

Chapter 1

I'm a Migrant Woman

With its poetic and picturesque allure, Jiangnan has left an indelible mark on my life during the three years I spent there. My innocence was lost amidst the misty rain of Jiangnan, and my dear sister, Ah Lan, passed away amidst the spring scenery. My first love slipped away like the flowing water under the small bridge in Jiangnan while my youth wandered through its bustling streets.

Last night, I decided to spend the night at an internet cafe. Please don't misunderstand; a man didn't confine me. I mean that I stayed at the internet cafe all night. It was affordable, only eight dollars for eight hours, from midnight until eight. I could serve three customers per hour at our establishment and earn at least a hundred bucks.

Lately, I've been feeling quite bored. I work the night shift from 4 PM to 12 AM and find sleeping difficult after work difficult. So, I turn to the internet for entertainment. Surprisingly, I've made many friends online who want to video chat with me, complimenting my beauty. I know I'm attractive, but is it my fault for being pretty? They ask for my phone number, claiming they want to meet me in person. But I refuse. I don't trust men on the internet. Nowadays, newspapers and television reports are filled with stories of people being robbed, raped, and encountering strange and scary situations when meeting online acquaintances. Frankly, I find such men foolish. In this day and age, why would anyone still resort to rape? What fools they are! For a few hundred dollars, there are plenty of girls available.

I don't have a high level of education, so don't expect me to be eloquent. But if you want to listen to my story, I'll share it with you patiently and truthfully. I wrote "junior college" under my education section when filling out job applications. Although I didn't attend high school and only completed technical school, even university professors are plagiarizing papers and flaunt false degrees. I've decided to embellish my qualifications a bit. After all, who wouldn't want to hire an undergraduate degree holder as a receptionist?

Degrees have become essential in today's society. Fake flowers, counterfeit money, and even phony emotions exist. It's even rumored that it's possible to clone someone precisely like you. How ridiculous! Who is the original? Who is the clone? How can you tell?

Now, I'm writing this diary. I can't give you a definite answer. It was a spontaneous idea. Once I start something, I wouldn't say I like giving up halfway. Since I've begun, I'll continue writing. I know I'm a massage girl, not a writer. This diary won't make me famous or wealthy. It's more exhausting than providing massages. But I'm willing to do it. Sometimes, we do things without an apparent reason. Women are like that. Please, my enthusiasm won't wane after five minutes. I will diligently write this diary for myself, for Ah Lan, and my fellow sisters.

I'm a straightforward person. I say what's on my mind and don't beat around the bush. I'll authentically present my personal experiences without any modifications. I was an honest girl, but now I've become accustomed to flattery, especially when it comes to men's lies. I've developed a solid immunity to them. If men don't play their tricks, I won't be fooled. One day they're millionaires. The next day they're penniless. One day they're charming. The next day they're disgusting. My experiences serve as undeniable proof.

Allow me to introduce myself properly in case we meet face to face. I'm Xiaojing, 22 years old this year. Although young, I've been "aged" by three years. Xiaojing is an uncommon surname, not found among the hundreds of names. I'm from Chongqing, a city of half mountains and half urban areas. We had to pass through countless mountain roads of varying elevations to reach my classmates' homes. Walking through the hills daily contributed to our good physique in us Chongqing girls, especially our slender legs. Unlike the delicate Jiangnan women, we possess a more substantial presence, captivating men. People say I'm beautiful, and although beauty is no longer highly valued these days, it still brings me joy. My parents may appear ordinary, but they raised a beautiful daughter. Two negatives can create a positive outcome.

Have you ever tasted the hot pot in Chongqing? It's numbingly spicy and hot! But don't worry, I'm as hot as a hot pot, just not as spicy. I'm not the fiery red chili pepper; I'm more like the mildly spicy bell pepper. They say when in Rome, do as the Romans do. Since coming to Jiangnan, my character has undergone significant changes. It has been three years since I left home. The road I've traveled and my experiences during these three years often flash through my mind like a movie. Both my body and soul have become somewhat numb. I yearn to regain the purity of the past, but those days have become like a tear-stained calendar lost in the wind. I can only move forward, one day at a time, living a happy life despite the contempt of others.

I originally arrived in Nanxun, Zhejiang province. Several years prior, a fellow villager named Wu Yumei came here, and I heard she made a lot of money. She sends tens of thousands of yuan back home every year, which most people in our village can't earn for several years. Naturally, I became envious. My parents urged me to find her and ask her to help me earn a fortune. At the time, I was 19 years old, fresh out of school, and ignorant about the world. Beautiful Nanxun town became the turning point in my life. It was here that my fate took a different course. Shortly after arriving, I lost the most precious thing a maiden possesses. It was also here that my first love ended in silence. The stone bridge in Nanxun has been wetted by my tears, and my shadow once roamed the long old street. It was here that my massage career began, erasing the pure dreams of my girlhood, leaving no trace behind.

Later, I left Nanxun and came to Suzhou. I found work at a shop called "Haitang Spring Foot Bath Room" in the northern part of the city. The boss is a local with a specific background. The employees and my fellow sisters fear him, but I'm not afraid. As the saying goes, "If you have a place to go, you can leave another." If needed, I can easily find another place to continue my life. My brother's name is Xiaolong, and he works in an electronics factory in Guangdong. He works tirelessly, often doing overtime. His boss is a stingy Taiwanese man, and the workers toil away for little pay. My brother only graduated from junior high school, and finding a job was challenging. He fears losing his job if he leaves the factory, so he swallows his pride and stays. It has been five years, and I returned home twice during that time. Our parents grow older each year, and we, as their children, have grown up and must rely on our efforts. Our father once said, "Children are like birds. They must use their wings to fly on their own."

It's widely known that reality is mocking the poor, not just the prostitutes. You can only do something with money. This is the wisdom of young people. When I mention diseases, I'm not discussing common ailments like the common cold. For us girls, the most dreaded diseases are of a certain kind. Accidentally contracting such an illness would be tragic. Once the boss found out, we would be fired immediately, and we would lose this hard-earned source of income. I have my own saying: "It's difficult to be a human being, even more so for a woman, and being a massage girl is the hardest of all." Please don't laugh at me; I'm speaking the truth. Good and bad people aren't absolute distinctions. Even in a mud pool, lotus flowers can grow.

Being a good massage girl depends on appearance, skills, and effort. Our appearance is a natural asset, and we must utilize it wisely. As for our craft, we learn from our masters and fellow artisans, but we must also rely on our careful reflection and accumulation of experience. While we're not explicitly soliciting, we follow the unwritten rules and regulations that have naturally evolved in this profession. If a customer is generous, the boss won't intervene and will ask the massage girls to socialize. We're willing to be selfless if we encounter a man we genuinely like. However, finding good men is rare, as most seek sensual stimulation. Given these circumstances, what can we expect to see in the vast sea? The good guys rarely come here, either. Some wealthy bosses handle large sums of money. Some sisters are enticed by their wealth and when in need, consider offering themselves generously to reap the benefits.

The massage industry is like a mixed bag, with only a few establishments dedicated to genuine massage. Most operate on the fringe of pornography and sexual services, with some openly engaging in money-for-sex transactions. Masseuses work hard on their own, and their business thrives within a specific range of visibility. Men who frequent sauna cities are often driven by malicious intent. Whenever I see customers entering, I think: "Money is coming." They are willing to spend generously to please us, and some even demand our services at high prices. Men are bizarre creatures. If their wives were unfaithful or cheated on them, they would be unable to bear it and would keep complaining. But when they encounter famous young ladies in entertainment establishments, despite being played by many men, they feel no shame; instead, they take pride in it.

We are not singing stars who earn hundreds of thousands of dollars in "after-tax income." We are not shameless women who loosen their belts to be showered with money. We are not fortunate enough to have considerate husbands acting ATMs for us. We are just humble masseuses. We do not pretend to be anything else or have grand ambitions. We earn our income by providing massages that relax and satisfy men. We work hard and occasionally take on odd jobs to improve our lives. When heterosexual massage services were briefly suspended, we migrated like birds for a suitable place to live. But as soon as the restrictions were lifted, we returned from all corners to resume work.

In the past, singers, writers, artists, and police officers, among others, used to take their roles seriously in front of the "public." Even officials were called "public servants." At that time, "serving the people" was deeply ingrained. But times have changed. Many people have forgotten about the people and act superior, thinking they were born to be above others. They have forgotten their roots! As massage girls, we may not be seen as respectable or elegant, but at least we dare to admit that we are serving the people and are unashamed to say that we also perform for money!

You might be curious about how well our foot bath business is doing. Well, it's thriving! From the "shampoo rooms" of the past to the current "foot bath shops," there is an air of grandeur. Some may say it's just a name change, but for me, I'll continue to be a masseuse. It doesn't matter what the establishment is called; what matters is that I provide massages. As the saying goes, "A journey of a thousand miles begins with the first step." Foot baths are believed to be beneficial for health. I've heard that they have long been popular in South Korea. By soaking the feet in warm water infused with herbs or massaging specific acupoints connected to various organs, one can experience fatigue relief, refreshment, and nourishment. I still have much to learn to perfect my skills. As they say, there are 360 professions, and being the best in your field is an achievement. I still have many areas to explore.

How I'm doing in life? I appreciate your concern in advance! Fortunately, I'm doing well! I'm in a much better state of mind now. Even if you criticize me for being shameless, I won't argue. I know exactly who I am and don't need to explain myself to anyone. I may be dirtier than some, but I'm also cleaner than others! With one glance, I can tell who returns to life and who truly knows themselves. If you believe in me, hold me in high regard, and treat me as a friend, I will never forget your kindness. By the way, if you treat us respectfully, we will treat you even better. But if you despise us, then you are nothing but a piece of shit to us! If you continue reading my diary, please raise a glass for me. Women love to hear compliments. It's a natural weakness.

Tonight is another night shift. We rotate shifts every week. Nothing noteworthy has happened lately, so I went to the internet cafe. Coming back from there, I feel disorganized and unable to sleep. I scribbled down these thoughts. Would you like to read them? I will continue writing. Starting tomorrow, I will document my three years of experiences, which include bitterness, tears, joy, genuine emotions, and amusement. If you're genuinely interested, please continue to follow along! Tomorrow, during my night shift, if you have the time, you can visit "Haitang Spring Foot Bath Room." We can chat while I give you a massage.

Chapter 2

Lost in the Red-Light District

Working the night shift and not getting proper rest during the day has left me slightly lethargic. These days, there's no one to take care of me. Although I'm not a supervisor in the Begonia Spring, even the supervisors show me a lot of respect. Wu Fang and I work together. She's in the second massage department, which is more flexible than my position. She gets to accompany the guests. Wu Fang's sister was the first one to come out. When I arrived in Nanxun, she sent over 100,000 yuan back home. For people in our hometown who have never seen that much money, it's astonishing! I stayed with Sister Wu for half a year before Wu Fang came from Guangdong, and Sister Wu sold Wu Fang's virginity for 5,000 yuan. Our families back home have no idea what we do. We lie to them, saying that we work in factories and live good lives.

Writing this diary is like rummaging through dusty memories, and I'm trying to stay calm and not let myself get overwhelmed by unpleasant experiences. Even though I attended a technical school, it was just a diploma mill. I didn't learn much but excelled in Chinese class, and my teachers praised my compositions. With dedication and perseverance, anything can be achieved. I want to take some time off to organize my past experiences and document my real-life massage career in the form of a live broadcast.

In July 2003, I arrived in Hangzhou by train. I knew West Lake was there, but I wanted to avoid visiting it. I only had three hundred dollars, and every penny counted until I found a job. There were many girls my age in the railway station square, desperately seeking someone to provide them with shelter during the day. I thought they lacked courage. How could they beg like that? People have their dignity, and losing it like that makes life not worth living! However, after half a month of being penniless, I realized how naive my thoughts were. When you don't have a penny to your name and can't even solve the fundamental problem of food, as long as someone is willing to give you money, you'll do anything! Trees have bark to protect them, but what do people have? What's more important than survival?

I'm a good-looking girl venturing out for the first time and afraid of encountering bad people. So, I didn't dare to stay in those rundown places where they pull in customers, nor did I dare to get into those unmarked cars that shout out to passersby. Carrying my luggage, I found the bus station and took a bus to Nanxun. When I arrived, it was four o'clock in the afternoon, and Wu Yumei was there to meet me at the station. I saw she was wearing a revealing halter top that was almost see-through, with a barely visible black bra. It looked small, and her breasts were bulging out. The top was pitifully short, with half of her waist exposed. The skin around her waist, possibly tanned from the sun, was rusty, much darker than mine. Her belly button was also flashy, with a flower tattooed around it. She had dyed her hair brown, wore bright red lipstick and eyeshadow, and her eyes were cunning, lacking the clarity they once had back home.

Timidly, I said, "Sister Wu, you look so beautiful!" I wouldn't say I liked her appearance, but my livelihood depended on her, so I knew how to say something nice. Wu Yumei is five years older than me. After she graduated from junior high school, she stopped studying and went straight to work. Before me, she had brought several girls from our hometown, and they reportedly made a lot of money. My parents went to beg her parents, asking Wu Yumei to help me find a job and take me in. Wu Yumei promised over the phone, so I left home to find her.

Sister Wu stared at me and smiled, saying, "I may dress sexy, but you are beautiful." I smiled shyly. Sister Wu enthusiastically said, "What's the use of staying at home? You have to make money! The earlier, the better! I said, "I'm not well-educated. Where can I find a good job? This time, I hope Sister Wu can help me more." Sister Wu replied, "I must go to work at five o'clock, so I can't chat for long today. But we'll be together for a long time in the future. If you work hard, you can make a lot of money! Come on, let me show you to my place first."

I followed Sister Wu through the old streets of Nanxun town. In a narrow lane, Sister Wu stopped in front of a courtyard, took out a key, and opened the door. I followed her inside. It was an old house with a yard, a well, and a grape trellis adorned with clusters of emerald-like grapes. There were three bungalows with black brick walls and white exteriors. Sister Wu led me into the house, saying, "This is my outer room. You can stay in the inner room, and there's another girl with you named Xiao Hong. She's from Leshan, Sichuan province, and'll return to sleep at night. There's a flushing toilet here, but there's no bathing facility. It's hot now, so if you want to bathe, you can wash at the well in the courtyard. If you want to eat, there's a snack bar on the corner.

Xiaojing, I must work, so I can't keep you company today. Here's the key to your room. You must be tired from the journey, so take a rest." Gratefully, I said, "Thank you, Sister Wu! I understand."

I placed my luggage on the floor, took out a change of clothes, towels, toothpaste, and other items, and pushed my bag under the bed. I looked around the room. It was a bit dim and had a peculiar smell, like a dirty sock or something indescribable. After searching for a while, I discovered a bulging wallet in the corner of the room. Curious, I opened it and found it filled with dirty, unwashed clothes. I thought about washing those clothes for her. Since I'm new here and she's accompanying me, we must care for each other. However, it was almost dusk, and there was no place to dry the clothes overnight, so I decided to wash them the next day.

Feeling tired from the journey, I decided to take a nap. Thousands of miles away from home, this was where I would be living. I grabbed a towel, soap, and a basin and prepared to wash up. As I filled the basin with cool water and started undressing, I realized I was in the courtyard. The walls were bathed in the reddish glow of the setting sun, and the courtyard's wooden gate was wide enough for a finger to fit through the gap. I turned around, took off my dirty pants and shirt, quickly washed them, and hurried back inside, shutting the door. I changed into clean underwear in the room and placed my dirty clothes aside to wash them with Xiao Hong's clothes tomorrow. I felt hungry but didn't have much appetite. I just wanted to get some rest. Perhaps I was too tired, as I lay down on the pillow and quickly fell asleep.

I'm still determining when I woke up. Maybe it was because I was hungry? I could hear my stomach rumbling. When I opened my sleepy eyes and stretched, I suddenly noticed a figure lying beside me. Her body was curled up like shrimp, and she was almost naked. On closer inspection, I realized she was wearing only a pair of panties. She's pretty thrifty. Why doesn't she buy looser underwear? She must be Xiao Hong, the one Sister Wu mentioned. Since there was no alarm clock or cell phone, I wondered what time it was. I needed to find something to eat. From when I left home until now, I only had a bowl of ramen in Hangzhou. After sitting on the train for over a day, I couldn't buy expensive food onboard. Those "instant noodles in a bucket" were being sold for five dollars, such a rip-off! Back in my hometown's small shop, they were less than three dollars.

I carefully got out of bed, afraid of waking Xiao Hong. I pulled out my luggage and took out the remaining half bag of cookies. As I started eating, I realized my mouth was becoming too dry. I would chew a cookie until it was swallowable, but it wasted so much saliva. I quietly opened the door and planned to fetch water from the well. As I passed Sister Wu's room, I heard strange noises coming from inside, and Sister Wu was shouting with apparent delight. Although I had never experienced sex before, I had a feeling it had something to do with that, and the sound of clapping hands was oddly enticing, causing my heart to beat faster. At 19, I didn't know what I was doing. I was both curious and skeptical about Sister Wu's profession.

It was an attractive house, with a skylight on the roof that let in bright moonlight at night, making the interior luminous. Like a thief, I quietly opened the hall door and went to the courtyard to fetch some healthy water. I drank it heartily, and the coolness refreshed me instantly. Any fatigue I felt vanished, and the heat in my mind subsided a little. As I returned to my room, I strained my ears to listen for Sister Wu's symphony, but it had ceased, and I could only hear muffled voices that were indiscernible. Unable to fall back asleep, I waited for dawn.

When Xiao Hong woke up the following day, I noticed she was a lovely girl around the same age as me. Later, I learned she was a year older and worked as a dancer in a nightclub with Sister Wu. She greeted me calmly and didn't question my presence. Through our conversation, I discovered her name was Xu Xiaohong. A year ago, another girl had been living in this house, but she met a boy at work, fell in love, and left with him, leaving Xiao Hong alone. Now that I had arrived, she had a sister to share her bed. Xiao Hong was friendly towards me, perhaps feeling less lonely now that she had someone to live with.

I couldn't help but think about the noises I had heard at night and wanted to ask Xiao Hong about Sister Wu's activities. I told her, "I'm a newcomer, Sister Wu's fellow townsman. My name is Xiao Jing." Xiao Hong nodded and replied, "Sister Wu mentioned you. From now on, you can sleep in the same bed as me. Besides, I don't bring clients here." I didn't quite grasp the meaning behind her words, so I asked, "You work with Sister Wu? Is your job okay? Is the salary good?" Xiao Hong smiled and said, "What do you mean 'okay'? It's not just good, and it's excellent! We're earning our living now. As long as we keep at it, the money will flow!"

Sister Wu came to check on me, accompanied by a man who appeared to be around forty years old. I wondered if he was the one who had slept in Sister Wu's room at night. Sister Wu smiled and introduced him, "Xiaojing, this is Boss Sun. He owns a large store. Today, you can go with him and take a look. I didn't expect Sister Wu to arrange a good job for me so quickly. I was overjoyed and said eagerly, "Okay, I'll see if it suits me. If it does, I'll work there." Boss Sun chuckled and replied, "The question isn't whether you can do it, but whether you want to do it." Sister Wu reassured me, saying, "Don't worry. Please ask Xiao Hong or me if you have any questions or need help. We're fellow villagers, and I'll support you."

I followed Boss Sun as he took me to the commercial street outside town. We arrived at a luxuriously decorated establishment called "Haitang Paradise Sauna City." Boss Sun said to me, "Here it is. This is the largest sauna center in Huzhou. With your looks, as long as you're willing to learn, I guarantee you a bright future!" Feeling somewhat confused, I followed him inside. He instructed a young woman in the lobby, saying, "Xiao Qin, show her around. Sister Wu introduced her." I realized Sister Wu had quite a reputation; everyone knew her name. I secretly felt envy and admiration for her accomplishments over the years.

Xiao Qin guided me through the three floors of the sauna city, explaining each area as we went along. She pointed out the sauna rooms, massage rooms, service hall, rest hall, VIP boxes, and regular boxes. Xiao Qin mentioned, "Business is slow in the morning, but in the afternoon, customers start coming in one after another. Evenings and holidays are the busiest times. It's a great place to work. The pay is good, and the tips are generous. You won't regret it if you choose to work here." I felt a flicker of temptation and asked, "If I decide to work here, what would be my role?" Xiao Qin replied with a smile, "That's up to you. The division of labor here is very detailed. Waitresses are divided into different levels, each providing different services. Those of us introduced by Sister Wu are all excellent at our jobs. With your attributes, I'm confident you can do just as well."

Realizing that having a job meant earning money, I said, "When can I start?" Xiao Qin explained, "If you want to work here, you must sign an agreement with the establishment. Come with me to the manager's office to complete the formalities. Once that's done, you can start working in the evening." Grateful, I said, "Thank you! I want to start today."

Chapter 3

An Accident at Work

I respected and felt grateful to Sister Wu. She was a woman too, but I knew she was much more capable than me. I understood that finding a job was challenging in the current times, but Sister Wu made it easy for me, and I was pleased about it. When I returned to Sister Wu's place, she was still asleep. At noon, when she woke up, and I told her about my decision to work at Sea Paradise Sauna City, Sister Wu nodded and said, "If you want to earn more money, you should work the night shifts. There are more customers during that time, and you must be open-minded and not too conservative." I replied, "I'll do my job." Sister Wu smiled and said, "If you're willing to put in the effort, you'll earn good money."

I arrived at Sea Paradise Sauna City in the late afternoon, around half past four. Xiao Qin took me to the manager's office to sign the agreement, but I didn't read it. As we reached the second floor, Xiao Qin called, "Ah Lan, come here!" A sweet-looking girl emerged from the locker room and approached us. She glanced at me and asked, "What's the matter?" Xiao Qin replied, "This is Ah Jing, the newcomer. From now on, you'll be working together." Seeing my confusion, Xiao Qin explained, "Here, all the waitresses use stage names. It's better not to reveal your real identity to the guests to avoid unnecessary trouble." Ah Lan smiled and said, "Yes, Sister Jean is right. We all use stage names to greet the guests. Come on, let's switch places." I was amazed that someone as young as Ah Lan was the foreman.

In the dressing room, I changed into my work uniform. It consisted of a short-sleeved top and a short skirt, both sky blue and comfortable. Ah Lan told me, "Jing, you don't have to work formally today. Just observe and familiarize yourself with the environment. Watch how the other sisters do their tasks. Remember, though, you should never enter rooms with closed doors. Disturbing guests in those rooms will lead to severe punishment." I thought to myself, "Exactly! Why should I be there if someone is showering or receiving a massage? Since I'm new, I don't know how to do anything yet. Let's observe the other sisters first."

I was assigned to the men's section on the second floor, where I noticed that most customers were men over 30. I had seen the service prices at the front desk, which included bathing, pedicures, massages, and leisure services. The male visitors were regular customers. After bathing, they would use the internal calling system to request a waitress's service. The waiter or waitress, called by name, would go into the box or VIP room with a cheerful demeanor. Business was booming that evening, and I peeked through a corner of the curtain to see a parking lot filled with cars. Our hostesses were quickly summoned. Ah Lan had yet to explicitly instruct me on what to do, and I didn't see anyone going to or leaving the service rooms. I stood in a corner of the lobby, feeling almost redundant.

At eight o'clock in the evening, Ah Lan came to me and said, "Jing, come and help." I followed hesitantly and entered the innermost room. Inside were four men wearing bathrobes, laughing and chatting. Ah Lan said, "You take care of them here. We're short on staff, but I'll arrange for someone to come later." I nodded and stood inside the room, my hands by my side. The man's eyes were fixed on me, making me uncomfortable. One said, "You're new here, aren't you?" Another remarked, "Regardless of whether she's new, she's here to serve us, brothers." Another added, "Well, why are you just standing there? Come and pour us some tea!"

I followed their instructions, and when I handed the tea to the man sitting in the corner of the sofa, he cautioned me, "Don't fill it up too much, just a little over half. If it's too full, the water might spill and scald the guests, and you'll get scolded." I smiled gratefully at him. The man in the first seat maliciously commented, "Brother, it would be nice if the water spilled. It's better to have it diluted rather than strong!" The man sitting in front of me said, "Old Four, be a bit gentler. Use the Meijia brand to clean your teeth!" I almost burst out laughing. The man by the window was the youngest, probably in his mid-twenties, and the most mischievous. As I poured tea for him and turned around, I was startled when he reached out and touched my buttocks, a susceptible area. I almost dropped the teapot in surprise! I glared at him, and the other men laughed. The young man remarked, "Don't act innocent. We're all here working. Who hasn't been through such experiences?" I didn't understand what he meant by "such experiences." It was a time of peace, after all. What could he be referring to?

One of the men said, "What a lovely lady! Look at her thighs, so close yet unseen. She's a newbie!" The man called Old Four remarked, "Hey, miss, can you give a massage?" I shook my head and said, "No, I'm new here." Old Four proudly declared, "Brothers, did you see that? She hasn't even had training yet!" The young man interjected, "Massaging isn't important. Come here and give the eldest brother a back rub. Can't you at least do that?" Although Xiao Qin had mentioned the services offered at the sauna city, and I had some idea of what they entailed, I never imagined that I would be massaging a man on my first day of work. I hesitated and said, "I'm sorry, it's my first day, and I don't know how to do it." Old Four said, "Then do something simpler. Pass each of us a cigarette. That should be doable, right?"

I couldn't refuse, so I removed the open cigarette pack from the tea table. I handed one to the man sitting outside, but he didn't take it. He pursed his lips, indicating I should place the cigarette in his mouth. I followed his gesture, intending to give a cigarette to the second man, but the first man called out, "Light it for me! Do you want me to smoke it raw?" I quickly grabbed a lighter and lit it for him. He took a puff and blew the smoke in my face. I held my breath and waved the smoke away. Old Four was next, and I knew he was up to no good. He asked me to light his cigarette, but after striking the lighter twice, it still didn't ignite. Old Four said, "Come here. Let me help you." He leaned towards me, and his hand brushed against mine. My heart raced with nervousness, but I heard a snap—the lighter's flame appeared suddenly. Old Four exclaimed, "Ah!" in pain. I realized it was not a good situation when I saw him touching his face, and the man sitting next to him exclaimed, "Old Four, you've burned half your eyebrow! Haha, it looks ugly!"

I started to panic. I quickly apologized, "I'm sorry! It was an accident; I didn't mean to!" Old Four flew into a rage and shouted, "You little girl! You purposely burned me, Zheng Old Four! Do you think you can get away with it?" His voice hadn't faded when I felt a stinging pain on my face—I had been slapped. It burned immediately! How could I be treated like this? My parents had never laid a hand on me. Why should this unknown man, with unclear intentions, strike me? Holding back tears, I defended myself, "Didn't you ask me to light your cigarette? Didn't you touch my hand and get so close that your eyebrow got burned?" Zheng Old Four angrily retorted, "Are you still arguing? I touched your hand, so what? I've touched hundreds of women, and none of them ever dared to lay a finger on me! If you don't explain yourself tonight, I, Zheng Old Four, will never let it go!"

The man sitting in the corner, whom they called Second Brother, stood up and said, "Old Four, let it go. She didn't do it on purpose." But Zheng Old Four ignored the advice and continued angrily, "A young girl like you, how dare you take action against me, Zheng Old Four? Do you want to become a laughingstock among us? How will I ever show my face again?" I panicked and said, "I truly apologize! It was an accident; I didn't mean to!" This unexpected incident could jeopardize my chance of keeping the job and even harm Sauna City's reputation. What could I do? In my silence, the courage I once had to argue vanished.

Ah Lan must have heard the commotion from the room. She opened the door and entered along with the manager. Ah Lan said, "This is our manager. Boss Sun isn't here tonight. If you have any issues, report them to Manager Tian." Tian offered each of them a cigarette and lit them before addressing the situation, "I apologize on behalf of Sauna City for what happened tonight. Ah Jing here was personally brought in by Boss Sun. Please consider Boss Sun's reputation and let her off this time. Sauna City is willing to offer you VIP treatment and a 20% discount for future visits as compensation for your loss. What do you say?" Zheng Old Four replied, "Forget it. Money is not an issue for us. But it would be best if you enlightened this little girl. If she doesn't learn her lesson, she will become a thorn in our side!" The four men left after their conversation. As Zheng Old Four passed me, he brushed his arm against my chest and lewdly said, "You got off easy today, but next time, you better be careful!" I let out a sigh of relief. The incident made me nervous, and I didn't know how it would end if they continued to harass me.

Manager Tian came over and scolded, "Are you Ah Jing? What's wrong with you? On your first day of work, you're causing trouble! If not for them giving face to Boss Sun, you would be in real trouble. We can't protect you from those hooligans!" I replied, "I came here to be a waitress, not to be harassed. I can't tolerate their rude behavior!" Manager Tian said, "Wrong! Don't act so high and mighty when you come here as a waitress. Your job is to serve the guests and make them happy and satisfied. Sauna City thrives only when the guests are satisfied, and you'll earn good money. Understand?" Ah Lan interjected, "Jing, you had a close call tonight. Regardless of the reasons, offending customers is unacceptable. Be careful next time." Manager Tian instructed Ah Lan, "Take care of her. She has good potential. We're short-staffed, so guide her and let her start her regular duties early."

On my first day of work, due to the incident, Ah Lan, as the foreman, didn't blame me but let me finish work at ten o'clock. She told me to rest well and start my regular duties the next day. On my way back, the more I thought about it, the worse I felt. It was chaotic. I witnessed some waitresses flirting with customers, but I didn't want to compromise my innocence. Something inside me told me that this sauna city wasn't quite right and that something else was going on. I wanted to quit the job and find work in a factory. A stable monthly income of several hundred yuan would be satisfactory for me. When I returned to Sister Wu's place, she hadn't finished work yet. Xiao Hong watched the black and white TV, and the image was surprisingly straightforward. Xiao Hong noticed me and asked, "Finished work so early?" I replied, "I don't want to work there anymore."

Xiao Hong looked surprised and questioned, "Why? Isn't business booming there?" I explained, "I can't handle it. It's a bit chaotic." Xiao Hong glanced at me and said, "Who is born knowing everything? If it's chaotic, it's a good thing. No one is paying attention. Maybe you're just too sensitive. Don't give up after just one day." I responded, "I don't think I can learn much there. I'd rather work in a factory." Xiao Hong chuckled, "Don't be foolish. Working in a factory is the least desirable option. It's tiring, and you have no freedom. Don't be indecisive. I advise you to stick with it. I'll tell you honestly; there's a lot to gain from working there!"

Chapter 4

The Woman's Capital

I couldn't sleep that night, waiting for Sister Wu to come back. I knew I had to talk to her about my decision not to work at the sauna city. Since she had helped me with the introduction, seeking her advice and avoiding any misunderstandings was necessary. Early in the morning, Sister Wu returned, looking exhausted. I hesitated but couldn't hold back any longer. As she entered her room, I called out from the doorway, "Sister Wu." She turned around and replied, "Oh, Xiaojing, why aren't you sleeping? Are there too many mosquitoes? No mosquito repellent coil?" I said, "Sister Wu, I need to talk to you." She gestured for me to come inside and sit down while she washed up.

As Sister Wu undressed and cleaned herself in front of me, I noticed her full breasts and well-maintained figure. Her skin wasn't fair, and her face lacked a youthful glow after being washed, appearing slightly dull. Trying to offer comfort, I said, "Sister Wu, you are still beautiful." She smiled and responded, "Don't flatter me. My muscles are loose and dull. It's young and pretty girls like you that men like." I hesitantly continued,

"Sister Wu, I don't want to work there." Sister Wu was taken aback and asked, "What did you say?" Afraid of her anger, I quickly added, "I don't know much, but it just doesn't feel right to me." Sister Wu understood. She put on her black underwear and said, "Xiaojing, do you mean you don't want to work there?" I nodded. "Why?" Sister Wu inquired. "I always thought it was a bit unprofessional, and the customers were very aggressive," I explained. Sister Wu said, "Really? The working environment and benefits there are comparable to Nanxun." I replied, "I don't know why, but I don't like it. I want to find another job." Sister Wu looked at me in surprise and said, "So, you came to me just to get a job in a factory? Do you think it's easy to make money at a factory? Do you think it's easy to get a good position there? Do you think having money alone will lead to success at a factory?" I mustered my courage and asked, "Can you please tell them I won't be going to work tomorrow?" Seeing my determination, Sister Wu said, "Did you sign the agreement with them today?" I replied, "Yes, just a signature, nothing more." Sister Wu laughed, "What do you think you're signing? Just a name is enough to bind you for life!" I was surprised by her words, and Sister Wu explained, "According to the agreement if you unilaterally break the contract and don't show up for work, you'll have to pay them 5,000 yuan all at once." I felt dumbfounded and nervously said, "I only have 200 yuan, and I need it for living expenses. How can they be so ruthless? 5,000 yuan just for a name?" Sister Wu said, "Since we're fellow villagers, fellow villagers should help each other. If I don't help you, who will? Don't worry too much. I won't force you if you don't want to work there. I don't want your family to think I forced you. Tomorrow, look for another job, and I'll talk to them about keeping your position. If you find another job, I'll find a way to explain it to them. Boss Sun is my friend and won't make things difficult for you. You can still go back there if you haven't found another job. What do you think?" I felt proud to have Sister Wu as a fellow villager. Little did I know, her intention was more like "fellow sees fellow, deceive you without discussion!" Sister Wu helped me get the job with a generous referral fee. Later, she even arranged for me to sell my "first night" to clients, taking the majority of the earnings while I only received a fraction. All her so-called kindness turned out to be a facade. In the end, she even got involved with her sister's partner, almost causing an accident. That's why her sister, Wu Fang, and I left Nanxun and sought a new life in Suzhou.

The next day, I went out to find a job. I visited several factories and approached their offices, but they all said they needed to be hiring. Some didn't even let me in after seeing my graduation certificate. In the current job market, where even college graduates struggle to find employment, a vocational school student like me faces even more difficulties. After several days of searching, my legs grew heavy, and I had no hope of finding a job. Many unemployed people like me roamed the streets with no purpose or direction. Making a living on my own was becoming a real challenge. With only 100 yuan left, it would last up to a few days. If I couldn't find a job soon, I wouldn't have enough money to return home.

Moreover, I couldn't bear the shame of returning empty-handed after setting out with such ambition. During these days, although I didn't work at the sauna city, I continued to stay with Sister Wu. I couldn't afford to stay in a hotel, and if Sister Wu didn't allow me to stay, I would be left with no choice but to live on the streets. I was a stranger in this town, and after more than a week of searching, there seemed to be no hope. With summer, many factories were laying off workers rather than hiring. Finding a job could not be solved in a day or two. I realized that there were many others who hadn't found jobs and were stuck in the same situation. I saw people loitering on the streets, doing nothing all day. It was becoming clear that making a living was going to be a real challenge. Sometimes, Xiao Hong would bring me a few fresh buns or freshly fried lamb kebabs. She sympathized with my situation but couldn't offer much help. I survived on those meager meals, understanding that survival was the priority, and I couldn't afford to worry about my pride.

Xiao Hong advised me, "Pride is important, but money is even more important! Talk to Sister Wu and return to work at the sauna city." Xiao Hong and I both knew that she and Sister Wu worked at a nightclub. Xiao Hong used to work in massage rooms, which was challenging. It seemed that Sister Wu, Sister Wu, was a dancer in the nightclub known as "miss maybe." They danced, drank, and sometimes engaged in other activities. Xiao Hong said that the sauna city's hostesses often only provided massages and didn't engage in different services, but many willingly provided extra benefits for additional money. I understood what Xiao Hong was implying, but I didn't want to compromise my virginity in that way. I respected their choices but didn't want to follow in their footsteps. I thought maybe I could focus on massage services instead. I decided to speak to Sister Wu and inquire about the situation. Xiao Hong shared everything she knew with me. She said, "There are different types of massages. The common ones include Chinese massage and Thai bone-setting massage. As for the oil massage and chest massage, those are more explicit services. In reality, very few masseuses truly focus on massage techniques. Most of the time, it's about pleasuring men. No matter which method you use, as long as you make the man happy, you're done. After all, we are women, and men pay for our companionship, right?" I considered following their path and entering this line of work, feeling unwilling and helpless.

I waited for Sister Wu to return and boldly expressed my decision,

"Sister Wu, I've thought about it, and I want to return to work at the sauna city. Can you please talk to them for me?" Sister Wu agreed, smiling, "Finally, you've come to your senses. A woman should understand her circumstances, seize opportunities, and maximize her youth and beauty." I pretended to nod in agreement and said, "Yes, Sister Wu, you're right! I want to learn massage well and earn more money." Sister Wu smiled, "Xiaojing, you can stay here for the night. Let's rest and have a chat. If you have any questions, feel free to ask. I will treat you like my own sister." I replied, "Okay, I want to seek Sister Wu's guidance."

Sister Wu seemed to be energized at night, accustomed to the nightlife. We lay in bed, the electric fan oscillating, tirelessly blowing the warm air. I found the breeze a little hot yet slightly cooling, but without the fan, it would be even stuffier, and the mosquitoes would feast on my skin, leaving behind itchy red marks. Sister Wu, still lively, took out a bag of sausages from the bedside drawer and handed me two, saying, "Eat." Seeing Sister Wu munching on the thick sausages with relish, I felt a bit queasy. I remember watching a film at a classmate's home in technical school, where I secretly witnessed a woman engaging in an unpleasant act using her mouth. Seeing Sister Wu eating the sausages reminded me of that scene, making it difficult for me to have any appetite for food.

Sister Wu, with confidence, said to me, "You shouldn't be too naive now. The more naive you are, the more you'll suffer. With your beauty, you shouldn't waste your advantageous resources. It's a pity. Our women's youth is short, and what do men desire in us? Isn't it just a pretty face and a young body? With the right approach, we can earn any amount of money. It's easier than you think." Sister Wu was skilled in influencing my thoughts, and her words that night alleviated many of my concerns while laying the necessary psychological foundation for my future career in the entertainment industry. Deep down, I had some hidden insecurities that made accepting Sister Wu's teachings easier. Yes, beauty fades quickly, and youth is fleeting. If we don't develop and use them to our advantage, we're like unknown flowers blooming in obscurity. Sister Wu said, "I wonder if Xiao Hong has spoken to you about it? To put it mildly, a masseuse is essentially an escort. Massages are just a cover. Xiaojing, don't be shocked or nervous. Listen to what I have to say, and you'll understand. This is where the true value of women lies." I admitted that I didn't fully comprehend what Sister Wu was implying. She continued, "Our true value lies in providing a pleasurable experience! When you're in this line of work, men will spoil you. They will take you shopping, buying you fashionable clothes and jewelry to please you. Later, when things turn cold, you can sell those items and convert them into cash. And then, there's the real treasure, when men offer you money to spend time with them. If you like them, you can engage in intimate activities, and the money will flow in." I finally understood. Sister Wu had earned hundreds of thousands of dollars by following this path. She said, "Once you're in this business, you'll experience the luxuries provided by men. Those men, in order to please you, will take you to shopping malls and willingly buy you fashionable clothes and jewelry. When they're gone, you can sell those items and get cash. Men will always be attracted to you and shower you with money. Another trick is to find a wealthy man and tell him your birthday is coming soon. He will buy you an expensive birthday gift. You can do the same for another man and make up any date, claiming it's your birthday. Men are more willing to spend money on women they're involved with. They may not buy home furniture or a single dress for their wives, but they'll always be generous with the women they're interested in. Men are more generous than women." I could sense the implication behind Sister Wu's words: if you want to make money, don't be concerned about preserving your dignity. But could I do it? Could I sell everything for cash, disregarding morals and shame?

I was left speechless, realizing how easy it was to make money. But then, why did a customer slap me on my first day of work? Sister Wu comforted me and said, "Xiaojing, Sister Wu knows you're a smart girl. You'll understand how to handle things. I know you're still a virgin, and we can start with the first step of looking and touching. When the opportunity arises, Sister Wu will help you sell yourself at a good price!" Was Sister Wu trying to manipulate me? Why did she say she would sell me at a reasonable price? I was puzzled, and Sister Wu explained with a smile, "Don't worry, I won't sell you off. I meant you can sell your 'first night' to a wealthy boss and then make a fortune!" Selling that? Can a woman really do that? I was astonished! Sister Wu said, "Who in your family would know what you're doing here? When you return, everything will be fine in a few years, won't it?"

Chapter 5

Massage For the First Time

There is a saying: "A single word from a gentleman is worth more than ten years of studying." Sister Wu's words resonated deeply with me as if she had shown me a path when I felt lost. I could almost feel the bright future calling out to me. When faced with the dilemma of survival, how many rational choices does one have? Sister Wu told me, "Xiaojing, you have such a good physical condition! It's a pity you're not a masseuse." Her words boosted my confidence, and I even imagined that I was born to be a masseuse. If I hesitated again, it would be paranoia!

How excited and grateful I was! It took me a while to wake up and realize that Sister Wu's words were misleading and damaging. I went to work at the Sea Paradise Sauna City, thinking that if there was no grass in front, I could eat the grass behind. Xiaoqin and Ah Lan treated me politely, but the manager warned me, "Next time you leave without authorization, you'll be fined ten thousand yuan! Do you understand?" I replied, "Last time, I was busy and forgot to ask for leave." Manager

Tian said, "Work well here, and it will be good for you!" Since I'm willing to work here, I will do well. Who would want to earn less money?

Ah Lan took me into the dressing room and handed me a key. She pointed to a cabinet and said, "This wardrobe is yours from now on." I changed into overalls, and Ah Lan smiled and said, "Today, you will be the official masseuse. Don't be nervous. Learn on the job, and try to meet the guests' needs. If you don't know something, don't show it. You can recommend other services to the guests instead. Don't tell them that you don't know. You can learn from the other sisters. Also, try not to wear a bra when wearing your fatigue dress. You'll look sexier without it." I nodded without overthinking. Since I had come this far, there was no point in being afraid. As Sister Wu had said, let them see and touch. It was just the last line of defense that I needed to protect. I didn't want to lose it quickly.

Ah Lan gave me a brief introduction to the personnel on the second floor and some basic skills for the service items. There were techniques like trample back, knock back, push oil, and chest push. Ah Lan said, "They come here to play anyway, and the bath is just an excuse. Your goal is to make them happy, nothing else. Also, if they request special services, it's up to you, but make sure to use condoms. It's for preventing diseases and pregnancy." I took mental notes, but my face turned red. Using my hands to push oil and touching men explicitly made me uncomfortable. Pushing my breasts against a man during the chest push seemed tiring. It was easier to step on someone's back, but it felt cheap. No wonder I had heard waitresses refusing foreplay and preferring to go straight to the main act, as it was more accessible and lucrative. However, I decided I wouldn't do that. I would focus on the massage and take it one step at a time.

The second floor was where men could enjoy the sauna. The reception was handled by young ladies, numbering over 20. The competition seemed fierce. There weren't many guests in the early evening, so I had time to chat with some of the idle waitresses. I got to know sisters Fang, Yu, Mei, Chun, and others. They came from different provinces, mostly Sichuan, Hunan, and Anhui, and some from northern Jiangsu. There were no local girls. After more than ten days of searching for a job, I gained a preliminary understanding of the entertainment industry in Nanxun. The entertainment services in this small town on the border of Jiangsu and Zhejiang were as thriving as in the city itself. The bathhouses, recreational centers, and nightclubs along the main street were bustling with activity when night fell. The lamplights were hazy, and the young ladies, dressed provocatively, added to the atmosphere. Yet behind the scenes, who knew how many dark secrets were concealed? Standing here today, wasn't I already one of those women being sold, or one of those "women who bet their youth on tomorrow"?

Ah Lan seemed to take care of me. After a while, she called me and said a customer wanted a back-stepping service. I took the number plate and entered a spacious massage room. Two neat rows of massage tables had handle rings and snow-white sheets. Each bed was occupied by men and waitresses performing back-stepping services. Ah Lan informed me that my customer was in bed number 12, a man in his fifties. I said, "Excuse me, I'm here for the back-stepping service." The man, with his face obscured, nodded without saying a word. I couldn't see his face as he slumped on the bed, wearing loose underpants. I began using my hands to gently massage his feet, moving up to his thighs, waist, back, and neck. I didn't know much about massage techniques or acupoints, but I stroked his body with my hands. It was my first time touching a man's body. He was middle-aged, but his skin was smooth, and his flesh was plump. He seemed like a pampered individual. He didn't move when I ran my hands over him, probably still relaxed from the bath. His skin felt slightly warm, and I noticed that he was ticklish as his body trembled when my hands rested on his waist.

After warming up, I removed my slippers and climbed onto the bed. Holding onto the rings, I was unsure where to start. Maybe he had been waiting for a while, but seeing that I didn't move, he turned to look at me. Our eyes met, and I saw his gentle gaze devoid of accusation or immorality. It put me at ease. I thought wherever I stepped, and I should start somewhere. I placed one foot on his hip, gradually increasing the pressure until it was firm, then I put the other foot on the opposite hip. I used the tips of my toes to mimic the sisters' movements on the adjacent bed, dancing on his back, stepping back and forth from the bend of his legs to his shoulder blades. I thought this was like feeling my way across a river, not knowing what lies ahead.

Luckily, the man seemed okay with it. I wondered how he felt. Was it uncomfortable or pleasant for him? He was the first client I worked with in the massage industry, and was cooperative. On other beds, I saw some guests rolling over and groping the waitresses, and one even lifted the skirt of the woman stepping on his back. I could see that the waitresses were used to this behavior and didn't seem surprised. One of the sisters asked the guest, "What are you looking at? The more money you have, the more powerful you feel. Don't play tricks here!" The young man, likely lacking funds, dared not move further. This must be what Sister Wu referred to as "letting them see."

After about 20 minutes, I felt his skin turning red from the stepping, and I became a little tired and started panting. Sweat formed on my forehead. I didn't think of massage as enjoyable but as paying for suffering, letting people step on my body. I couldn't understand what made it comfortable.

I got off him and went under the bed to grab a clean towel to wipe him down. As he rolled over, I caught a glimpse of the height between his legs, and my face turned red. He stared at me, looked deeply, and said, "You're new here?" Not wanting to lie, I replied, "Yes, I'm new here. Please take care of me!" The man smiled kindly, put on his bathrobe, and left the massage room.

When I emerged, Ah Lan smiled and said, "Jing, you did a good job. Congratulations!" I felt embarrassed and said, "But I didn't do well. Didn't he say anything?" Ah Lan smiled and said, "No, he gave you an extra 100 yuan!" I was overjoyed. I didn't expect such a clumsy back-stepping session to earn me such a generous reward. It was truly surprising. I learned that each time a waitress stepped on a customer's back, she received 10 yuan as a service fee. If there were any additional tips, I would receive half, 20% would go to the head waitress as a commission, and 30% would be charged as the "cost of work" by the establishment. I was curious to know how much they set for my services. As for the money for the head waitress, it was fair. If she didn't arrange for customers to give it to me, I might come to work for a day and not earn a penny. Ah Lan brought me more customers, and I had to work harder in return. It seemed fair. Being too obvious in favoritism would only stir up resentment among the other sisters.

Ah Lan pulled me aside and whispered, "I just received a call from inside. There's a customer who wants an oil service. Can you handle it?" I knew what "push oil" meant. Although I wasn't too worried, I readily agreed, thinking I needed to learn anyway. Ah Lan whispered, "But you need to get him to finish quickly, okay?" I attended health classes and saw those videos at a classmate's house. I knew what it meant, and it involved the essence of men. If released inside a woman's body, it could create new life. I didn't have much experience, but there must be a way.

When all else failed, I could treat it like squeezing toothpaste, right? No matter what, I had to give it my best shot. I grabbed the necessary ointments and towels and headed to Room 16.

It was a small single room, about seven or eight square meters. Besides a bed, there was a TV cabinet and a neatly folded towel on a platform. A man in his thirties, wearing a bathrobe, leaned on the bed, waiting for me. I closed the door and approached him, trying to mask my guilt. I spoke gently, "Sir, please lie down." As the man saw me, a glimmer of interest flashed in his eyes. However, he was taken aback by my words and said, "Just let me lie down? How will you push me if you don't help me undress? How can I take off my clothes?" I didn't realize that pushing oil on a man also involved undressing him. Wasn't he capable of doing it himself? But my lack of experience left me unable to argue back. He opened his arms, and I proceeded to remove his bathrobe. He was left in his red underpants. I smiled and said, "Now may I lie down, Sir?" He sighed and mumbled, "What's the matter? Why did they send a newbie like you? You don't know anything!" He took out a towel from under the TV cabinet, spread it on the bed, and lay down on the towel, legs bent, directly in front of me, unexpectedly removing his underpants! I saw everything, including the dark hair surrounding it, and my mouth hung open in shock. I didn't expect him to be so audacious, exposing himself like that in front of me. I was startled, but then I realized I was there to provide the oil service. How could I do that if he wasn't naked? I was so uninformed!

I gathered myself and massaged him with a professional demeanor. It was still a massage, but my hands were swimming and touching him. After a while, when I felt his skin warming up, I applied the black ointment to his body and spread it with the palms of my hands. As I used it to his thighs, I couldn't help but notice that he stood tall and imposing like a snake's head. My heart raced. I could thank this job for opening my eyes to things I wouldn't have experienced otherwise.

After a few minutes, I became more involved and massaged him attentively. Strangely enough, I felt a sense of professional accomplishment within me. Despite being faced with his nudity, I had no erotic thoughts. I heard him say, "What's your name? You look innocent but in a cute way!" Innocent? Did he call me innocent? I smiled and replied, "My name is Jing. If there's anything I'm not doing well, please let me know. I would be grateful for your feedback." The man chuckled and said, "Well, I must tell you the truth. Your massage skills didn't pass the test! Don't you know that 'genital massage' is in demand these days?" What? My face turned pale, shocked!

Chapter 6

It Feels Dirty

I was flushed and confused. Sister Wu and Little Red had told me that back-stepping was just for show, that a short skirt couldn't hide countless styles, and that men lying on the bed could sneak a peek at the waitresses' lower bodies. Ah Lan had also mentioned that we should wear revealing outfits, not wear bras, and bend over during massages to give men a view of the scenery and entice them. I knew that chest pushing involved using breasts instead of hands and often involved touching the guest's lower body to provide release. As for oil pushing, I knew it was a more explicit service involving using oil to stimulate the guest until they reached climax. But I didn't know that massage could be so varied and explicit. Was it essential for the waitresses to be naked?

"Sir," I said in horror, "are you joking?". The man smiled and said, "I'm a regular customer here, and when I first came for a massage, you were probably still a newcomer. Now things are more open and exciting. Didn't your trainer explain it clearly to you?" I replied, "I don't have a trainer, and I didn't know about this rule, sir. If possible, could you please make an exception?" The man chuckled and said, "I see, you're a novice. In this industry, full nudity is expected for the vacuum service. It enhances the transparency and sincerity of the service. I'm straightforward about what I want but don't worry; I won't violate the rules. Are you afraid I'll force myself on you?"

I knew that this type of heterosexual massage had a pornographic nature and would not be allowed to happen. However, I also knew I needed to compromise to survive. My heart raced, and I wondered what to do. Should I leave, or should I comply with his request and undress? I couldn't believe I was considering taking off my clothes in front of a stranger. It felt degrading. But my survival instincts kicked in, and I hesitated, unable to make a decision. The man noticed my red face and motionless stance and said with a smile, "Men come here for fresh stimulation; isn't that what you masseuses do for money? What's there to be ashamed of? Don't you undress when you go to sleep? Do you want me to undress you?" My heart hardened, and I thought, "Fine, I'll undress. Who's afraid of whom? I don't think you can do anything to me just by looking!"

Determined, I removed my jacket and let my skirt fall to my feet. I unclasped my white bra and pulled out my lace underwear, gritting my teeth and avoiding eye contact. I didn't dare look at him because I feared his gaze would strip away my courage. No man had seen my body before, but I was willing to expose myself. How cheap did I feel? I hesitated for a moment, neither advancing nor retreating. The man saw my red face and wooden expression and smiled, saying, "I've seen many women, both inside and outside the industry, but none as beautiful and sexy as you. This is the first time I've seen someone like you! Truly remarkable!" Hearing him praise me was becoming tiresome, but I couldn't help but feel satisfied when he described me as "perfect." He continued, "Some women are beautiful with their clothes on, but you're even more beautiful without them! Beautiful things are meant to be admired by everyone. Tang Jiali took artistic photos of the human body and caused a sensation, didn't she? Isn't it a shame to hide your figure? Come closer, little sister." Although I didn't know what he had in mind, I approached him unafraid. He stared at me for a while and suddenly reached out to touch my breast. As I was shocked by his action, he pinched my buttocks. It stung a little, and I glared at him, saying, "What are you doing? Keep your hands to yourself!" He laughed and said, "I apologize for getting carried away! Can I change my request? I want a special service customized just for me!" I knew he was trying to push his luck and take advantage of me, but I had already decided. The special service would come later, not now. I was still a virgin and wasn't foolish enough to give myself away so easily. I refused and said, "No way! Now lie down and behave!" I didn't know how I had summoned the courage to stand up to him, but he didn't push the matter further. I proceeded with the massage, starting with his inner thighs. During the massage, my hand accidentally brushed against his private area, and it instinctively recoiled. I held it in my hand and felt its warmth and heat. It was an interesting sensation devoid of any revulsion. I rubbed it with my hand. Was this what men referred to as their pride? Was this the weapon they used to conquer women? In my palm, it was nothing more than a toy.

Sometimes, when you break through a psychological barrier and let go of the knots in your heart, things that once seemed mysterious and powerful lose their significance. Gao had seen my body, and I had seen his. I didn't feel diminished. While massaging him, I could sense his pleasure, at least physically. He said, "Little sister, please hurry up. Apply more pressure. That's it, good!" I watched his body react to my massage, and it was amusing to see the changes. I could feel its hardness and temperature in my hand. My face grew warm as well. As I increased the pressure, I leaned forward slightly, and the man widened his eyes, panting heavily. His expression seemed to convey a mixture of pleasure and pain. I suddenly realized what was happening and tried to react, but it was too late. I saw a stream of white liquid shoot out, unable to dodge in time, and it sprayed onto my face. I sighed and quickly grabbed a towel to wipe it off. I also noticed a fishy smell. The man apologized, saying, "I'm sorry! I'm sorry! I couldn't hold back!" I understood that this was what "pushing oil" meant, the act of helping the guest reach climax. I wiped him off roughly, relieved that it was finally over. Although I was still confused, I had gained some understanding of the process. I told him, "Mr. Gao, please wash up over there."

I put on my overalls. Despite being "honest" with him, he behaved himself and didn't make any inappropriate gestures. When men and women are naked together, they feel a sense of closeness that isn't present when they're clothed. I wondered if I would feel embarrassed if I were to meet him during the daytime. But then I reminded myself he was a guest here, and I could pretend not to recognize him elsewhere. As long as I removed my clothes in front of a man once, it became much easier and less awkward. The beginning was always the hardest. Wasn't that how life worked?

Five minutes later, he returned, wrapped in a towel. I removed the ointments from the bed, and he lay back down. I dried him off with a clean towel and provided a gentle massage. I knew that the price for the oil service was 120 yuan for three "clocks," with each clock representing a service period. Some watches lasted 15 minutes, others 30 minutes, and the price needed to be standardized. The establishment belonged to the mid-range in terms of price, and in some simple roadside shops, the cost would be lower, with 120 yuan covering the company of a young lady. Although my skills were still rough, I wanted to provide a full hour of service. After all, the guests were paying, and I couldn't neglect them. Mr. Gao said, "Although your massage skills are not refined yet, I enjoy your technique. Some experienced masseuses tend to be lazy and finish the job quickly, but you took your time with the oil service, and I thoroughly enjoyed it. You have great potential, and I believe you'll become popular soon!" I felt grateful for his kind words. If a customer had criticized me initially, it would have shattered my confidence. "Thank you for your encouragement, Mr. Gao. I appreciate your support. Please feel free to visit again." Mr. Gao replied with a smile, "You're welcome. Whenever I come, I'll bring my friends along." I thanked him for his attention, and he added, "You're the talk of the town, the new girl who has caught everyone's attention. Keep up the good work, and you'll become the princess of the Seaview Resort in no time!" I felt embarrassed and replied, "Mr. Gao, you're overestimating me. I'm just an ugly duckling. Becoming a noble princess seems too far-fetched." Mr. Gao laughed and said, "Don't be modest. I trust my judgment. It won't be long before you experience the taste of stardom. Gold will always shine, sooner or later!" I smiled and said, "Thank you for your kindness, Mr. Gao. I truly hope I can rise to the top."

On my way back, I observed that the town was peaceful and quiet, but it seemed to hide false prosperity in the dim light. That night, I couldn't sleep. I saw both the beauty and ugliness of my first day at work. But what other choice did I have? There was no turning back once I was caught in this cycle, and it would be difficult to break free and live a clean life. I had a family, and how would my parents feel if they knew I was working as a masseuse? I still wanted love and marriage in the future, a good life. But as a lowly masseuse, did I even have the right to dream of sacred love? Being a masseuse was dishonorable and unsustainable. Could I ever live a bright life with such a stain on my past?

Looking at Little Red sleeping soundly, I wondered if she had any worries. Perhaps those who think less have fewer worries. After all, I was just a girl without a great sense of purpose. I was still determining what lay ahead or what I would do. I recalled a poem I had read online: "Life is but a play; what's the point of being so serious? The crimson autumn leaves and the lonely silence are enough. Maple red autumn will do, and loneliness will accompany the passage of time." Yes, life was like a play, and we should do what we wanted. Why worry so much? No matter how much we thought about it, it wouldn't change anything. The sun would still rise in the east tomorrow, and we would still need to eat and work. Nothing had changed.

Chapter 7

Apprenticeship in Wisdom

The next day, I continued to have a successful day at work. With Ah Lan's recommendation, I provided massages to three clients, and one even gave me a 50 yuan tip. I found that earning money as a massage therapist was relatively easy, although it could be tiring and lacking in dignity to be at someone's beck and call, being touched and examined. However, I had accepted this job and its realities, knowing I was here to earn money, so I had no complaints.

After all, we are in a market economy, right? Supply follows demand. If it weren't for so many "horny men" with their desires, we massage therapists wouldn't have a place to earn a living. So, if you have a son or a husband at home, never let them go to entertainment venues like saunas. What kind of business are they conducting there? It's all lies! Is that a place for conducting business? Remember the saying, "If you walk along the river, your shoes will get wet." Our customers include businessmen, powerful officials who hold real power, and ordinary men with wandering minds. Some visit saunas not with their own money but as someone else's guests. Their visits usually involve a range of services, from bathing to massages. These individuals are the financial gods of the sauna city, and we can't afford to offend them.

Ah Chun once told me about when she encountered a high school student who was still a virgin. Technically, he wasn't a virgin anymore, according to his own words. He claimed to have lost his virginity in junior high school but hadn't had intercourse with a woman yet. Women have that membrane that can verify their virginity, but what do men have to prove? Massage therapists usually judge whether a client is experienced or inexperienced based on their instincts. Ah Chun said that the young boy was seeking special services because, in his words, he wanted to share what it feels like to be with a woman. Ah Chun advised him to focus on his studies and not visit such places. The boy calmly said he was the only one among his male classmates still "untouched."

Others, like hair salon workers, had already been with female classmates or women from outside. This made him feel embarrassed and frustrated. Ah Chun reluctantly fulfilled his request, but he was nervous and finished quickly. The boy shamefully said, "If I had known it would be this unexciting, I wouldn't have come!" Ah Chun laughed and persuaded him, saying, "Focus on your studies instead. You can come find me when you graduate, and I promise you'll be satisfied." The boy agreed, saying, "Okay, it's a deal!" I sighed inwardly. How have today's high school students become so lackluster? We've tried to advise them, but their willpower could be more assertive. The youth feel lost about their future and need more compassion, confidence, and ambition. The responsibility lies with families, society, and the education system.

Regarding massages, I'm still a novice. Although I've asked my fellow sisters for guidance, they say it's not that they're conservative and unwilling to teach me; they genuinely don't know much either, just bluffing their way through with those clueless men. Xiaohong, who lives with me, knows quite a bit. She said she was trained by a teacher who was an experienced sister in the industry. She no longer works as a massage therapist but focuses on teaching others, which she claims is even better than doing a massage business. I've heard that many girls are lining up to learn from her. I also want to learn some basic techniques. To establish myself in the massage industry, I need more than looks and body; I need fundamental skills. People say that even as a "miss," one needs to have skills in bed. Although massage therapists are more reserved than "misses," we still need genuine skills and knowledge. Superficial skills will only last for a while.

Being harassed by customers who try to touch us inappropriately is unavoidable, especially during oil massages and chest rubs. Some uncultured men try to take advantage. However, such behavior is strictly prohibited in the establishment. If massage therapists engage in private transactions with customers without proper documentation, and if the customers deny or refuse to pay, there is nothing we can do. The establishment knows that engaging in such "private activities" results in fines for the service providers. We don't want to do it because it's a thankless task. After all, the level of contact in "special services" is more profound, and the risks are higher. If we accidentally encounter someone with AIDS, it can cost us our lives. This is no trivial matter. Suppose a customer has solid demands, and the service providers want to avoid offending them. In that case, they usually adopt a compromising approach, using their mouths to extract their "oils" to retain the customers. It is said that almost all men enjoy this kind of approach, which leaves them infatuated.

After a few days, my relationships with the sisters improved. We are all here to earn a living, so there's no need to become enemies. I heard service providers fight over customers in some saunas, resulting in physical altercations. Let them have the customers instead of competing with them. I have only done essential services such as massages, back rubs, foot rubs, and oil massages, but I have yet to provide services involving oral actions or more tiring chest rubs. I will eventually have to experience them. As long as the customers need us, we must serve them wholeheartedly to ensure their satisfaction. Fortunately, although I have just started working, I haven't received any customer complaints.

On the contrary, I have received many positive reviews because, unlike other service providers, I don't demand tips. Tips are an extra reward from the customers, but whether they give them or not doesn't affect the enthusiasm and quality of our service. Although the commission from tips is high, I don't care about it. Since I will receive my salary on the 5th of next month, I borrowed 100 yuan from Ah Lan. She said, "Do you have free time tomorrow? I want to take you to meet someone."

The next day, I accompanied Ah Lan to a residential area in a small town. She pressed the doorbell, and the door opened with a click. I was excited because the person I was about to meet was the teacher mentioned by Xiaohong. She had taught Ah Lan before, and the massage therapists in this town and those in the Jiangsu and Zhejiang areas had received her training. Ah Lan knew I wanted to learn more, so she especially accompanied me to pay respects to her as a mentor. I recalled the saying, "At home, rely on your parents; outside, rely on your friends." It was true. I would be sleeping on the streets if it weren't for Wu's sister's support. Without Xiaohong and Ah Lan's guidance and help, I wouldn't have become adept at this job.

The door was opened by a woman in her thirties with a charming figure and captivating charm. Ah Lan affectionately said, "Sister Xu, you are getting younger and more beautiful daily!" Xu's sister laughed, saying, "A woman turns to bean curd at thirty. I'm already thirty-two, so I'm getting old." I sincerely said, "Sister Xu, you are lovely! You look no older than twenty-seven or twenty-eight." Xu's sister smiled and said, "I heard from Ah Lan that your name is Xiaojing, right? She said you are ambitious and good-looking. You indeed have the potential to become a beautiful woman!" Being praised by the teacher made me both happy and a bit embarrassed. I said, "Where, where? I'm far from being on the same level as Sister Xu. You are the queen of massage, and I'm just an ignorant young girl who doesn't know anything. So, I would like to ask for your guidance!" Xu's sister said, "You are Ah Lan's good sister and my younger sister. Although Ah Lan and I have a teacher-student relationship, we have always been like real sisters. You don't need to apprentice formally. If you have any questions, feel free to ask, and I will tell you everything openly."

I was delighted that Xu's sister was willing to teach me. With her guidance, my massage skills would significantly improve. I said, "I would like to ask Sister Xu about the general techniques used in formal massages. What should we pay attention to in massage services at saunas like ours?" Xu's sister smiled and said, "You are someone who cares about details." She gestured for Ah Lan to lie on the massage bed in the living room. I noticed several massage chairs and fitness equipment in the room. After Ah Lan lay down, Xu's sister demonstrated a few moves on her while explaining, "Formal massages require a bAh Lance of finger pressure, lightness, heaviness, slowness, and speed. It would be best to accurately target acupoints and gently use your fingers to stimulate those points, relaxing the tendons and promoting blood circulation. Various techniques include bone loosening, skin tightening, backstepping, cupping, scraping, spine pinching, and more. Some techniques involve tapping, pressing, kneading, rubbing, and more. However, as massage therapists at saunas, we don't have to adhere to these standardized techniques strictly. We have the freedom to use different movements while keeping our focus intact. When gently stroking, stroke with purpose; when tapping, tap with force. Guide the customers to have a mix of relaxation and tension, openness and relaxation so they can reach a state of physical and mental well-being." I said, "So, during a massage, I shouldn't let the customers lead me around like a puppet; instead, I should take the initiative and let them follow my lead?" Xu's sister said, "That's about right. Xiaojing, do you know what the highest level of massage is?" I asked, "Is it about helping them completely relax or releasing their desires?" Xu's sister smiled and said, "Your understanding is one-sided. The highest level of massage is not about massaging the body but massaging the soul!" I was puzzled and asked, "How do you massage the soul?" Xu's sister smiled and said, "Even as massage therapists, we must understand psychology. When you massage a customer, don't be silent. Instead, be proactive and engage in conversation. The massage itself is a form of communication. You can feel whether the customer is enjoying it or being indifferent, whether they are happy or troubled through their reactions. Sometimes, a single sentence from you can have a more significant and immediate effect than half an hour of massage. It can make them feel comfortable and happy." Xu's sister's words were like a beam of sunlight in the fog or a bright moonlight shining into a dark room, illuminating my heart. Yes, if massage therapists become friends with the customers, if we can share their burdens and worries, then massage takes on a more positive meaning, opening up a broader world and bringing happiness.

Gratefully, I said, "Thank you, Xu sister, for your guidance. Your words have truly benefited me."

Ah Lan joked, "Ah Jing, you have great influence. Xu's sister even shared her most valuable techniques from her treasure trove of skills with you. I followed Xu's sister for several years, and she kept those techniques a secret from me." Xu's sister laughed, saying, "I feel a special connection with Ah Jing. She's such an intelligent and beautiful girl. She shouldn't just stay at the level of an ordinary massage therapist. I believe she will excel!" Although being a massage therapist is a profession I chose out of necessity, being valued by Xu's sister, a renowned figure in the field, filled me with pride and a sense of potential. Being a massage therapist may be stigmatized, but why can't I strive to improve? There's no need to equate massage therapists with a specific type of woman. We can not only embark on a path to wealth but also a path to enlightenment and happiness!

Chapter 8

Forget Shame

The environment one is in will have a significant influence on one. Although I had dreams in my heart, just like the customer with the surname Gao said, I wanted to become the princess of the sauna city, to be loved, respected, and gain more benefits. But how could I stay untainted in this murky environment? Sometimes I think about it. I work hard for a few hours giving massages, but Ah Fang and the others can make more money by visiting a room with a customer after work. It's unfair. What makes me inferior to them in terms of appearance, figure, temperament, and service attitude? In this sauna city, I have gradually become outstanding. They even envy me a little. But my income is much lower than theirs, not to mention the extra money. My salary and commission rank near the bottom. I'm climbing the stock market, gaining points but not making real money. Even though we all claim to be college students, their education level is probably lower than mine. I suspect some of them might not have even finished middle school. The way they talk and write is genuinely disappointing.

I have repaid the money I borrowed from Xiao Hong and Ah Lan. I revealed my current work situation to Xiao Hong when we went to bed that night. I told her I was doing well, but my income was low. I earned 1,500 yuan in the first month and felt good about it. But when I compare myself to others, I feel like a novice. I still need to buy new clothes, repay the money, and cover next month's living expenses. I have very little money left. I won't be able to send any back home for a few months. I still need to pay the rent and electricity bill to Sister Wu. Xiao Hong said, "You don't need to worry about the rent. Even if you give it to her, she won't accept it. This amount of money is nothing for Sister Wu. It's not even enough for her to buy a bra." I said, "Thanks to Sister Wu for taking me in, but I still feel indebted to her. It doesn't sit well with me." Xiao Hong laughed and said, "It's fine. Sister Wu is good to fellow villagers. The person who stayed here before you was also her fellow villager. It's not easy outside, so we should support and keep each other company."

I suddenly remembered what Sister Wu told me last time and asked Xiao Hong, "Before you came here, did you sleep with men?" Xiao Hong was puzzled by my question and asked, "Why do you ask?" I said, "Sister Wu mentioned that a woman's first time can be sold at a high price. Is that true?" Xiao Hong laughed and said, "You're naive. Everyone knows about this. How many women nowadays wait until their wedding night? Either they give it to their lovers, or they sell it." I asked, "So, it's true. What about you? Did you give it away for free or sell it?" Xiao Hong said, "In our line of work, sooner or later, something will happen. Instead of being cheated, it's better to sell it at a good price. Initially, Sister Wu arranged for me to meet an older man who gave me 2,000 yuan. Sister Wu has been in this industry for a long time and knows many people. If you're willing, she can find a rich boss for you. What's the use of keeping it? It's better to sell it early and open the door for more customers."

You can make 2,000 yuan in one go? That's more than what I earn after working hard for a month! It sparked some interest in me. After all, there would be a first time sooner or later. Xiao Hong said, "Nowadays, girls who are pretty and still virgins past 20 are rare." Although I didn't quite agree, her words made me feel like keeping my virginity wasn't honorable but rather shameful. I thought about those online auctions for purity. It was truly outrageous. I just wanted to get something in return for it. Xiao Hong suggested, "You can talk to Sister Wu and ask her for help. You can sell it at a good price if there's an opportunity." I nodded, "Yes, Sister Wu will help me with that. She mentioned it to me before."

Xiao Hong said, "But I advise finding someone a bit older. Younger guys are inexperienced and reckless. They only care about their pleasure and don't care about your well-being. Older men, like married men in their thirties or middle-aged businessmen in their forties and fifties, understand the value of a woman's first time. They will cherish you and be generous." At that moment, I began to fantasize. It would be a process of transforming from a girl to a woman, and I would earn a substantial amount of money. It seemed like a win-win situation. Xiao Hong added, "It might be a bit painful the first time, but as long as the man isn't forceful, you endure it for a while, and it will pass. Some experienced men can even make you feel comfortable." I curiously asked, "You can feel comfortable even when a man is on top of you?" Xiao Hong laughed, saying, "Yes, it's hard to explain. It's like being in a cloud or having an itch, and someone vigorously scratches it. Doesn't that feel good?"

The next day at noon, I bought some cooked dishes and a bottle of red wine to treat Sister Wu and Xiao Hong. It was the first time I was treating someone because I didn't have money before. Although I had never drunk alcohol, I knew Sister Wu and Xiao Hong did. Sometimes when they returned from work, I could smell alcohol on their breath. Sister Wu smiled and asked, "Xiao Jing, why suddenly try to please me? Do you need something from me?" I smiled and said, "You have taken care of me a lot. It's only right for me to express my gratitude to you now that I have received my salary." Sister Wu said, "Oh, your salary? How much did you receive?" I said, "1,500 yuan. Is that alright?" Sister Wu smiled and said, "Just 1,500 yuan? Did you earn any extra money?" Xiao Hong said, "She's too honest. She stays at home during the day or goes online. How could she earn extra money?"

1,500 yuan was quite good. In the factories back in my hometown, I would only earn five to six hundred yuan per month, so I considered myself better off. But from how Sister Wu and Xiao Hong spoke, it seemed they looked down on that amount. Sister Wu said, "Xiao Jing, you're smart, but 1,500 yuan is nothing. If you do well, you can earn 1,500 yuan in just one encounter." I was eager to learn and quickly asked, "Sister Wu, how can I earn more money?" Sister Wu said, "Aren't you planning to go online? When men see your appearance on the webcam, they swarm toward you like bees. You can arrange to meet them, have a meal together, and if you're willing, you can go to a room with them. You can easily make a few hundred yuan each time." I felt worried and said, "I'm afraid of meeting strangers. I've heard they kill many girls who meet people online." Sister Wu took a sip of wine and laughed, "In today's society, the daring ones will survive, and the timid ones will starve. You're too conservative. Didn't the central leadership advocate for progress and reaching new heights? If you remain conservative, won't you be left behind? We're not home anymore, so what's there to worry about?"

Xiao Hong interjected, "Sister Wu, Xiao Jing is still a virgin. She wouldn't casually fool around. Maybe you can find a way for her. Why don't you introduce her to a big boss? What's the point of keeping it? It's better to sell it early and attract customers." Sister Wu looked at me and said, "You organized this meal today for that, right? Why didn't you say so earlier? Some of my clients have already reserved a virgin half a year in advance. Tomorrow, I'll arrange for you to meet one!" I was both shocked and delighted. I was about to lose the pride that girls cherished—their virginity. But at the same time, I could let go of my worries and earn more money! I shyly said, "Sister Wu, is it possible?" Sister Wu said, "In this world, anything is possible as long as you desire it. Xiao Jing, are you in your safe period these days?" I nodded, "I just finished my period the day before yesterday." Sister Wu smiled and said, "Then get ready. Tomorrow, I'll accompany you to meet the client."

I had seen men before and knew that thing of theirs could be flexible and long, but when it got hard, it felt like a little iron rod. The thought of it entering my body made me a bit scared. Xiao Hong laughed and said, "Xiao Jing, from now on, you must always carry three things. Don't be careless and forget them." I was puzzled and asked, "What three things?" Sister Wu said, "Contraceptive pills, condoms, and tissues. These three small things are indispensable." Xiao Hong said, "When you're with a man, whether you're in your safe period or not, you must make sure he wears a condom to prevent any diseases from being transmitted to you. If you have some regular customers who don't like using condoms and you're certain they are healthy, you can go without them, but you must remember to take the contraceptive pill to avoid pregnancy. As for the tissues, I don't need to explain their purpose, right? Afterward, you must clean up properly; otherwise, it will feel sticky and uncomfortable."

We were discussing these things while having a meal, and we even had smiles. It was pretty unbelievable, but that's how it was. I decided to sell my first time for a reasonable price, and they were my best allies. Later, I found out the truth that day. The price for my first time wasn't 3,000 yuan, as Sister Wu had said; it was 8,000 yuan! Sister Wu had secretly kept 5,000 yuan for herself.

Chapter 9

Unforgettable First Time

We arrived at a luxurious hotel in Huzhou, and Sister Wu told me, "I won't accompany you inside. He's waiting in Room 502. Call my phone when you're done." I nodded nervously and walked into the lobby without paying attention to the disdainful gaze of the receptionist. I headed straight to the elevator and went up to the fifth floor. In the corridor, I found the door to Room 502, adjusted my clothes, lowered my head, and lightly knocked on the door.

Seemingly, the person inside was waiting behind the door. When I knocked twice, the door silently opened, revealing a refined middle-aged man. I smiled faintly and said, "Mr. Zhang, hello!" Mr. Zhang had an amiable smile. He said, "Hello, please come in!" Since I had come this far, I wasn't afraid anymore and followed him into the room. I noticed that he was tall and much taller than me. His shoulders were broad and reminded me of my father. His face was handsome, and if it weren't for my personal experience, I couldn't imagine that such a dignified middle-aged man could also be the type to seek pleasure.

He picked up a bottle of Farmer's Orchard from the table and politely handed it to me, saying, "It's hot weather. Are you thirsty?" I accepted it and said, "Thank you," but I didn't drink it. I feared he might have tampered with the drink, like adding drugs. What if he drugged me, and I fell into trouble as a weak woman? He seemed to sense my suspicion and chuckled, "Are you afraid that I will harm you? Do you think I'm that kind of person?" I spoke frankly, "In today's world, it's hard to tell. Faces don't have words written on them. Who knows who's good or bad?" He laughed and said, "Good, I really like your straightforwardness. It's much better than those dishonest people."

I sat on the edge of the bed, feeling a bit uneasy, wondering how he would start with me. Mr. Zhang asked, "Do you want to watch TV?" Since I felt bored just sitting there, I nodded. Mr. Zhang picked up the remote and turned on the TV, revealing a smile. He said, "It's so hot. Would you like to take a shower?" I wanted to calm my mood and accept the impending reality, so I said, "Sure, I'll go wash up." I took off my outer shirt and skirt in front of him. Everything may become natural with habit. Ever since I became a massage girl, undressing in front of men has become as casual as doing it at home. As I walked towards the bathroom, I caught a glimpse of his gaze upon me—a look of satisfaction and appreciation. I hoped this man would be gentle with me.

In the bathroom, the water from the tap was at a constant temperature. I showered using the handheld showerhead. Hotels have a mixed crowd, so if you bathe in the bathtub and the person who used it before had any diseases, or if the hotel's disinfection wasn't thorough, there's a chance of infection for the person who bathes afterward. Therefore, girls usually choose safety showers, as water doesn't enter the body. After about ten minutes of washing, I dried myself with a towel and put on my panties. I didn't wear a bra since my breasts were firm and didn't sag. I thought that sometimes I had to take off my clothes during an oil massage, so I was practically naked at this moment.

Returning to the room, I felt the pleasant temperature. The air conditioning had cooled it down just right. I saw Mr. Zhang lying on the bed, covered by a thin towel. His shirt and pants, which he had taken off, were on the nearby chair. I hesitated briefly but eventually walked to his side, blushing and smiling. A towel covered my lower body, and I leaned against him. Although the room felt comfortable, like spring, I could still feel the warmth emanating from Mr. Zhang. He turned his head slightly, glanced at me, and skillfully reached out his arm to embrace me. I said, "Do you want to take a shower?" Mr. Zhang shook his head and said, "I already did."

After a period of adjustment since entering the room, my mood had calmed down. I knew what was about to happen and was prepared to accept it. I obediently nestled in his embrace, like a daughter embracing her father affectionately. With his other hand, he caressed my body, and the breath that escaped his mouth smelled of Green Arrow chewing gum. His hand lingered on my chest, gently exploring my breasts. When his hand gripped my breast, I heard him exclaim, "Hmm, you're so beautiful!" Perhaps he had touched many women's breasts, but his compliment still made me smile. After all, which woman doesn't enjoy a man's praise? He said, "Your skin is so smooth, like the silk from our Jiangnan region." His eyes were filled with admiration and affection, different from the sensuality of the clients in the massage parlor. This gave me a new understanding of men.

I was glad that this middle-aged man was genuinely lovely. If he had acted like a wild beast from the beginning, I would have been frightened and felt scared. I preferred his gentle and refined approach, and I was willing to accept and cooperate with it. To showcase my massage skills and make the subsequent intimate process easier for both of us, I made a move and said, "Please lie down." Mr. Zhang misunderstood my intention and asked, "Are we starting now?" I smiled and replied, "Please lie down, and you'll find out."

Mr. Zhang lay flat on the bed, and I uncovered the towel, revealing his well-maintained body. His abdomen wasn't protruding like some bosses. There was a slight bulge between his thighs, and it was apparent that he wasn't fully aroused yet. I later learned that middle-aged men are generally slow to warm up. There's a process from attraction to impulse, unlike some young people who quickly charge into battle and lose interest just as fast. But middle-aged men also have their advantages. They have good skills and endurance. They understand women's psychology and know what women need. They excel at bringing women to the peak of pleasure. This might be the difference between "skillful and brutal" experiences. Based on my later experience, I preferred enjoying the care and consideration of middle-aged men. I didn't particularly like the immaturity and rudeness of young men.

If the client is sitting, I usually start by massaging the neck. Now that he was lying down, I planned to start with his feet. The feet not only serve the purpose of walking but also significantly impact the human body. Many older people's rheumatism is caused by the invasion of cold in the feet. Soaking your feet in warm water before sleeping can bring comfort, calm the mind, and improve sleep quality. Those thriving foot massage parlors have their existence justified, apart from exaggerations and false claims. Foot massage indeed helps with relaxation and healing. In our sauna room, we usually start with the feet in massages and then move upward to the legs, abdomen, waist, hands, neck, etc. Since the feet are the farthest from the heart, their nerve endings and blood circulation aren't very flexible, so they require massage to activate them. Sister Xu mentioned that some massage parlors perform full-body massages from top to bottom. Different places have different training methods, just like other martial arts schools—Wudang and Shaolin.

I massaged Mr. Zhang's body, alternating between light and firm pressure. I was attentive and dedicated. He was my client, and today, he was a particular client who paid a price far higher than the regular "special services" in the massage parlor. It was only natural and willing that I provided him with better service. I said, "Mr. Zhang, you must be very busy with work, right?" Mr. Zhang replied, "Yes, I'm busy every day, to the point of being overwhelmed. It's rare for me to have the opportunity to relax." I was just casually chatting with him to help him relax without trying to verify the truthfulness of what he said. I continued, "According to Sister Wu, the mall you manage is famous in Huzhou. It shows that your management skills are excellent, right?" A man, like a child, usually enjoys compliments. A smile appeared on his face as he said, "Yes, in Huzhou's commercial system, it can be considered one of the best." I added, "You must be working very hard, then?" While engaging in casual conversation with Mr. Zhang, I didn't neglect the massage at all.

I could feel that Mr. Zhang was utterly enjoying the massage. He had an expression of pure pleasure. He must be wholeheartedly savoring my massage movements. When I massaged his lower abdomen, my thumbs and index fingers applied slight pressure on either side of his "manhood," albeit through his underwear. I saw his heated reaction, but I didn't remove his underwear, and he didn't make any obvious moves. When I leaned over his head with my upper body and massaged his shoulders, I noticed his passionate gaze. I realized his inner desire. I asked gently, "Are you feeling comfortable?" Mr. Zhang nodded,

"Mmm, very comfortable!"

If I had completed this series of movements in a massage room, and the client still had other needs, the next step would naturally be to provide an oil massage. However, Mr. Zhang wasn't just interested in an oil massage; he wanted to indeed "invade" me. My first time was about to begin. I knew that Mr. Zhang was ready to take action at this moment, like a bird about to take flight. In my heart, I had a mix of anxiety and anticipation. Whatever was coming, I would face it without regrets. Since I had made my choice, I had to confront reality.

Indeed, before I could finish the final massage movement, Mr. Zhang opened his arms and embraced me, pulling me onto his body. I felt his heavy breaths, and he kissed my face anxiously. He found my lips and explored them with his palm pressed against my head. I didn't resist; I thought this man had gained a lot already. He had taken my virginity and my body! Ironically, my first kiss had become a "buy one, get one free" deal in the shopping mall. In return, he bought my body and also received my first kiss! Oh my, how did it come to this?

While he kissed me, his other hand glided across my smooth back. I didn't experience the electrifying feeling described in novels; it felt comfortable, like a small hand cradled in a warm palm, exuding a sense of paternal tenderness. I slipped to his side, and he freed one hand to stroke my smooth lower abdomen. It gradually warmed my heart. There seemed to be a fuse he had found there, and under his teasing, I started to feel a vague desire. I thought, "If it's going to happen, just let it happen. Let's get started!"

Mr. Zhang removed his underwear and mine, and now I was completely exposed in front of him. The moment had arrived, and I didn't feel any fear. Instead, I felt a sense of heroic sacrifice. I secretly glanced down and saw that he was already very aroused, and I thought I was already wet as if drenched by rain. I wasn't confused and remembered Xiao Hong's advice to prioritize safety. I reached out my hand and found a small packet near the bed. I opened it and took out a condom. Believe it or not, although I had it with me, I had never used one before. In other words, I had no idea how to put it on a man's thing.

Mr. Zhang noticed what I was holding in my hand and swiftly took it from me, tossing it to the other side of the bed. I heard him pleadingly say, "Little sister, don't use it today, okay? Let me experience the feeling of being with a virgin. Please, let me know the taste of a virgin, okay?" He, a respected mall executive, must be accustomed to giving orders to his subordinates, and he was almost the same age as my father. Yet here he was, speaking to me in a pleading tone. I couldn't bear to refuse him! Perhaps he wanted that genuine feeling, unobstructed by a thin layer. I silently consented to his actions, stretching my body as much as possible to welcome his fiery invasion through my passageway...

Chapter 10

Gentleness in Middle Age

The refined and gentle nature of the middle-aged man, Mr. Zhang, was fully reflected in his actions. He was meticulous until I relaxed and slowly adapted to him. I couldn't help but feel a bit nervous as Zhang approached the untouched and sacred place within me. With his hands supporting him, he seemed reluctant to transfer his weight onto me. Every time I opened my eyes, I could see his plump face. I could feel his strength and warmth, and I wanted to accommodate him like a welcoming king, but his repeated attempts failed to breach my defense.

Instead of getting angry or embarrassed, Mr. Zhang remained patient and kissed my face while I gently closed my eyes. I knew that I belonged to him, and at this moment, I wanted to complete the mission and return to work as soon as possible. There was always a sense of shame in a straightforward transaction.

The attraction between the opposite sexes is a natural phenomenon. I, too, had some desires and longings deep within my mind and body, waiting to be fulfilled. Timidly and confusedly, I said, "You can go ahead!" Mr. Zhang, acting like a general receiving the charging order, moved toward me. I felt his forceful advance while my heart resisted and welcomed him at the same time. Mr. Zhang suddenly whispered, "Relax, don't be nervous. Every girl has to go through the first time." I let out a soft moan as I felt him forcefully enter me, experiencing a momentary sharp pain that felt like a knife cutting through me. I couldn't help but exclaim, "Ouch!" My cry of pain flashed like a red traffic light, causing him to stop abruptly!

Mr. Zhang was panting heavily, and I felt drops of sweat from his forehead land on my face. I didn't know if he was nervous, excited, or tired. Nevertheless, he didn't withdraw but remained inside me. Strangely, the pain I felt only lasted a moment and quickly disappeared. Mr. Zhang noticed my expression wasn't one of agony and softly asked, "Can I continue?" I didn't answer or object; I silently consented to his continued "violation."

Gradually, I began to experience the pleasurable sensation Xiao Hong had described—the comforting feeling of being "tickled." My body trembled involuntarily, yearning for his thrusts and pressure. I wondered if I was being debased. But then I thought, isn't the fusion between a man and a woman meant to be enjoyed rather than endured? Don't parents also experience this to bear children? I finally understood why Adam and Eve in mythology couldn't resist the temptation of the forbidden fruit.

After a while, I felt like I was about to float away. Faced with Mr. Zhang's attack, I didn't retreat but felt a sense of entanglement. Mr. Zhang seemed to understand my excitement and continued pursuing me relentlessly. I felt like I was swinging on a swing, exhilarating and liberated. Suddenly, I felt a shudder from him and sensed a rush of heat inside me! I went weak momentarily, clutching the bedsheet tightly as my boiling emotions gradually subsided.

Mr. Zhang lay beside me, his warm palm caressing my face as he whispered, "You're so beautiful! I won't forget you!" Sister Xu mentioned that it was a one-time transaction in this line of work. Continuing contact with clients would only lead to complications, as they might demand more from future encounters due to their higher initial payment. Moreover, men's words in bed often need to be more reliable. Regardless of whether he genuinely wouldn't forget me, I decided not to meet him again.

I got up and cleaned up the battlefield, and Mr. Zhang also sat up. He looked at the bedsheet stained with my blood and smiled happily. He put the money back into his wallet and then took out a business card, which he handed me sincerely, saying, "This is my business card. If you encounter any difficulties, feel free to find me. I believe I can help you." I took the business card and said, "It has your work and home phone numbers. Aren't you afraid that I'll inform your wife?" Mr. Zhang chuckled and said, "I trust you're not that kind of person, and you told me your true identity. It's just a gesture of goodwill." I hesitated and said, "This is too much. I'll take 100 yuan." I took one bill and returned the rest to him.

Mr. Zhang didn't insist and took the money, putting it back in his wallet. Then he took out an envelope and handed it to me, saying, "This is for you." I wondered if it was another gift. He took out a stack of 100-yuan bills and handed them to me, saying, "This is 3,000 yuan for you." Confused, I said, "But Sister Wu said you already paid." Mr. Zhang smiled and said, "I did pay. Consider this a tip for your massage services." I hurriedly said, "It's not necessary. It's what I should do." Mr. Zhang smiled faintly and said, "I know life is tough for you. Consider this a small token of my appreciation. Please accept it." I hesitated and said, "This is too much. I only need 100 yuan." I took one bill and returned the rest to him.

Mr. Zhang didn't insist and put the money back in his wallet. Then he took a business card and handed it to me, saying sincerely, "This is my business card. If you encounter any difficulties, feel free to find me. I believe I can help you." I took the business card and glanced at it mischievously, saying, "It has your work and home phone numbers. Aren't you afraid that I'll inform your wife?" Mr. Zhang laughed and said, "I trust that you're not that kind of person, and you told me your true identity. It's just a gesture of goodwill." I was ready to bid farewell and said, "Mr. Zhang, I should go now." He pointed at the bedsheet stained with my blood and said, "What a pity. I can't take this bedsheet with me as a lasting memento. Can I see you again, Xiaojing?" I didn't answer, and I couldn't answer. Who knew what would happen after today? Huzhou and Nanxun were close. Who could say that we wouldn't meet again?

Leaving the hotel and walking on the street, I called Sister Wu. She appeared beside me in no time, seemingly out of nowhere. Sister Wu asked, "How did it go? Smoothly?" I smiled but didn't say anything. Sister Wu continued, "There's nothing significant about it. With your first time behind you, you won't have any concerns in the future." We hailed a taxi and quickly returned to Nanxun. When we arrived at our place, Sister Wu took 3,000 yuan from her bag and handed it to me, saying, "This is yours. Keep it." I took the money and counted 1,000 yuan, handing it back to Sister Wu, saying, "Thank you for taking care of me. This 1,000 yuan is to show my gratitude."

Sister Wu pushed the money away and said, "Why be polite? We're sisters. Don't be formal with me. I'm here to help you, and it's only right. No need for these formalities!" Sister Wu firmly refused the 1,000 yuan I offered, so I hid the "selling myself money" of 3,000 yuan in an envelope under the bed. I plan to buy a mobile phone with the remaining money and send the rest home tomorrow. It was time for me to go to work, and as I was locking the door, Sister Wu said to me, "Xiaojing, did you take the necessary precautions?" I knew Sister Wu was referring to condoms and contraceptives. I said, "He didn't want to use them, so I didn't. Do I need to take the pill?" Sister Wu said, "Just in case, you should take one. An accident could harm your health, and you might even lose your job!"

Chapter 11

Helpless Descent

I deliberately went to the pharmacy and bought a box of Yuting, a contraceptive pill said to be effective within 72 hours after intercourse. But as soon as I left the pharmacy, I suddenly remembered that I was in the safe period of my menstrual cycle and didn't need any protection. It turned out I was worrying for no reason. Well, it's always good to be prepared. I don't know how others feel after their first time. I only remember from novels and movies that the female protagonists had a face full of pain. But I didn't feel any pain at all. On the contrary, I felt very relaxed, like a butterfly after breaking free from its shackles. I was beaming with happiness, feeling as light as a butterfly.

I eagerly and thoughtfully served the customers, speaking softly and attentively. Ah Lan took care of my business, and I already had regular customers. Mr. Gao, whom I served last time, kept his promise and brought a group of friends who specifically requested my massage. But I only provided full-body oil massage to one person, and my sisters took care of the others. The first customer I served in the massage parlor was a middle-aged man, and I hadn't seen him since then. It was strange how deep an impression he left on me. At that time, I was completely clueless, just randomly stepping on his back, but he didn't blame me and even gave me a tip. I was deeply grateful for his generosity.

Tonight, for the first time, I also tried chest massage. It was tiring, but luckily, I was in a great mood, and it went smoothly. Not only was the customer satisfied, but I was also proud of myself. In our sauna city, many massage services have a sexual undertone. Even if it's not explicit, there's a teasing element. Like today's chest massage, it was quite stimulating, and I could barely contain myself.

Among us sisters, a little rhyme goes, "A jade won't be polished without carving, a knife won't be sharp without grinding, and a chest won't be beautiful without being touched." It's a playful way to refer to chest massage. Tonight's customer was a man in his forties, a private business owner, and he had a sturdy physique, probably weighing around 180 patties (90 kilograms). Perhaps because of his weight, his skin was elastic, and my breasts glided smoothly and gracefully on his body, like playing the piano. My emotions rose and fell with every movement. A man his age must have become indifferent to women's charms, but when he saw my body, he still exclaimed, "You have a well-proportioned and sexy figure, truly a rare beauty!" At that time, I didn't fully understand what he meant by "rare beauty." Later, I learned that men use an adjective to describe a woman's stunning and seductive appearance.

I've always been confident about my figure, especially my breasts. They're not something I'm proud of, but they are well-shaped. When I go to bed at night, I caress my breasts to promote blood circulation in the erectile tissue. When I used my warm breasts to perform the massage on the customer, not only did the customer feel comfortable, but I also felt good. When taking a bath, rubbing the body with a towel feels refreshing, but using breasts to massage the skin is much more interesting. My touch and pressure were just right, teasing the skin like grass brushing against it, creating an itchy sensation that reached the heart, making me want to sing.

Initially, I thought of myself as a massage girl serving others passively. But when I entirely devoted myself to the job, I realized that while serving others, I also experienced happiness and a sense of accomplishment. When the customer was satisfied, I was comfortable too. It was mutual. Of course, the higher level is what Sister Xu calls "mental massage," which I haven't achieved yet, but I will strive for it. In my subsequent experiences, I learned that men don't like women who are too proactive or passive. Being too proactive makes them feel pressured, while being too sedentary is like being with a wooden person, lacking excitement.

The main part of chest massage is the finishing touch, using breasts to stimulate and extract his "oil." I wasn't skilled in this massage service and had to put in much effort. It took me nearly half an hour, using various teasing techniques, to finally make him unable to endure any longer and ejaculate like a slaughtered pig. Because chest massage also involves skin-to-skin contact, even though it's only the upper body, there can be some emotional fluctuations during the massage. But as a service provider, I had to restrain myself and eliminate sexual intent. In a legitimate massage, whether it's male or female service providers, it's part of professional ethics not to have any "wayward thoughts."

Through conversations with this customer, I learned that he was from Jiaxing and ran a thriving luggage factory. Although I hadn't been to Jiaxing, I knew that according to history books, the first National

Congress of the Chinese Communist Party was held on a boat on the South Lake in Jiaxing during the White Terror period. They say that the ship is still there. He said his surname was Gu, and his relationship with his wife was average. Sometimes, when they got bored, they would go to entertainment venues for recreation, but he had never hired prostitutes. He found them dirty, so he preferred going to the sauna for erotic massages, where he could find release for his body and mind. I somewhat understood men of his age. They had to support their families and businesses, and after being married for over ten years, their wives usually lost their allure and attractiveness. So, despite their outward success, they also felt frustrated deep inside. In the massage room, there were no ulterior motives, deceit, hierarchy, or age barriers. There were only men and women who were strangers to each other, and they could freely express their frustrations to me. At least at that moment, they could treat me as a friend.

Who can resist the temptation of money? Seeing my sisters coming back with smiles after going out with customers now and then, I couldn't help but feel a little restless. In the following days, I boldly decided to join the ranks and make some extra money. I was no longer a virgin, and there was no practical difference between once and a hundred times. Besides, I had already entered the massage business, so pretending innocent was pointless.

Most importantly, I needed money. Who wouldn't get along with money? When I massaged customers, I would give them my newly purchased mobile phone number if they showed interest in me and wanted to pursue further relationships. I planned to develop my business and earn more money based on my image and excellent service. It shouldn't be a difficult task to improve my life and provide some financial support for my family.

Soon, several customers contacted me, inviting me to dinners and tea. I knew their intentions weren't about food or drinks; they wanted to sleep with me. I chose those who looked pleasing to my eyes and had conversations with them, knowing that they were financially well-off. After dressing up carefully, I willingly went on these dates. Sometimes we went to hotel rooms, and other times to apartments or villas. They achieved what they wanted, and I got what I deserved. Due to my night shift work, I only met clients every few days. I wasn't willing to be with just any man. The clients I "targeted" were mostly men in their thirties or older, primarily wealthy private business owners who enjoyed having fun. Some men wanted to maintain a long-term arrangement with me or have me as a short-term lover, but I refused. I knew engaging in such transactions might bring me a large sum of money quickly, but it would also make me lose more dignity and freedom.

It is ridiculous to say that a massage girl has dignity. Does sleeping with men come with dignity? I believe it does. We massage girls, and those self-righteous clients are equal in terms of personal satisfaction. No one has the right to insult us. If the "seller" is considered lowly, then the "buyer" is equally lowly! In the past, there were Li Xiangjun, Liu Rushi, and Dong Xiaowan—weren't they courtesans? But who didn't admire them? We cannot spend our whole lives in this profession. We entered this place for specific reasons and at a particular stage. We also hope to have an everyday life, to experience love, and to have a happy family. The despicable ones are those men who, on the surface, pretend to be upright and look down on us, but in reality, they use their own and public money to indulge in debauchery and corruption. We are just withering flowers and willows; they are even more despicable than us!

Chapter 12

The Rogue Wu Fang

I didn't work hard to earn more money. Including my side income, I only socialized a few times a month. I know money is a good thing and need it, but I'm not foolish enough to sell my blood and work myself to death for money. Women need maintenance, especially those of us in this line of work. Working night shifts, our sleep and rest are not adequately guaranteed. If we recklessly squander our youth, we will age quickly. After a few years, we will look haggard and unrecognizable. I refuse to engage in such a losing business. I would instead take on fewer clients during work and avoid being too exhausted. For example, doing chest massages only earns us around ten yuan, disproportionate to our effort. It's less profitable than doing full-body oil massages, although sometimes we have to sacrifice a bit of modesty by taking off our clothes. But there's no harm in letting them have a look.

My skin has become thicker and thicker. I can undress in front of men without batting an eye. It's not that I can't pretend to be innocent, but I don't want to. Why should people wear masks in their lives? Some may say I lack self-respect, but have you ever considered my situation? If I didn't have to worry about food and shelter if I had a secure life, why would I come out to work? Why should I lower my head and be submissive? You're just talking nonsense, saying it without experiencing it! I don't need cheap sympathy; I need your understanding and respect! Every penny we earn is hard-earned. We are not like some officials who use their positions to embezzle money. We are not like some civil servants who receive various subsidies. We have low education, and it's difficult for us to find jobs. How can a meager 600 yuan monthly salary be enough if we work as dishwashers? Not to mention supporting our families! We must spend money on rent, meals, water, and electricity. Even a month's worth of sanitary pads costs several yuan! We still need to buy a few sets of clothes for washing. And there are various daily expenses. If we fall ill, it's even worse. A minor cold or flu requires us to spend dozens of yuan visiting the hospital. Who will reimburse us? How do you think we should live? I'm not complaining; I hope that everyone can understand our difficulties. We also have siblings. No one wants to degrade themselves and become a massage girl willingly. It's a last resort. Once I earn enough money, I will wash my hands and return home to be a good girl!

Today, Wu Fang asked for a week off. Others didn't know the reason, but I did. She secretly told me last night that she had developed small bumps in her private area, which was slightly painful and itchy. She took off her underwear in the bathroom and showed me. I saw many red and white bumps there. I knew that if these bumps were on her face, they would be pimples. What are they when they appear in the genital area? Wu Fang told me that recently she had been quite active outside, and some men refused to wear condoms. She hadn't insisted, and now she was afraid of getting some sexually transmitted disease, especially the dreadful AIDS. She heard that there were still many people getting infected with it. I comforted her and said, "This must be a minor issue. Go to the hospital tomorrow to get it checked. Then you'll know." Since becoming a massage girl and having relationships with clients, I have been taking my health very seriously. I bought several books on physiology and sexually transmitted diseases from the bookstore. I know that the initial symptoms of AIDS are similar to a cold—fever, dizziness, and weakness. Wu Fang's condition seemed more like genital warts. I told her, "You should go to the hospital for treatment as soon as possible. Take a few days off until you recover, then return to work."

Wu Fang's incident, although it was just a minor issue and there were no significant problems, served as a warning to me. I stayed clean for more than half a month. When clients contacted me, I refused them because I did not feel well. It was already deep autumn of this year. I had been in Nanxun Town for four months and had saved nearly 20,000 yuan. Of course, I wouldn't have had that much if it was just my salary. The primary income came from socializing. I agreed with clients on a price of 1,000 yuan per session within three hours. I knew my worth. After all, I had just entered this line of work and had an excellent physical condition and decent appearance. The critical parts were still tight. I couldn't be compared to those women who walk along the main road, catering to all kinds of people.

I wanted to distinguish myself from the girls in roadside shops by setting a higher price. They only charge one or two hundred yuan per session, some even as low as thirty or fifty yuan. But they mainly cater to migrant workers and low-income individuals. I targeted men who were at a moderate income level. They were willing to spend more. They were looking for quality rather than quantity. I considered myself somewhere between a respectable woman and a prostitute. We are a means of self-rescue in the face of life's difficulties. This world has no savior; we can only rely on ourselves. But we don't have capital; the only thing we can count as our capital is our youthful body. We utilize our grassland to attract investment and manage the "profit and loss" ourselves. We rely on ourselves. We should not be subject to much criticism. In real life, with all the fakes, evils, and horror, not to mention the opportunistic actions of specific individuals, are they not more despicable and shameless than us?

Wu Fang, the sister of Sister Wu, came over. She is one year younger than me and went to Guangdong last year to study beauty. She worked at a beauty salon there but returned home this year because she didn't have the capital to open her shop. Additionally, business in her hometown of Chongqing could have been better, so she came to live with her sister. Sister Wu introduced her to work at a beauty salon where the salary was based on commission. The beauticians receive 40% of the total spending when they wash customers' hair or provide beauty treatments, while the boss takes 60%. The beauty industry is highly competitive now, with low prices everywhere. Wu Fang earns about 1,500 yuan per month, similar to my salary. However, she gets paid daily rather than monthly. As a result, she spends the money she earns daily, and by the end of the month, she only has a few tens of yuan left.

Wu Fang lives in the room with me and Xiao Hong. She also bought a separate bed. Sister Wu lives alone. Xiao Hong and I know the reason. Sometimes she brings men home. Wu Fang is now aware of the situation. Living with us, she has learned what we do. She asked me secretly, "Do you make good money doing this? How much can you earn in a month?" I had no reason to lie to her, so I said, "I earn over 1,000 yuan in salary and over 2,000 yuan in side income." She exclaimed, "Wow, that's a lot! I want to do it too!" Sister Wu initially didn't want her sister to follow in our footsteps, but she couldn't resist

Wu Fang's insistence, so she let her join me in working at the Sea Paradise Sauna City. Sun, the boss of Sea Paradise, had a deep relationship with Sister Wu even before he opened the sauna city. Later, their relationship evolved from a romantic one to a business partnership. Several of the massage girls in Sea Paradise were either brought by Sister Wu from their hometown or recruited from other nightclubs. Of course, Sister Wu, as the "professional intermediary," didn't do it for free; she received a referral fee.

In January 2004, Wu Fang experienced a similar incident to mine one afternoon. Sister Wu sold her virginity to a cloth merchant from Wujiang for 5,000 yuan. However, Wu Fang's client was a shop owner from the Oriental Silk Market. He had a low education level and was quite rough in his actions, which resulted in tearing and injuring her private area. Wu Fang was so much pain that she was gritting her teeth and hated the man. She would have fought back long ago if it weren't for the 5,000 yuan he paid! Wu Fang wasn't as good-looking as me, but the price she received for her first time was higher than mine. I felt a bit dissatisfied. Later, I discovered my price was 8,000 yuan, but Sister Wu had skimmed off 5,000 yuan.

From then on, Wu Fang became unrestrained. She was bolder and more open than me. In the massage rooms of the sauna city, she would quickly agree on a price with the clients and then go to a hotel with them after finishing work late at night, without returning to our place. I advised her to moderate her actions and not engage with men so frequently, but Wu Fang said, "Why not make money when we have the chance? I want to seize every moment to earn big money. Otherwise, no one will want me when I'm old!" Wu Fang bought a VCD player and watched adult films with great interest. She told Xiao Hong and me, "Foreigners are so open!" Wu Fang learned massage techniques from me. Although I only knew the basics, I kept some of the "massages of the soul" I learned from Sister Xu. Perhaps it takes a certain level of comprehension for anything. I considered myself reasonably insightful, so that I could understand some of Sister Xu's insights. However, Wu Fang was different from me. She treated massage as a stepping stone for making money. In the massage rooms, she only focused on the clients. The so-called massage was just an excuse to touch the sensual parts of men.

But Wu Fang's business was not less than mine because most clients were there to have fun. They were delighted when they encountered Wu Fang, who was direct and straightforward. Massage became an excuse for those men. They specifically requested Wu Fang for a massage because they were attracted to her body and wanted to have fun with her. On the other hand, I earnestly provided massages and only won the favor of a portion of honest clients. Once, when I was in the restroom, I unexpectedly found Wu Fang fooling around with a man inside. It was awkward for me, so I hurriedly exited and disturbed them. But they didn't care, which made me feel embarrassed. Another time, Wu Fang and I were in a couple's massage room, simultaneously providing massages to two men. My client made no special requests, so I continued wearing my uniform. However, Wu Fang's side was quite lively. During the client's warm-up, sitting on the client's lap while massaging is currently popular. Wu Fang seemed a bit impatient. She suddenly started dancing and made the client burst into laughter. It left me dumbfounded!

Chapter 13

Smiling Against the Illness

That day, I will never forget as long as I live. The memory of it wrenches my heart with pain. On the afternoon of January 18th, when I entered the second floor of the Sauna City, I saw many sisters gathered together, seemingly discussing something. When she saw me, Ah Fang rushed over with teary eyes and said, "Ah Jing, something bad happened!" Startled, I thought one of our sisters had been taken to the police station. I hurriedly asked, "Who? What happened?" Ah Fang didn't answer; instead, she burst into tears and hugged me tightly. I couldn't see Ah Lan, who was usually busy shuttling around the front desk. Where had she gone?

Ah Fang, Ah Lan, Ah Chun, and I were known as the "Four Beauties" among the girls. I glanced around and couldn't find Ah Lan or Ah Chun. Could they have also been caught? I gently patted Ah Fang's back and asked, "Is it Ah Lan who got into trouble?" She nodded while tears streamed down her face. I wondered why she was crying so much. After all, it was just a 5,000 yuan fine. Haven't you, Ah Fang, been taken in before? You didn't cry then, so why do you cry now that Ah Lan is in trouble? But I understood; our sisterly bond was deep. I said, "Does Manager Tian know? Let's quickly get her out!" Shaking her head while crying, Ah Fang said, "No, it's not that! Ah Lan is sick!" In our line of work, there's nothing scarier than hearing the word "sick." We either don't get sick or, if we do, it's never good news. But Ah Lan, as a manager who didn't have direct contact with the clients, how could she have been infected?

I said with some confusion, "If she's sick, she should go and get treatment. Where is she? Is she at the hospital?" Ah Fang stopped crying, and the sisters who were gathered around came closer. Seeing my puzzled expression, Ah Ju said, "Ah Jing, don't you know yet? Ah Lan felt dizzy today and went to the hospital for a check-up at noon. The doctor said she has uremia and is in danger!" What? Uremia? It felt like a bolt from the blue, and it stunned me! Isn't that a kidney problem? Isn't it something only men are related to? How can women get uremia too? I know people with uremia, and it's almost as serious as leukemia; in severe cases, it can be life-threatening. Ah Lan, such a kind girl, how did she suddenly get this dreadful disease?

I anxiously asked, "Which hospital is she in? I want to visit her!" Ah Fang replied, "She's at the town's health clinic, getting an IV drip. Manager Tian and Ah Chun are with her at the hospital." I said, "Then I'll go too! Manager Tian is at the hospital, and I'll ask him for leave." Ah Fang said, "Manager Tian has already taken care of it. After Ah Lan was admitted, he asked you and me to look after things temporarily here on the second floor. If you leave, I'm afraid I won't be able to manage it alone. If anything happens, the boss will blame me, and I can't afford that." I said, "Ah Lan is so seriously ill, and you want me to stay here? I can't focus!" Ah Fang said, "Ah Jing, don't worry. Let's go together after work."

January 18th, a day that sounded auspicious, as it rhymed with "want to prosper." However, fate could be so unfair. Ah Lan was in her early twenties, yet she was struck with such a disease. It was a fatal blow! Su Dongpo said, "Life is full of joys and sorrows, just like the moon's waxing and waning. Ancient times have shown that nothing is perfect." It seems to be true! The date seemed auspicious, and the Sauna City's business was surprisingly good. Customers kept coming, and the service girls on each floor ran around in a daze. During the day, several couples in formal attire and wedding gowns took photos on Nanxun's old streets to commemorate their happiness. In sharp contrast, Ah Lan had contracted uremia, a dreadful and hateful demon. Why did it have to target such a kind-hearted person?

The Lunar New Year was just a few days away. Our Sauna City would remain open until the eve, and everyone was busy bidding farewell to the old year and welcoming the new one. There was a surge in the number of people coming for baths. I couldn't take leave and return home for the New Year. It had been years since Sister Wu went back home too. She said, "Why bother going back? Getting train tickets is hard, and the trips are crowded and exhausting. I'll send money back home!" A few days ago, I sent twenty thousand yuan back home. My brother told me he had a girlfriend at the factory in Guangdong, a girl from Hunan who had come to work. If my brother gets engaged, they might marry soon. Our family is short of money; wasn't it my brother's hard-earned money that paid for my vocational school? Now that I can support myself, I'm sending money back home as a small token of appreciation.

Ah Lan's illness weighed heavily on my mind, and I was eager to visit her, but the work here was too busy to leave. When massaging the customers, I was absent-minded. Luckily, most customers knew me well; they knew my personality and skills. Seeing my troubled expression, they understood I had something on my mind and didn't blame me. Finally, when the workday ended, I pulled Ah Fang and hurried to the hospital. The supermarket and fruit shops had already closed, so we didn't buy anything and went directly to the hospital.

We first went to the inpatient department and consulted the on-duty doctor. The doctor said, "We conducted blood, urine, and kidney function tests. Combined with her clinical symptoms, we have tentatively diagnosed her with rapidly progressive nephritis, similar to acute uremia. This disease progresses aggressively and is very dangerous. Currently, there's no effective treatment. It would be best if you contacted her family. We asked her, but she wouldn't tell us, saying she didn't want her family to worry." Profound grief surged inside me. Ah Lan, a girl in the prime of her life, had just begun her journey, and now she had to endure such humiliation to survive. Now, her right to life was being cruelly taken away. Why did such misfortune befall Ah Lan? I couldn't believe what I was hearing!

I said, "Doctor, does she know about her condition?" The doctor replied, "She knows, but we haven't told her about the severity of the illness." I asked, "Is there hope for a cure? If there's hope, I want her to be transferred to a major hospital in the city." The doctor said, "Given her current condition, the outlook is grim no matter where she goes. Her life may not exceed half a year. If you don't believe it, I can help you arrange a transfer to hospitals in Hangzhou, Suzhou, or Shanghai." Upon hearing that Ah Lan only had half a year to live, Ah Fang burst into tears. I comforted her, "When we visit Ah Lan, you can't cry in front of her. We must give her confidence for a chance at a longer life." Though deeply saddened, I knew we had to face this with Ah Lan together if we were to have any hope of defeating the disease.

We found Ah Lan's bed when we arrived at the Intensive Care Unit on the second floor. She was lying there with an IV drip, and her eyes closed as if asleep. Ah Chun sat blankly beside her, lost in thought, while Manager Tian was not around. Ah Chun stood up when she saw us approaching. Afraid of waking Ah Lan, I whispered, "Is Ah Lan asleep? Did Manager Tian leave?" Ah Chun turned and gestured for us to step out of the ward. In the corridor, she sadly said, "The doctor said Ah Lan's condition is severe. What should we do?" I said, "Of course, we have to treat her! What did Manager Tian say?" Ah Chun explained, "Manager Tian said Ah Lan's illness is not considered a work-related injury and won't be covered by medical insurance. However, the sauna can provide 10,000 yuan as a compassionate gesture. Manager Tian paid the 5,000 yuan deposit for today's hospitalization." I muttered, "Such a ruthless business! How much money have we sisters earned for them? They won't even cover her medical expenses now that Ah Lan is sick. It's heartless!" Ah Fang said, "There's nothing we can do. The shop didn't provide medical insurance, so where can we claim?"

Ah Chun added, "Though we paid the 5,000 yuan deposit, the medical tests today were costly—blood tests, urine tests, kidney tests, and ultrasounds—quite a few things. The doctor already came to urge us about the remaining bAh Lance. It won't be enough by tomorrow, so we need to raise more money as soon as possible. The IV fluids being administered to Ah Lan are imported drugs, and each bottle of saline costs hundreds of yuan. It's been running all day, and it's still not finished. Manager Tian said he'd go raise more money and then left." I said, "Treating Ah Lan's illness may require a lot of money. She earned quite a bit over the past two or three years, but most of it was sent back home. Her mother's health isn't good, so we, her sisters, should help her a bit." Ah Chun asked, "How can we help?" I suggested, "We can take turns to take care of her, and we can each contribute some money. Maybe we can pool enough to help Ah Lan with her treatment and save her." Ah Fang and Ah Chun agreed, "Okay, I'm in!"

It was past two in the morning when the glucose drip was finally finished. When the nurse came to remove the IV needle, Ah Lan woke up. She saw the four of us and tried to sit up, but I quickly said, "Ah Lan, don't move. Just lie down." Ah Lan said, "Did you just finish work? Why aren't you resting at home? I'm fine, a few days' rest, and I'll be alright." I said, "We couldn't sleep knowing you were sick, so we came to see you." Ah Lan smiled and said, "Thank you!" The torment of the disease was astonishing. Ah Lan was still beautiful and lively yesterday, but now she appeared a bit pale and haggard. She would spend half a year lying on this hospital bed, and she might even leave this world. I couldn't help but feel sadness overwhelming me, and tears nearly welled in my eyes.

Ah Lan, my dear friend, why is your fate so unfortunate? I held her hand, unsure of how to comfort her. But she smiled and said, "It's alright; I'll be fine in a few days. When I called home a few days ago, my mom told me that a young man just returned from the army and wanted to meet me for a blind date. I plan to get better and meet that demobilized soldier. I've always respected soldiers. If he likes me, I won't work as a masseuse anymore. I'll go home and get married. You can come to my wedding as my bridesmaids." Hearing Ah Lan speak with a smile, my tears honestly couldn't be held back. Ah Fang and Ah Chun were also teary-eyed. I said, "Sure, we'll come! Ah Lan, you'll be the most beautiful bride in the world on that day!"

Chapter 14 Sistership in Times of Trouble

When the four of us were together, we could talk endlessly. While we couldn't chat during work hours, we sometimes had supper after finishing our shifts or went shopping together during the day. Those were the times when we were carefree and happy. But now, with Ah Lan falling ill, the "Beautiful Quartet" would be missing a beautiful leader, which truly saddened and worried us. We wanted her to rest well, but after waking up, she couldn't sleep anymore and insisted on us keeping her company. Ah Lan said, "I don't know what's happening to me. These past few days, I suddenly started feeling dizzy, my legs became swollen, and I felt weak overall. I came to the hospital for a check-up, and the doctor wanted me to be hospitalized for observation. I called Ah Chun, and she came immediately. Manager Tian also rushed here after hearing the news. The doctor asked for my family's contact number, but I didn't want to worry my parents, so I didn't give it to the doctor."

I wished we could always be so close and happy, but why did fate play such a cruel joke on us? I said, "Ah Lan, uremia requires rest and timely treatment. Don't worry too much, and stay in the hospital to recuperate. Believe that you will get better." Ah Lan replied, "Hospitalization costs a lot of money. I only have a little over 10,000 yuan in my account. I sent all the money back home, and my mother has been using it for medication." I said, "We all know that even though you are a leader, you have always treated us well. You have been frugal with your expenses. We are good sisters, so you don't need to worry about money. Ah Fang, I, and the others will figure something out." Ah Fang said, "Ah Lan, just focus on staying in the hospital and getting the necessary tests and treatment. We have been together for two years, just like sisters. If you encounter any difficulties, we will find a solution." Ah Lan smiled gratefully and said, "You all have been so kind to me. I'm sorry for causing trouble."

After midnight, when the glucose infusion was completed, Ah Lan needed to use the restroom. Ah Chun and I supported her as she got out of bed, but Ah Lan insisted, "I can walk on my own, no need to help." Ah Chun said, "Your legs are swollen, making walking difficult. Don't be stubborn." Inside the restroom, I noticed something unexpected. Ah Lan's urine wasn't clear or occasionally yellowish; it was milky white, like milk. I said, "Why is it this color? Could there be a problem?" Ah Lan smiled and said, "I noticed it a few days ago. How did I suddenly start producing milk? Ah Chun couldn't help but laugh and said, "This isn't milk, it's a sign of illness!" I laughed and said, "Ah Lan, what are you thinking? Are you a cow? This is a sign of nutrient loss! It's an illness!" Ah Lan protested with a smile, "Alright, Ah Jing, you call me abnormal. When I recover, I'll hold you accountable!" I laughed and said, "Sure, I'll be waiting."

None of us felt sleepy and spent the rest of the night chatting. In the morning, Ah Lan urged us to rest and said, "I'm fine. You all haven't slept all night. How can you work tonight? Falling asleep on the job will result in fines." I said, "Here's the plan. Let Ah Fang stay with you, and Ah Chun and I will return and rest. We'll take a short break in the morning, apply for leave in the afternoon, and come back to accompany you at night." Ah Chun said, "The Lunar New Year is coming soon, and the business at the sauna city must be busy these days. It might be difficult to get leave." I said, "It's only busy for these few days. After the New Year, we'll have a break until the eighth day of the new year. I'll talk to Manager Tian, and if we can't get leave, the three of us can switch shifts. We'll alternate between day and night shifts, so we can take turns to keep you company."

I left the hospital and didn't immediately go back to rest. Instead, I went to have noodles and bought some steamed buns and soy milk for Ah Fang and Ah Lan. When I returned to the ward, the doctor was making rounds. I asked about Ah Lan's condition, and the doctor said, "Her immune system and digestive function have weakened. Combined with electrolyte imbAh Lance, we will give her effective medication to eliminate viruses and provide nutrition. The patient may need to use the restroom frequently, so someone must always accompany her. Also, please go to the billing counter and pay some money to avoid discontinuing medication if the funds run out." Sigh, hospitals nowadays, like education, have become profit-driven institutions. They have downplayed their responsibility to save lives and heal the sick. Money is all they care about. They won't let you stay in the ward if you don't have money.

Ah Chun went back to rest first. Even though I hadn't slept all night, I didn't feel tired. I arrived at Sauna City, and as soon as I entered the front desk, Xiao Qin waved at me and called me over. She asked with concern, "I heard that Ah Lan has uremia. Is it true?" I nodded, "Yes, it's true. She's currently undergoing treatment at the hospital." Xiao Qin said, "I can't believe it. She was fine just a few days ago. How did she suddenly get so sick?" I said, "Yes, it's so sudden. Ah Lan is such a good person. No one expected her to fall ill." Upon hearing the news, the other receptionists expressed their sympathies as well. I said, "Thank you all for your concern about Ah Lan, but please don't act impulsively. Everyone should continue working as usual and not let Ah Lan's situation affect our work."

A girl named Ah Hui suggested, "Why don't we donate money to help her?" As soon as she mentioned it, many others responded, "Yes, let's donate money to help her get better and return to work soon!" They quickly returned to the locker room to fetch money, some giving 500 yuan, some 200 yuan, and some 100 yuan, all of which they handed me. Gratefully, I said, "Thank you all! Thank you for being so kind. Don't worry; let me register the donations." They said, "Why bother? We are all in the same boat. Helping her is only natural. We don't have much money now, but if we still fall short, we can donate again next time!" Though the amount wasn't large, their heartfelt solidarity weighed heavily on me.

I wasn't strong enough by myself, and I became anxious at the thought of Ah Lan's condition. I returned to Sister Wu's place, where she and Xiao Hong were having a meal. Seeing my worried expression, they both asked, "Xiao Jing, what's wrong? Have you eaten?" I said I couldn't eat, and Sister Wu said, "What's troubling you? Let's talk about it later. Come and have your meal for now." Xiao Hong also advised, "If something is bothering you, speak up. Keeping it inside isn't good. If you can't solve it alone, Sister Wu and I will help you." I told them about Ah Lan's illness and sadly said, "Ah Lan is only 23 years old. The doctor said she won't live more than six months. What can we do?" Xiao Hong said, "Fate is unpredictable. She has such a serious illness. Why didn't she go to a big hospital for treatment?" I said, "Big hospitals require a lot of money. Ah Lan sent all her earnings back home for her mother's medical expenses. We don't have money now. Can we watch her die?"

Sister Wu said, "Regardless of the effectiveness, it's better to go to a big hospital for treatment. They have better medical equipment and more skilled doctors. I have 5,000 yuan in cash here. Xiao Jing, please give it to her." Xiao Hong also said, "I have 3,000 yuan. Let's give it to her together." Sister Wu and Xiao Hong had no personal connection with Ah Lan and only saw her when she came to find me. For them to contribute such a substantial amount of money to help others deeply moved me. In the eyes of others, we might be lowly masseuses or dance hostesses in nightclubs, but we still possessed warm hearts and sincere love.

I withdrew 10,000 yuan from my bank account, added 8,000 yuan from Sister Wu and Xiao Hong, and the over 3,000 yuan donated by the sisters in the sauna city. We had more than 20,000 yuan to cover the medical expenses temporarily. In the afternoon, I paid the money into Ah Lan's hospital account and went to her ward. Ah Fang, Ah Chun, and several other sisters from our shift were there. Ah Lan tearfully said, "Thank you all so much. I never expected that when I fell ill, you would all be so concerned and worried for me. I'm sorry! Ah Jing, I have over 10,000 yuan here, which everyone brought. Can you go and deposit it?" I said, "The day shift sisters also gave me thousands of yuan, and Sister Wu and Xiao Hong, who live with me, also contributed. I've already paid it at the cashier's office. You can keep this 10,000 yuan for now, and we can deposit it in a few days."

Ah Lan said, "I'm sorry for causing you all trouble!" Ah Fang said, "Ah Lan, don't say that. We come from different places, but we can work together. Donating money to you is everyone's heartfelt gesture. Don't thank us; getting better is the most important thing." Ah Lan said, "Thank you all! You can go back to work now. Ah Fang will stay with me. It's almost the Lunar New Year, and I imagine the sauna city must be busy. Try your best to provide good service to the customers and let them have a joyful New Year."

Chapter 15

Desperate Doctoring

During the 2004 Spring Festival, the joyous celebrations were not for us. Ah Chun, Ah Fang, and I stayed with Ah Lan to welcome the new year. That stingy boss, Mr. Sun, didn't invite us for a New Year's Eve dinner or give us red envelopes. Although we couldn't reunite with our families for the feast or watch the Spring Festival Gala on TV in the hospital room, we still felt warmth and harmony. Ah Chun bought a small electric rice cooker, and we cooked dumplings in the ward. Ah Fang was thoughtful; she gave Ah Lan two sets of red underwear and bras, as it was her zodiac year, and wearing red undergarments was believed to ward off evil spirits. We prayed for Ah Lan's recovery, hoping we could work together again, go shopping together, and dream of the future.

We had time off work from the first to the eighth day of the Lunar New Year. Although Ah Lan was weak, she could walk with our support. We strolled through the streets of Nanxun together. The famous hidden library, Xiaolian Village, Zhang Jingjiang's former residence, and Baijian Tower were all tranquil and beautiful places. Despite working here, this was the first time we had thought of visiting these places. But now, due to Ah Lan's condition, we felt a sense of regret if we didn't explore them. Ah Lan had a positive attitude. I didn't sense any despondency from her; on the contrary, she comforted us and told us to stay optimistic. She said that after falling ill, she understood life's value and friendship's preciousness.

Ah Lan needed nearly ten bottles of glucose solution per day, from noon to midnight, without any breaks. Her daily medical costs and other medical and nursing expenses added up to several thousand yuan, which put us in a difficult situation. Her condition didn't improve; it showed signs of deterioration. Her urine was no longer clear but reddish, and she quickly got tired. Ah Lan seemed to realize the seriousness of her condition, yet she still smiled and chatted with us. To fight boredom in the hospital room, I bought magazines like "Reader," "Zhiyin," "Girlfriend," and "Family." Ah Lan liked reading "Reader," saying that she gained a lot of wisdom and strength from this thin magazine.

The Spring Festival passed quickly, and we resumed work. Manager Tian still handed me the 10,000 yuan, saying they had difficulties and couldn't set a precedent for employees to claim reimbursements for medical expenses. Although I looked down on such profit-oriented business people, I had to accept it without any reservations as Ah Lan urgently needed the money for treatment. Could she only wait for death in this small hospital? I couldn't bear to think about it. As sisters, we would try every possible means to save her life. We needed to raise money to transfer her to a better-equipped hospital, and it was also necessary to inform her parents. If something happened to Ah Lan and her parents were unaware, how would they go about living?

Sister Wu and Xiao Hong worked in a nightclub, accompanying guests for dancing, drinking, and "escorting." Escorting meant attending guests to other places and keeping specific activities unspoken. They earned much more money than me, but their work was also challenging. They had to learn to drink, smoke, play mahjong, and do various entertainment activities. Their primary source of income was "escorting"; they would accompany guests in any activity they wanted. My work was different—I mainly provided massages and could refrain from engaging in additional activities to earn extra money if I didn't want to. Now, I had been promoted from a regular masseuse to a massage therapist, and I was responsible for training new staff. My salary increased to 2,000 yuan per month, along with tips.

I quite liked this job. It may be my first job, and I felt attached to it. Work doesn't have levels; we were all striving for the same goal—survival. Moreover, I found pleasure in the art of massage. The smiles of satisfied customers were the most rewarding for me. Because of Ah Lan's situation, I once thought about quitting the sauna and following Sister Wu and Xiao Hong to earn more money. But with my efforts alone, it would be futile, and I couldn't demand that Ah Fang and Ah Chun also give up their massage jobs to do something they didn't want to do.

What I found laughable was that Wu Fang was still obsessed. Her salary from the sauna was not enough to cover her expenses, so she took on numerous private jobs to earn extra money, and all that money flowed directly to that man who fascinated her. I thought Wu Fang was unreasonable; nurturing a "toy boy" was something rich women did. Why would she join in this craze? But she wouldn't listen to my advice. She even said that the man liked her, and she planned to marry him shortly, having him all to herself. Wu Fang didn't know that her older sister also had a hand in this. Now it was a mess of sharing the same man among sisters. It's absurd! I had nothing to say; she seemed a bit crazy. Why do women act so foolish in front of men?

Life will not change one bit because of the joys and sorrows of us small people. February 4th marked the beginning of spring, and February 5th was the Lantern Festival, a time for happiness and harmony. However, did any of that concern us? Buddha said, "All living beings are equal," but how can we compare ourselves with others? We are so poor that we can't afford to get sick; we must watch helplessly as the disease overwhelms us. As we walk on the streets, the locals who recognize us point and gossip about us, spreading rumors. We are even cursed by some women who can't control their husbands, calling us names like lewd women, sluts, and prostitutes... We also have parents, siblings, and the dignity of our personalities; we deserve basic respect! Do you know we are swallowing back tears when you find happiness through us? We were all born into this world, and our lives are equal; the only difference lies in our fates!

After the Lantern Festival, Ah Lan's condition rapidly deteriorated. She developed edema, and her urine was dark red, almost like menstrual blood. Occasionally, she even fainted. I knew we could no longer delay; although the doctor said Ah Lan might live for another six months, who could guarantee that? As long as there's a glimmer of hope, we cannot give up on her treatment. The most pressing issue was the lack of money. The money paid for Ah Lan's hospitalization was almost gone. Although our colleagues at the sauna had donated some money, we had tried every possible means and still couldn't raise enough. As outsiders, we couldn't apply for local civil affairs assistance. Ah Lan's condition couldn't be postponed any longer, so we had to quickly raise a sum of money to transfer her to another hospital. Ah Lan understood the gravity of her situation and apologized to us, saying, "I know you are worried sick for me, and I appreciate your kindness. With such good sisters like you, I will die without regrets! Please focus on your work and stop running around for me. Let me wait alone in peace." We hugged and cried, letting the tears flow uncontrollably. We choked and said to Ah Lan, "Don't worry, nothing will happen to you. We will find a way to save you!"

However, what could a few girls from elsewhere and a few masseuses do? Where could we find hundreds of thousands of yuan for Ah Lan's treatment? I even thought about posting online, like some girls who sell themselves to save their mothers, but who would believe something like that on the internet? It could stir up a commotion and attract onlookers; nobody would think it's true. I regretted not staying in touch with the sauna's guests, many wealthy business owners. I should have thought about maintaining connections with them instead of just focusing on doing my job well and not bothering them. If I had done that, someone among them would have been generous enough to help us in this desperate situation.

At Ah Lan's bedside, we took shifts to keep her company. I had the late-night shift, meaning I would go to the hospital to accompany her after my shift ended at midnight. Ah Lan would usually be asleep by then, making my duty relatively easier, and I could nap by her side. Ah Fang would relieve me in the morning, and I'd go back to rest. Ah Chun worked the early shift, and after she finished at 5 PM, she would came to the hospital to take over from Ah Fang. Keeping her company was a small task; the main issue bothering us was the need for more money. When the hospital saw that our funds were running low, they would come to collect, making us quite miserable. This made Ah Lan repeatedly request to be discharged, saying it was a waste of money and that she could save it. She would feel uneasy if we had to borrow money and get into debt for her sake. Of course, we wouldn't listen to her. If a person is sick, they must be treated; there's no other way.

While massaging a guest and chatting with him one day, I learned he was doing business in Huzhou. Suddenly, I remembered someone from Huzhou—the man who took my virginity. Yes, it was Mr. Zhang! He had left me his business card, which I had kept in my bag, but why hadn't I thought of him earlier? He said I could find him anytime if I had any difficulties. Although I knew that many men say such things but never mean it, I decided to give it a try. I thought that with Ah Lan, Ah Chun, Ah Fang, and myself all penniless, desperately seeking medical treatment, why not ask him for help? After all, he was my first man, and my impression of him was still favorable, especially his fatherly gentleness, making him seem reliable and warm. Perhaps he could help me?

It was like seeing a glimmer of hope in the darkness, so I quickly called him. It was 9 PM then, and I thought that with his status, he wouldn't be asleep so early. Indeed, he answered, asking, "Who's this?" I said, "It's me." He didn't recognize my voice. After all, it had been several months; how could he still remember me? Mr. Zhang asked, "Little Jing? Oh, I remember now. It's you!" I smiled and said, "Thank you for remembering me, Mr. Zhang." He replied, "I never forgot about you. By the way, how's your life now? Do you need any help?" Sophisticated and straightforward, I liked men with both capabilities and refinement.

I hesitated momentarily and said, "Nothing urgent. I just suddenly thought of you and wanted to call to say hello." Mr. Zhang seemed surprised and happy. He said, "I've been thinking of you too, Little Jing. If you're free, I'd like to see you again." I needed something from him, so naturally, I wouldn't refuse. I said, "Sure, I have time tomorrow during the day." Mr. Zhang said happily, "Great, then call me tomorrow, and I'll pick you up." I suggested, "How about I come to the hotel where you saw me last time? I'll find you."

Chapter 16

Journey through Huzhou

After spending the night with Ah Lan, I rested in the morning. At noon, I took a taxi and arrived at the hotel I had visited before. It was an odd feeling to revisit the same place. However, I couldn't deceive myself; I had a natural affinity for this middle-aged man. Seeing him felt like meeting a relative, a trusted elder, or perhaps a close friend from years ago.

When Zhang saw me, he appeared genuinely delighted. He gently embraced me and said, "Xiaojing, I've missed you!" I playfully poured cold water on his enthusiasm, saying, "If you really missed me, you wouldn't have seen me again." He chuckled and replied, "Have you had lunch? Let's eat together." I explained that I was on a diet and only ate twice a day, breakfast and dinner. Zhang insisted, "Having a meal together won't hurt. It's just for the company. I've been waiting for you and haven't eaten yet." I agreed to dine with him but teased, "If people recognize us and tell your wife, what will you say?" He laughed, "If someone asks, I'll say you're my goddaughter." I laughed in response, "That's your idea; you mustn't entertain any other thoughts about me!"

We dined at the hotel restaurant, and Zhang ordered a table full of dishes and a bottle of red wine. I hesitated about drinking alcohol but ended up toasting with him. The taste was pleasant, with a sourness, sweetness, spiciness, and fragrance. No wonder Sister Wu and Xiaohong enjoyed drinking. After half an hour of eating, we received a bill of over 200 yuan. I exclaimed, "So expensive?" Zhang smiled and remarked, "Money is meant to be spent; using it brings value."

Back in the room, we lay on the bed, watched TV, and chatted. Zhang asked, "Xiaojing, what made you decide to call me?" I replied, "I just missed you." He laughed and said, "Really? I never thought you'd want to see me again." I explained, "You're a good person, and I've been busy with work, so I didn't want to disturb you by contacting you." Zhang suggested, "If you're willing, you don't need to work. Come to Huzhou." I jokingly said, "How will I survive without a job? Will you support me?" Zhang hesitated and said, "I can arrange a less demanding job for you." I playfully frightened him, saying, "I don't want to depend on others, nor do I want to be someone's mistress. If you like me, then divorce and marry me." Zhang was taken aback and awkwardly responded, "I'm not worthy of you, and I can't get a divorce." How could a successful businessman like Zhang not be worthy of a simple massage girl like me? I knew he was making excuses, but I didn't expose him.

I said, "Don't worry; I won't affect your life. I know men prioritize their careers. As for me, I'm just one of the many flowers you've encountered on your life journey." Zhang replied, "Occasionally, business acquaintances invite me out, and I attend for politeness. However, you left a profound impression on me, and I've been reminiscing about you. I haven't been with any other woman since you left." I teased, "Are you lying? Can you honestly say you haven't been with your wife either?" Zhang chuckled, "That doesn't count; we're an old married couple. I mean, I haven't been with any other woman." I said, "As a humble woman, why would I occupy Mr. Zhang's thoughts?" He sighed and said, "If I were twenty years younger and had met you, I would have pursued you regardless of anything. Unfortunately, that's not possible now. Reality leaves us with many constraints. One cannot always do as they please. Besides, I don't want to put you in a difficult situation. As long as we can meet occasionally, I'll be content." I didn't know if Zhang was speaking from his heart.

After resting for a while, Zhang went to take a shower. I felt conflicted; I was willing to do anything to raise money for Ah Lan. However, today, I didn't want any intimate relationship with Zhang. It wasn't about whether I liked him or not. I had already begun to regard him as a family member. If we crossed that line, it would ruin and violate my feelings for him. The respect and trust I once had for him would disappear. However, I also understood that since I came today, would Zhang easily let me go? Would he understand and respect my feelings?

After Zhang's shower, I said, "You rest for a while, and I'll massage you." There was no massage oil here, so I used gentle movements. Sister Xu once said that massage itself was reasonable and legitimate; it was just that some massage therapists changed the nature of the massage. She also said that the attraction between opposite sexes was a natural phenomenon. As long as the masseur provided heartfelt service, the customer would feel the sincerity and relaxed.

Outside, it was early spring, and the air was chilly. However, the room was warm and comfortable due to the heating. I massaged Zhang's skin, which turned white with a rosy glow. Most business owners lacked exercise, so I focused on massaging their joints, promoting blood circulation, and relieving stiffness. Although my skills were less refined than Sister Xu's, I still considered myself adept. I genuinely wished for his comfort and happiness.

Zhang lay on the bed for a while and then sat up. He looked deeply into my eyes and asked, "Xiaojing, tell me, have you encountered a difficult problem?" I fell silent, unsure how to open up. I needed a large sum of money. Even if I did, would he give it to me? Seeing my hesitation, Zhang continued, "Xiaojing, if you consider me a good person, just say it. As long as I can do it, I will help you." Who was a good person, and who was a wrong person? Could society divide us so clearly? There are no good or bad people; human beings are contradictory beings. There is no unconditional goodness or badness, no eternal goodness or badness. We cannot even understand ourselves, whether we are good or bad.

I mustered up the courage and told Zhang about Ah Lan's illness truthfully. Tears uncontrollably streamed down my face as I spoke about her having less than half a year to live. I said, "We are powerless and have nowhere else to turn. We can't wait any longer. That's why I thought of seeking your help, hoping you can assist us so we can take Ah Lan to a big hospital for treatment..." Zhang listened attentively, and I could see a hint of surprise in his eyes, but it wasn't suspicion; it was genuine sympathy! He looked at me intensely and said, "Xiaojing, what do you want me to say?" I thought he might blame me and quickly added, "Zhang, it's alright if you can't help. I won't hold any grudges. I know I might have been delusional!" Zhang nodded and said, "Xiaojing, you don't know. I'm not blaming you. Your actions move me! The sacrifice you're willing to make for a friend, someone with no blood ties, is truly admirable. I apologize for my rudeness towards you! Please forgive me!"

I sincerely said, "Zhang, thank you for understanding! It's nothing. Between people, there should be more understanding and compassion. Zhang, I recognized you as a good person from the moment I met you. You're different from other men. Whatever you did to me, I won't blame you; it was my choice." Zhang's expression became somewhat emotional. He swiftly put on his clothes, grabbed his bag from the sofa, and said, "There are only a few thousand yuan in this bag, not much use. I brought my credit card. Let's go to the bank right away and withdraw some money. Let's not waste any more time!"

With joy, I followed Zhang to the nearby Bank of China. He withdrew fifty thousand yuan and stuffed it into his wallet. Then, he handed me the wallet, saying, "Take this wallet. It's safer." As I received the wallet, gratitude overwhelmed me. I said, "Thank you. When I have the money, I'll repay you." Zhang smiled and replied, "We'll talk about repayment later. A personal bank card can only withdraw up to fifty thousand at a time. If you need more, let me know, and I'll help you." I hesitated and asked, "Is this your money, or is it from your company?" Zhang gently touched my head and said, "Of course, it's my money. Can't I do good deeds without becoming Lei Feng?" For some reason, a surge of tenderness rose within me. I opened my arms and embraced his waist, saying sincerely, "Thank you! Thank you!" At that moment, the bank hall was full of people, and some might have recognized Zhang. Nevertheless, I embraced him before everyone, and tears blurred my vision.

It was a complex emotion, containing gratitude, reliance, and positive regard between a man and a woman. However, I knew this wasn't love; I was leaning on his broad shoulder. I wished I were his daughter, and I even had the urge to yell, "Dad!" I was in dire need of affectionate care. But I remained clear-minded; I had my path to walk. I wandered through the lower ranks of life, and my dear friend Ah Lan needed the nurturing of sunshine and rain. Spring was the blooming season, and I couldn't bear to see her wither prematurely!

Chapter 17

Love Saving a Buddy

Mr. Zhang was the first benefactor I encountered in my life. Although he took my first time, I don't resent him. He knew I was a massage girl but didn't discriminate against me. He showed me care and warmth like a family member when I started working, making me feel a subtle emotion that wasn't solely because of the money he gave me. Even though I claimed it was a loan, I knew he wouldn't ask me to repay it. How long would it take for me to repay such a sum? Money is a lifesaver for people like us with limited means, but for wealthy individuals, it might just be colored paper. Mr. Zhang did me a great favor, but I brought him misfortune in return. He ended up divorcing his wife because of me. However, he never came looking for me. Not because of our age difference but because we knew we were merely passing strangers in each other's lives, not a harbor.

I wanted to take a bus back to Nanxun, but Mr. Zhang was concerned and said, "What if you encounter a bad driver who wants to rob you?" I replied, "In broad daylight, who would dare to do such a thing?" Mr. Zhang chuckled and said, "You never know. Even if you had 50,000 yuan or just a bundle of straw paper in your bag, they might still rob you if it catches a thief's eye. Let me be your guardian." Respecting his concern, I allowed Mr. Zhang to drive me to Nanxun. Luckily, the bank was still open, so I deposited the money into my account. Mr. Zhang noted my account number and said he would transfer another 50,000 yuan to my account the next day to avoid any inconvenience. His generous help moved me to tears, and I couldn't find the right words to express my gratitude.

Mr. Zhang dropped me off at the sauna city and apologized, saying he had other matters to attend to, or else he would have accompanied me to see my friend. I replied, "I'll convey your concern, and on behalf of Ah Lan, I want to express heartfelt thanks to you!" Mr. Zhang replied, "Why be so polite to me? By the way, have you decided on transferring your friend to another hospital?" I said, "We're not sure where to transfer her yet. Her condition is quite severe, and she often falls into a coma with severe swelling. I don't know what to do." Mr. Zhang thought momentarily and said, "You should have her checked out immediately. Suzhou No. 1 Hospital has a friend of mine, a chief physician specializing in kidney diseases. If you transfer her there, I can arrange for him to take care of her." Mr. Zhang gave me a phone number and said the doctor's surname was Shen. I felt grateful for meeting him; it was as if heaven was looking after me. As Mr. Zhang got into his car and drove away, the familiar tune of an old song, "A good person lives in peace..." drifted from the music store nearby. It was the most beautiful blessing for Mr. Zhang and Ah Lan.

That night, I told Ah Chun that I had raised the money. She was both surprised and happy, repeatedly asking where the money came from. I said, "Don't worry; it's from a wealthy boss who promised to give me the money to help treat Ah Lan." Ah Chun said, "Can rich people be so kind-hearted? That's rare. But can we repay the money in the future?" I smiled and said, "Of course, but he didn't set a deadline, which means we can repay it whenever possible." Ah Chun playfully punched me and said, "I know what's going on. Did he 'buy' you and give you advance payment?" I replied, "No way! I don't want to be someone's kept woman; that would mean losing my freedom and becoming a canary, right?" Ah Chun said, "I still can't believe he would give you money for no reason." I said, "The money is in my hands; believe it or not, it's up to you. Let's arrange for Ah Lan's transfer tomorrow, and the day after tomorrow, we'll take a day off and move her to the hospital in Suzhou."

Ah Lan WAS STILL AWAKE when I arrived at the hospital late at night. The doctors had just checked her weight, temperature, and blood pressure. Her condition was being closely monitored 24 hours a day to respond to any unexpected situations and provide timely treatment. While I didn't doubt the quality of the clinic's service, I felt that a larger hospital might offer better treatment and more skilled doctors, increasing Ah Lan's chances of survival.

Filled with joy, I told Ah Lan, "Tomorrow, we'll transfer to a larger hospital in Suzhou with better medical facilities." Despite her weak physical condition, Ah Lan's mind was clear. She shook her head and said, "Ah jing, please don't trouble yourselves anymore. I've burdened you enough, and I'll feel uneasy about it." I replied, "Ah Lan, what are you saying? We are like sisters, and spending some money is nothing compared to life itself. We're fortunate to have the money now, so focus on getting better, and I'm still waiting to hear you sing." Ah Lan had a beautiful voice and could imitate Liu Ruoying's singing style. She sang "Love You So Much" and "Later," which sounded so authentic that it could draw applause even in leisure time at work.

Ah Lan looked puzzled and said, "Where did you get the money? You've spent all your money on me; I haven't seen you buy new clothes in a long time." I laughed and said, "When I finished work at night, I encountered an old man with a white beard. He handed me a bag and disappeared in an instant. When I opened the bag, wow, it was filled with money!" Ah Lan laughed, saying, "Are you kidding me with these dream-like stories?" I said, "It's true. Why would I lie to you?" Ah Lan reached out her hand, covered with needle marks, and said, "Where is the money? Seeing is believing. Let me take a look at that bag." I said, "I deposited it in the bank." Ah Lan smiled bitterly and said, "In the middle of the night, is the bank open?" I chuckled and said, "Yes, there are many 24-hour self-service banks now." Ah Lan said, "Ah jing, I know your kindness, but you don't need to console me. Even if there's money, I won't go." I joked, "You're the leader in the sauna city, and we should follow your lead, but now you're the patient, so you should listen to us."

When Ah Fang came to take my shift the following day, she brought someone with her. As soon as Ah Lan and I saw her, we exclaimed, "Sister Xu!" It was indeed Sister Xu, our massaLady Gester, and also our sister! I asked, "Sister Xu, why are you here too?" She barked, "Xiao Jing, why didn't you tell me earlier? I had no idea Ah Lan was in such a state!" I said, "We've been quite busy and didn't want to bother you." Sister Xu gave me a stern look and said, "You're such a clever girl; why are you being polite to me? Why didn't you call me? If I hadn't passed by the sauna city today and wanted to see you and Ah Lan, I wouldn't have known she was in the hospital. When did all this happen? You two are too much. With Ah Lan's serious condition, you should have transferred her to a bigger hospital. How can this place do?"

Sister Xu went to the bedside and saw Ah Lan, who was intelligent and capable, lying in bed, her face swollen and slightly changed due to edema. She couldn't help feeling sad and said, "Ah Lan, how did this happen?" Ah Lan replied, "Sister Xu, don't blame Xiao Jing. She's worked so hard for my sake, losing weight and spending all her hard-earned money. It's all my fault..." Sister Xu said, "Well, you should have told me earlier. I just bought a shopfront recently and paid all my money for it. If necessary, I'll get a refund. Treating you is more important." Ah Lan said, "No, I'm fine here. I don't want to transfer." I said, "Sister Xu, don't worry about the money; I borrowed some already. We have 50,000 yuan now, and another 50,000 may come tomorrow. I plan to arrange for Ah Lan's transfer today and move her to the hospital tomorrow." Sister Xu said, "Xiao Jing, I knew I didn't misjudge you. You really can do things!" Ah Lan glanced at me and said affectionately, "So what you said was true, Xiao Jing? I've troubled you too much!" Sister Xu said, "We shouldn't delay any longer. Let's arrange for the transfer this afternoon. Xiao Jing, you should take a day off and inform Ah Lan's family to come. It's unfilial not to let them know their daughter is sick."

With Sister Xu by my side, I felt more at ease. She was older than us and had rich social experience, making her quite skillful in handling things. Sister Xu took care of the discharge procedures here, and I had already spoken with Dr. Shen in Suzhou on the phone. He said, "Your call came at the right time; we have an available bed. I'll reserve it for you, so come as soon as possible." Ah Fang and I got a few days off from Manager Tian, and together with Sister Xu, we moved Ah Lan into the ambulance and headed to Suzhou. Nanxun was part of Zhejiang province, but the distance to Suzhou was much closer than Hangzhou. After a two-hour drive, we arrived at Suzhou University Affiliated Hospital and found Dr. Shen. He gave Ah Lan a preliminary examination and reviewed her medical records, immediately arranging her admission.

Being a large hospital, the nursing was more standardized, and the doctors were meticulous in inquiring about the patient's condition. The nurses' service was gentle and intimate, making you feel like you were not in a hospital but back home. Dr. Shen called me to his office and said, "Let's start with some treatment and perform blood, urine, and kidney function tests to determine the next treatment plan. She'll probably need blood dialysis. If there's a suitable kidney source, kidney transplantation would be best, although it's costly." I asked, "Can her condition be cured?" Dr. Shen smiled and said, "For uremia, according to the current medical level, it's incurable, but with proper medication and surgery, we can extend the patient's life." I hadn't expected that there was no absolute guarantee of survival even after transferring to a bigger hospital. I couldn't help feeling disappointed. Dr. Shen said, "Please rest assured, we'll do our utmost!"

Why do people get sick? Why did Ah Lan have to fall ill? She was so young, yet she contracted such a severe disease. It seems that even the heavens can nod off sometimes and be indifferent to human life and death. Although I knew death was inevitable, I initially thought hospitals could cure all illnesses. It seems that doctors aren't gods, either. Some diseases may be beyond their abilities, and all we can do is pray for miracles to happen and hope that Ah Lan can live a healthy life!

Taking care of Ah Lan here is much easier than in the clinic. Nurses frequently visit the ward to check on her condition and provide attentive care. I told Ah Fang and Sister Xu, "You two should go back; I'll be enough here." Sister Xu said, "Your eyes are bloodshot; you probably haven't rested properly for days. It would help if you went home.

Besides, I'm not on duty, and the training doesn't matter. I'll stay here." How could I leave? Ah Fang didn't want to go back either. Ah Lan mentioned that she had a slight headache and felt too exhausted to open her eyes. I hurried to call the on-duty doctor, who said it was a normal phenomenon for patients and advised her to rest. They told her condition would improve after dialysis. Ah Lan struggled to open her eyes and asked, "Ah jing, have my parents come? I miss them so much, and I'm afraid I won't see them again." I replied, "I've already called them, and they might come at night. Yancheng to Suzhou isn't far. Ah Lan, please don't overthink. You will get better!"

Chapter 18

The Lady-killer in the Rainy Night

At eleven o'clock at night, Ah Lan's parents rushed over from the rural area of Yancheng. They were ordinary farmers in their fifties. When they saw their daughter lying on the hospital bed with her face and body swollen, they couldn't help but burst into tears, crying out, "Lan Lan, how did you become so sick? Why didn't you tell your parents earlier? Don't you miss us?" Ah Lan's hand was attached to an IV drip, feeling cold to the touch, while her other hand was swollen, and pressing down on it would leave an indentation that took a while to recover. Ah Lan was weak and struggled to sit up but couldn't manage it, so she gave up her efforts and lay on the bed, eagerly looking at her parents.

Moving her lips, Ah Lan said, "Dad, Mom, are you hungry?" Ah Lan's mother wiped her tears and said, "We're not hungry, but are you hungry? How about Mom buying you some food?" Ah Lan shook her head and said, "I'm on a drip, I don't feel hungry. Mom, please thank them for me.

They've been with me all this time, not sleeping for several days and nights." Ah Lan's mother turned back, about to kneel before us, but Sister Xu held her back. Ah Lan's mother said, "You've all taken such good care of my daughter; you're all kind-hearted people!" Sister Xu said, "Who doesn't have their health issues in this world? We're all sisters; it's natural to help each other. Don't be polite." Ah Lan's father said, "As soon as we received the call, we brought eight thousand yuan from home and rushed here quickly. I hope it's enough." I said, "Please rest assured, Uncle and Auntie. We still have the money for Ah Lan's treatment, so you don't need to worry."

The next day, I checked the card's bAh Lance and found an additional fifty thousand yuan. I thought about calling Mr. Zhang to express my gratitude, but ultimately, I decided not to. What would I say to him? Thank him? Unlike our first transaction, I knew that Mr. Zhang helped me out of goodwill. He wanted to be a good person, and I only needed to understand his intentions. A woman's gratitude to a man usually involves intimacy, and Mr. Zhang and I were both ordinary people. Our hearts were not noble, but from my perspective, I didn't want to have any ambiguous relationship with Mr. Zhang. I could treat him like family or even be his goddaughter, but I didn't want to get entangled in a transactional relationship. I could accept sleeping with other men because I had no emotional attachment to them, but with Mr. Zhang, a sense of affection had sprouted, and I didn't want to muddy the waters.

I only left a few thousand yuan for my living expenses and deposited the rest into Ah Lan's hospital account. The doctor performed blood dialysis on Ah Lan, essentially placing an artificial kidney outside her body to replace her failing kidneys and take over the function of filtration and detoxification. Although Ah Lan had difficulty moving, her complexion improved a bit. Sister Xu said, "Ah jing, Ah Fang, you both return and rest before work. We're taking care of Ah Lan here, and there are nurses too. You can rest assured, and if there's any situation, I'll call you."

I had heard that Suzhou was a paradise on Earth, but now we were burdened with heavy thoughts and had no mood for sightseeing. Moreover, I hadn't slept peacefully these days due to worrying about Ah Lan. After returning to Nanxun town with Ah Fang, we were met with concern from Sister Wu and Xiaohong. They asked, "How is your little sister? Is she feeling better?" I said, "She has been transferred to a hospital in Suzhou and is getting better." Sister Wu said, "This poor girl is suffering from kidney disease. In this world, good people seldom receive good in return, while the wicked live long lives!" I casually asked, "What about Wu Fang? Why haven't I seen her?" Xiaohong pouted and said, "She's always out having fun. She doesn't even come back after work." Sister Wu said indignantly, "If I had known she was so wild at heart, I wouldn't have let her work here! She's bound to get into trouble sooner or later! It would be best if she got kidnapped!"

I slept for an afternoon, and when I went to work in the evening, many sisters gathered around, asking me inquisitively, "Is Ah Lan feeling better? Did she have surgery?" Friendship was much needed in a foreign land; otherwise, I'd be lonely and helpless. Ah Lan was cared for by so many sisters, which showed that she was a good person in her daily life. I said, "She's receiving treatment and will get better. Ah Lan asked me to thank everyone. She will remember your contributions." Aju said, "I hope Ah Lan can come back to work soon. We came in together and used to be together every day. It feels strange not to see her for such a long time." When Ah Fang came to work, she was already ten minutes late. Rushing in, she said to me, "I overslept. It was already five o'clock when I woke up, so I hurried here." I told Ah Mei, "Let's drop the record of her late. She's been exhausted these days." Ah Mei was the temporary team leader now because of Ah Lan's illness. The team leader position was vacant, and Manager Tian wanted me to take it, but I declined politely as I tried to accompany Ah Lan.

Many wealthy people are now, and the sauna city's business is booming. Boss Sun rarely comes, as he's said to be investing in other businesses. Manager Tian mainly manages the place. Ah Chun told me, "Ah jing, you weren't here these past few days, and many old customers came and left. They insisted on having you massage them, as it's uncomfortable when it's not you." I smiled; although my job wasn't respectable, customer appreciation and recognition still made me feel content. True to her words, several customers came that night, saying, "Ah jing, where have you been? We thought you'd changed jobs. We've been to several massage parlors, but you're the best; even our bones feel comfortable after your massage. If you change workplaces, please let us know. We're your loyal customers and will follow you to support your business." I laughed and said, "Sure, once I have the money, I'll open a sauna parlor, and don't forget to come and support me!"

I was joking; opening a place like that requires a minimum investment of tens of thousands, while a place like this, the Sea of Heaven Sauna City, costs at least a few million with the rent, decoration, equipment, steam rooms, and private rooms. With our massage therapists' salaries, we won't be able to earn that much in a lifetime. Moreover, I don't plan to be a masseuse my whole life. "Necessity is the mother of invention." In the future, I might do what Sister Xu did, privately run a training center to earn money, or change jobs and work in a legitimate company. Alternatively, if I find a man who loves me, becoming a virtuous wife and mother would be even better! Serving my husband is blissful while serving other men is just a compromise.

Late at night, the rain was drizzling outside as I left work. None of us had brought an umbrella, and we hurriedly went through the light rain to head home. Heaven Sauna was located in Xin Town, while my rented place was on the old street, about a fifteen-minute walk away. At first, the raindrops were light and floating, but my body and face became damp after a while. It was a typical spring rain in Jiangnan, and I recalled a line of poetry: "Silently following the wind into the night, moistening things without a sound." The scene indeed carried that kind of artistic conception. I held my bag over my head and strolled through the streets of the small town.

In a few more minutes, I would be home. I had already considered Sister Wu's place as my home in Nanxun. The sky was quite dark, and the dim yellow streetlights illuminated the puddles on the ground, creating a pale reflection. Walking into the old street, I hugged the wall and moved forward. I was very familiar with this road: Xiao Lian Zhuang and the Book Collection Pavilion were ahead. There was an alley, and passing through it and walking a short distance further, we would arrive at the courtyard where we lived. The rain seemed to intensify, and I quickened my pace. Late at night on the street, I was the only one, like a wandering ghost, walking hurriedly through the rainy night, and the sound of my lonely footsteps felt urgent and cold.

I had just reached the corner of the alley when two dark figures suddenly rushed out from the side. In an instant, everything turned black, and a black cloth bag covered my head, hands, and bag. Under the cloth bag was an elastic band that tightened around my neck, making me feel uncomfortable, so I instinctively struggled. From inside the bag, I shouted, "Let go of me! What do you want?" I felt a sharp knife pressing against my back, and it seemed as if the tip pierced through my clothes, reaching my flesh. A deep voice threatened, "Don't shout, be obedient!" I was terrified, and my body was trembling. Regardless of the consequences, I wanted to call for help, but my throat felt as if it had gone mute; I couldn't produce any sound! Despite the shock, I knew that I had encountered some bad people! What did they want? Money or something else? How should I resist?

One of them tugged at the cloth bag, and the other held the knife, pushing me toward the alley. After walking a dozen steps inside the alley, I remembered that there was a public restroom, and it seemed like they were pushing me toward it. From inside the bag, I shouted, "Let me go! If you want money, I'll give it to you!" If they didn't have a knife, I would have fought them!

A man chuckled, "Who cares about your measly money? Beautiful lady, Big Brother has been thinking about you!" His voice sounded familiar; I seemed to have heard it somewhere. Suddenly, I remembered: this was Lao Si, who tried to take advantage of me on my first day at the sauna city! They hadn't come to the sauna city for a long time, and I had forgotten about them, thinking they had disappeared. Who would have thought they still hadn't forgotten about me and would use such despicable means to bully a vulnerable woman? The other man must be his accomplice, and I was both angry and nervous. At the moment, I was lost and didn't know what to do.

I felt the cloth bag on my head loosen, so I used my hand to push it up, and the black bag came off, revealing my head and hands, freeing me. The two men were startled, and Lao Si held the knife, threateningly saying, "Don't move. If you're not obedient, I'll stab you to death!" The other man grabbed my shoulder and whispered, "Listen, stay still!"

The public restroom was dark, and I couldn't see their faces. Among them, one was undoubtedly Lao Si—two big men against me. If I were to fight back, I would surely be at a disadvantage. Escaping was also challenging, as they had a knife, and they might harm me.

In their eyes, I was still that innocent little girl, unaware of the many changes I had undergone. At this critical moment, a calm mindset saved me. Smiling, I told the two men in the darkness, "Gentlemen, be more polite. Being so fierce, who'd want to accompany you? Put down the knife and your hands, and I'll agree to your request."
They didn't expect me to compromise, but they also hesitated. They began to argue intensely over who would get intimate with me first. What I wanted was precisely this effect. While they were distracted, I could find an opportunity to escape. Facing a formidable enemy, I couldn't make any pointless sacrifices and had to figure out how to protect myself.

Indeed, they were quarreling so intensely that they even got physical. Seeing this chance, I made a run for the door! Lao Si quickly caught up with me! I loudly cried for help, "Help! Help!" The night in the small town was so quiet, and I ran as if my life depended on it. My shouts were particularly clear in the deep night. If someone could hear my call for help and open the door or call the police, I could escape their pursuit!

Chapter 19

Night of No Return

The rain poured relentlessly, obstructing my view, but I paid no attention and ran desperately ahead! Out of panic, I didn't head toward my nearby rental place but instead ran along the old street toward the new town. The small town was eerily quiet at this moment, except for me and the thugs relentlessly pursuing me. No one else was in sight, and I didn't know if they were all chasing after me. I yelled a few times but stopped shouting; it would only drain my energy and slow me down. Zheng Lao Si closely followed me, trailing about ten meters behind. It seemed he was fearless of residents coming to my aid. My speed was fast, and I felt the wind whooshing past my ears; the rain was icy cold. I dared not hesitate momentarily; I feared Zheng Lao Si would catch up to me and harm me.

The outskirts of the small town were the commercial district, with wide roads and bright street lamps. I ran towards the outside, hoping to encounter people and passing cars on the road. The bright lights might deter them from doing anything to me. I ran to the intersection, with Zheng Lao Si only a few meters behind me. I could feel his anger and murderous intent. He shouted from behind, "Stop! Stop right there! Let's see where you're running!" He didn't seem afraid of being noticed; these villains were too audacious nowadays! If it were daytime, uninformed people might think I was a thief and he was chasing after me!

Later, I realized that maybe I was just lucky, so they would often turn into blessings in disguise whenever I faced difficulties. When I ran to the road outside and saw a 110 police patrol car approaching, I immediately ran to the center of the road and shouted, "Help! Someone is trying to kill me!" Usually, when I encountered police cars or officers on the road, I would feel guilty and try to avoid them. Although my profession was not illegal, some of my massage services were inevitably associated with sexual favors. Of course, the primary responsibility lay with Boss Sun; we masseuses were just under his employ, earning meager wages while he profited from our cheap labor.

The patrol car screeched to a halt beside me, and two officers jumped out of it. I noticed their ages, one was around forty, and the other in his twenties. The older one asked, "We saw you running. What happened?" I turned around and pointed, saying, "Someone is chasing me! Please, he's right behind me! Look!" But no one was behind me; Zheng Lao Si must have slipped away when he sensed trouble. The older officer said, "Calm down. Tell us what happened." I briefly explained, "Just now, two men tried to attack me on my way home. I managed to escape, but one of them kept chasing me. He was right behind me just now. Where did he go?" The younger officer said, "Do you want to file a report? Come with us to the police station and make a statement." Go to the police station? Make a statement? No, I couldn't do that; if the police remembered me, it wouldn't be good for me. I said, "No, I won't file a report. Can you please escort me home? I'm a bit scared to go back alone."

The rain eased a bit, and I walked with the two officers along the old street where I had just fled in terror. When we reached the narrow lane, I said, "This is it. They suddenly appeared and used a cloth bag to trap me." The older officer, Lao Zhao, said, "Oh? That's concerning. What happened next?" I said, "They pushed me into that toilet, trying to harm me. I took advantage of their distraction and managed to escape!" The younger officer, Xiao Ge, said, "Lao Zhao, we should report this to our superiors. The old street is too dark at night, and residents lack a sense of security. We must send more patrol officers to prevent criminals from taking advantage." Lao Zhao replied, "Alright, I'll talk to the station chief. Young lady, can you take us to the toilet?" Still trembling from the experience, I said, "There was another man with them. I don't know if he's still there." Xiao Ge said, "Let's go take a look. If he's still there, we'll apprehend him!"

Armed with flashlights, they followed me into the toilet, but no one was inside, and the cloth bag was gone too. There was no evidence left. Lao Zhao asked, "Did you see their physical features?" I replied, "One was taller, the other shorter, both around thirty years old. One had a knife, but it was dark, and I couldn't see their faces. I remember that they called each other Lao Si and Lao San." Lao Zhao said, "Lao Si? Could that be Zheng Lao Si? They are a vicious gang of criminals. The last time we tried to apprehend them, they even stabbed one of our officers." Xiao Ge said, "They disappeared for a while but are back. Lao Zhao, we need to increase patrols on the old street. They might have committed another heinous crime if this clever young lady hadn't escaped!"

They accompanied me back to my rental place, and I said, "Thank you both. This is the first time I've encountered such a situation. I never expected villains to be lurking on the streets at night. It isn't very comforting! You've escorted me home today, but what about tomorrow? The day after tomorrow?" Lao Zhao said, "We'll strengthen nighttime patrols, so please rest assured. Such incidents won't happen again." I said, "The bad guys hide in the shadows while I'm in the open. How can anyone be vigilant against that?" Lao Zhao turned to Xiao Ge and said, "Xiao Ge, why don't you accompany this young lady from now on?" Xiao Ge chuckled and pretended to strike Lao Zhao, saying, "Lao Zhao, we're on official duty. We can't joke around." Lao Zhao laughed, saying, "Once is an acquaintance, twice is a friend. Police officers are also humans; they date, marry, and have children. Making friends is normal. I think it's suitable for you to accompany her, a perfect match made by fate." I couldn't see the young officer's face clearly in the darkness, but I could tell from his figure and outline that he was a handsome young man in his mid-twenties. If I had someone like him to escort me, I would be worry-free, but did I have such luck?

Lao Zhao chuckled, "What's not suitable about it? You have to protect the lives and property of the people. Privately, you are both young people, making friends is normal." Xiao Ge playfully raised the flashlight as if to hit Lao Zhao and said, "Lao Zhao, we are on official duty. We can't joke around." Lao Zhao laughed, "Familiarity breeds affection, policemen are also human beings. They date, get married, have children, making friends is normal. I think it's appropriate for you to escort her, a match made in heaven." Unexpectedly, even the severe police officer had a playful side. I opened the door and said, "Thank you both! I've arrived home."

I opened the room door and found that Xiao Hong had yet to return, and

Wu Fang was also missing. I knocked on Sister Wu's door, but there was no response. Where could they have gone? Wu Fang not coming home at night was a common occurrence, but what about Xiao Hong and Sister Wu? They should have finished their night shift and come back by now. Why were they still not back? I tried calling their phones, but they were both switched off. I got along well with them, living together in the same rented house, almost like a family. Moreover, Sister Wu and Xiao Hong were my fellow townsmen, so it was only natural to care about each other.

I couldn't sleep well that night, tossing and turning in bed, thinking about many things. Sometimes, I thought about Ah Lann and wondered if she was feeling better. Other times, I worried about Xiao Hong and Sister Wu, wondering what happened to them and why they hadn't returned home. Could they have gone to some nightclub or entertainment venue? Then, I also thought about myself, how I almost fell into the hands of those two bastards! It's not like I'm overly proud, but I despise men who try to force themselves on me. And what about that young police officer? Would he come to escort me after work, or was it just a joke? I would be uneasy at night if no one came to pick me up.

Morning came, and the rain had stopped, but the ground was still damp. Sister Wu and Xiao Hong still had yet to return. Usually, they would have returned by now if they spent the night out. I tried calling them again, but their phones were still off. Sister Wu's younger sister, Wu Fang, came back humming "The Most Romantic Thing" and laughed when I told her that Sister Wu hadn't returned home. She said, "It's normal for her to be out all night." I replied, "The problem is that her phone is off. She never turned it off before. Xiao Hong hasn't come back either. They work together. Why can't we reach them?" Wu Fang nonchAh Lantly said, "You're making a fuss over nothing. It's just a dead battery. They probably spent the night out. What's the big deal? Women need nightlife too!" I couldn't help but laugh and cry, saying, "She's your sister. Why don't you care at all?" Wu Fang smiled and said, "Do I care about her? Who cares about me? Little Jingjie, stop being so nosy. They won't have any problems."

In the afternoon, I called Sister Xu and asked about Ah Lann's condition. Sister Xu said, "Ah Lann's condition has improved somewhat, but the doctor said that dialysis alone won't be enough. The best option is a kidney transplant. Finding a healthy kidney donor is a problem, and the expensive medical expenses are also a headache. The kidney transplant surgery and post-operative recovery treatment are estimated to cost 300,000 yuan, and I can't come up with that much cash right now." I was surprised and said, "300,000 yuan, that much?" Sister Xu replied, "It's not just about money. Dr. Shen said that Ah Lann's disease is terminal and already in the late stage. Even if she undergoes a kidney transplant, it will only give her a few more years to live. In the end, she still has to leave us..." The thought of Ah Lann's life, at only 24 years old, ending due to this illness made me feel heartbroken. Why is human life so fragile? Despite our best efforts, we still couldn't save her. Her flower was about to bloom but withering before its time. How could this not be heart-wrenching?

So that's what happened. Sigh, last night was an inauspicious day. Sister Wu and Xiao Hong were detained, and I almost got into trouble as well. I asked, "What happened afterward?" Xiao Hong said, "Several of us from the nightclub were taken in. Luckily, it was just for exposing ourselves, not caught in the act, so the problem wasn't severe. It would not have been good for us dancers if they had caught us in the act, and the nightclub would have been shut down! This morning, the boss went to the police station and paid the fine, so we were released." I said, "Your boss didn't have good connections. In our sauna city, the boss, Sun, always receives a heads-up, and everything goes smoothly." Sister Wu replied, "Connections? For running an entertainment venue, who doesn't have connections? You would have closed down long ago if you don't have a background. The police usually don't come to inspect unless there's an event or someone reports. Last night, someone called 110 and reported that our nightclub had adult activities, so the police came. They only arrested a few of the staff and released them today."

I called Sister Xu in the afternoon to ask about Ah Lann's condition. Sister Xu said, "Ah Lann's condition has improved somewhat, but the doctor said that dialysis alone won't suffice. The better option is a kidney transplant. Finding a healthy kidney donor is a problem, and the expensive medical expenses are also troubling. The kidney transplant surgery and post-operative recovery treatment are estimated to cost 300,000 yuan, and I can't come up with that much cash right now." I was surprised and said, "300,000 yuan, so much?" Sister Xu replied, "Money is not the main concern. Dr. Shen said that Ah Lann's disease is terminal and in the late stage. Even if she undergoes a kidney transplant, it will only extend her life for a few more years. In the end, she still has to leave us..." The thought of Ah Lann, just 24 years old, having to face the end of her life due to illness made me feel profoundly touched and heartbroken. Why is human life so fragile? We tried our best, but we still couldn't save her. Her life was like a flower that hadn't fully blossomed but was withering prematurely. How can one not be moved by such a sight?

At nine o'clock in the evening, I, along with Ah Chun and Ah Fang, discussed retaking leave to go to Suzhou to accompany Ah Lann. The head attendant, Ah Mei, hurriedly said, "Immediately inform the private rooms to stop the massage activities. Ask the service staff to dress neatly and persuade the customers to leave immediately. Don't bother with the bill!" We all dispersed to notify the private rooms that any massage with erotic elements must stop immediately. All the service staff should put on their work uniforms and dress appropriately. Within five minutes, ensure the customers' safe departure, and be vigilant against any issues. This included removing the names from the price list and hiding them discreetly. We finished all these tasks systematically and stood respectfully in the lobby. We knew that the police were about to come and inspect the place!

Chapter 20

Massage for Relaxation

Adapting to the routine inspections or surprise visits by the police, we were well-prepared and rarely showed any flaws. Moreover, we often received advance notice, allowing ample time to cover up any suspicious activities. Unlike other saunas that panicked when the police arrived, we wished they would come and go quickly so we could resume business as usual. Sometimes, unreliable information leads us to unnecessary worry.

Five minutes later, two police cars stopped at the entrance, and several officers and community patrol members stepped out, some staying outside and others entering the sauna. For entertainment venues like ours, police visits were unfavorable as they scared away potential customers. However, as law-abiding citizens, we had to cooperate with their inspections. The first floor housed the public baths, with separate sections for male and female customers and shower rooms. The second and third floors were dedicated to sauna baths and private spaces. Since they had checked before, they went directly upstairs.

Around a dozen masseuses stood in the lobby, warmly welcoming the police with smiles. Three officers entered, and I felt familiar with one of them. When his gaze met mine, he seemed momentarily startled. They inspected the private rooms but found nothing, of course. One of the officers commented, "Business seems pretty quiet; how can they keep it running like this?" We stifled our laughter because we knew that the police's unannounced visit had frightened away the customers. Another officer smiled and said, "Novices watch the excitement; veterans observe the doorways. It looks like the boss was well-prepared, knowing we were coming. If business were this slow, they wouldn't be able to last a month, let alone several years."

The officer who looked familiar to me walked up to me and smiled, asking, "Are you working here?" I nodded, glancing at him. While masseuses might feel less nervous than criminals when facing the police, it was still hard to avoid some anxiety. I hadn't seen his face last night, but now I noticed he was a handsome young officer with precise eyebrows and a sunny smile. He might have become a movie star if he weren't a policeman. His companion called him, "Wei Ming, let's go!" So I learned his name; he was called Ge Wei Ming. He replied, "Got it!" Then he smiled at me and asked, "What time do you finish work?" I suspected that only I understood the meaning behind that smile. Could it be that he took Old Zhao's advice and came to see me off after my shift? I met his gaze and smiled faintly, "noon." He said, "Goodbye!" and turned away with his partner, leaving the second floor.

When they turned the corner, my colleagues gathered around, teasing me, "Ah Jing, you're quite charming! When did you become friends with the police?" Some said, "Cooperate to get leniency, resist and face strictness. Ah Jing, come clean!" Even Ah Fang said, "I can't believe it! Ah Jing, you're so secretive; you didn't even tell me!" I hadn't shared yesterday's frightening experience with them, so no one knew about the scare I had endured. What was my relationship with Ge Wei Ming? In reality, we had none! I replied, "Let's get back to work, everyone!" Ah Ju said, "No way, we won't start until you spill the beans." I chuckled, "There's nothing to tell. I've just met him like all of you." Some masseuses said, "We don't believe you; you're lying! Look at how he looked at you; you must have known each other before!" I said, "Let's return to work; the customers are coming soon!"

I discussed with Ah Chun and Ah Fang, "Sister Xu asked the doctor, and it seems that treating Ah Lan's illness is quite challenging. What do you think we should do?" Ah Chun said, "I'm broke; I can't help." Ah Fang said, "Yeah, we're all out of money, but money isn't the main issue at this point. Shouldn't we spend more time with her?" I said, "Ah Fang has a point. Now that the three of us are back, even though Sister Xu and Ah Lan's parents are here, it's better to take turns keeping her company. You two go first and stay with her for a few days, and then I'll go for a few days. It's better that way; what do you think?" Ah Fang and Ah Chun agreed.

After finishing work late at night, I walked out of the sauna, and a motorcycle pulled up in front of me. The rider wore a helmet, and I couldn't recognize him at first. But when he lifted the transparent windshield in front of his eyes, he smiled and said, "Come on, I'll give you a ride home." I couldn't believe it, "Is it you? Did you come?" It was the young police officer named Ge Wei Ming, and he had indeed come to see me off after my shift. He smiled, "We are short-staffed, and the street patrols haven't been arranged yet. I just got off work. This is my motorcycle, and for your safety, let me take you home." During the night inspection, he had already learned my identity but didn't look down on me. Instead, he still came to escort me home, and I was grateful for that.

I sat in the back seat, and he said, "Get closer and hold on tight; I'm starting the engine." He stepped on the gas, and the motorcycle went onto the road. The distance from the sauna to my rented place was a fifteen-minute walk, but the bike arrived in just a few minutes. When we descended the bridge, my upper body leaned forward unconsciously, and my chest pressed against his back. Even though clothes separated us, I sensed him tremble, and the motorcycle hesitated momentarily. Due to inertia, I leaned against his back, causing him to lean forward, almost falling onto the handlebars, to avoid my chest. I couldn't help but chuckle inside: Look how mighty you are, but you're pretty shy!

Time passed too quickly; he brought me to my rented place in just five minutes. I got off the bike and said, "Thank you, Ge Wei Ming!" He smiled and said, "You know my name? What's your name?" I replied, "I'm Xiao Jing. Thank you for taking me home." Ge Wei Ming said, "Oh, Xiao Jing, that's a lovely name, quite rare." I smiled, "Rare things are precious. Because it's uncommon, people tend to remember me." Ge Wei Ming said, "That makes sense. So, what's your schedule? Are you working tomorrow night?"

Having a handsome police officer as a boyfriend is undoubtedly an honor. I have a bit of vanity as well. As a 20-year-old girl, my dreams are rosy. Who wouldn't want to meet a handsome boy and have him as their true love? Like the opening scene in a movie, our relationship has just begun, and I don't know what will happen next. Judging by my understanding of men, he probably doesn't have a girlfriend yet. I'm curious what impression he has of me. He's a police officer, so he must know about the sauna. I'm the kind of girl associated with such places, so why would he be willing to escort me home after work? Is it just his sense of responsibility?

Xiao Hong is an attentive girl. In the early morning, she woke up and saw that I couldn't sleep, so she asked, "What are you thinking? Do you have something on your mind? Don't tell me you're thinking about men?" I smiled, "Who would I be thinking about? And who would think about me?" Xiao Hong said, "People like us can't expect love. Men only see us as playthings, and we see them as merely satisfying our needs. There won't be any true love for us from a man." I said, "We can't keep doing this job forever; we must get married and have children." Xiao Hong said, "That's right. So, we'll work hard and make money in these few years. Our families don't know what we do; they think we have regular jobs. We'll return to our hometown and marry a decent man when we've earned enough. That's how life will be." Sigh, that seems to be our fate. I feel reluctant! I asked, "Xiao Hong, have you ever had a customer fall in love with you, or have you fallen in love with a customer?" Xiao Hong laughed, "In our work, who talks about love? Otherwise, we're the ones who will suffer!"

Honestly, will I fall in love with a customer? Most likely not. If I were to find a partner, I'd either choose someone from a different profession or, as Xiao Hong suggested, marry a decent man from my hometown. Men won't truly love us, and we don't have much faith in men either. For both men and women, what happens before marriage can be overlooked, but mutual respect and love are essential for a good life after marriage. Otherwise, it would be like constant changes in the weather or living with different dreams, making the marriage meaningless. In ancient novels, there were many stories of talented men falling in love with courtesans and redeeming them from their profession, but in reality, it's improbable. The men who visit entertainment places like ours are skilled in sweet talk and experienced in flirting; there's no room for deep affection and unwavering loyalty.

The sunlight and spring breeze are gentle and pleasant in this sunny spring season, with peach blossoms and willow trees. This southern town is genuinely delightful with its small bridges and flowing waters. Coming from the mountainous region of Chongqing, the scenery here is vastly different from the lush green hills of my hometown, but living here and having a peaceful and fulfilling life is a good choice. You don't realize it until you leave, but I used to think that the verdant mountains of my hometown were the most beautiful scenery. But after seeing this place, although small, it's incredibly charming. Bai Juyi once wrote, "The morning sun turns the river flowers red like fire, and in spring, the river water appears blue like indigo. How could one not yearn for Jiangnan?" This shows that the beauty of Jiangnan intoxicated poets over a thousand years ago. Of course, some aspects of this place, such as the social atmosphere, could be more satisfying. It lacks the sincerity and straightforwardness of our hometown, and people here are less trusting of one another. There are also many entertainment venues here, especially at night, with neon lights flashing and so many men and women mixing in them. A trace of impurity is blended into the spring breeze, making it somewhat regrettable.

If it weren't for Ah Lan's illness, which made us feel down, I would have considered life in Nanxun quite good. At work tonight, Ah Mei asked me to help train two new service attendants and teach them some basic techniques. As a masseuse and a trainer at the sauna, it's funny how I've gone from knowing nothing about massages a year ago to becoming a well-known masseuse now. However, I'm keeping my wits about me; I can't teach them everything I know. I'm only showing them some common knowledge; if I taught them everything, I'd be out of a job once they start working.

I entered one of the massage rooms where two new girls were massaging a customer. They were called Ah Yu and Ah Zhen. Seeing their clumsy techniques and bewildered expressions, I recalled that I was once like that. I told them, "When you massage a customer's back, straddle their waist with your body leaning forward. Besides using the correct techniques, your body should sway rhythmically. This way, you can interact with the customer and give them a pleasurable experience." Although the two service attendants nodded frequently, they hesitated and said, "Wouldn't it be painful to sit on the customer?" I chuckled, "When you make love with your boyfriend, do you feel heavy? A true masseuse not only satisfies the customer but also enjoys themselves." The two girls blushed, and the customer lying on the massage bed laughed, "Well said! No wonder you're the famous masseuse of Paradise on Earth!" I chuckled: I've heard of peonies and chrysanthemums, but who knew there were "massage flowers" as well?

Chapter 21

Take Me Home

Can I have a sweet love? I dare not hope for it. What is love? Is it the trailing wedding dress worn during the marriage? Is it the expensive diamond ring on the ring finger? Is it the fragrant rose that blooms quietly in the heart? Or is it the warm embrace yearned for in the middle of the night? I work in the sauna city, not to mention the men I come into contact with, and there are also many men I have socialized with outside to earn some extra money. Some come from affluent families, but none have left a lasting impression on me. Yes, I don't lack men; what I lack is love.

Ge Weiming still comes to pick me up after work at night, and I am very grateful and happy, but at the same time, I feel a bit uneasy. I know that, theoretically, people are equal, but they are often far from equal. I am a masseuse, and he is a police officer. Can it be bAh Lanced if we stand on opposite ends of the scale? He treats me with kindness and friendliness. I'm not afraid that I will fall for him, but I'm worried he will develop feelings for me. I don't mind being an outsider, but it might bring him unfavorable consequences. Rumors can be dreadful, and he is, after all, a police officer. If everyone knows he is getting close to a masseuse, let alone being in a romantic relationship, there will inevitably be gossip even if he escorts me home. If it affects his future, won't I become a notorious sinner?

Ge Weiming's appearance has caused the girls to tease. Ah Ju said, "Jingjie, this is great. We don't have to worry about being investigated anymore. With your boyfriend as a protective umbrella, he can release us if we ever get locked up." Their thinking needs to be more complex. Even if something is between me and him, can he unilaterally release someone? That would be breaking the law. You bunch of troublemakers! I smiled and said, "He's currently my free chauffeur. Other than that, there's nothing else. Don't get any funny ideas!" Ah Ju and the others didn't believe me. "Why would he be your chauffeur? Aren't you lying?" I chuckled, "He is a police officer serving the people!"

Ge Weiming and I don't interact much in ordinary times. We have spent less than two hours together, but I don't feel unfamiliar with him. I find him very familiar like an older brother taking care of me properly and uprightly. His gaze towards me has changed. It has shifted from straightforward directness to discreet glances. Since becoming a masseuse, I may not have learned much else, but I do have some level of understanding when deciphering men's words and expressions. I know that ripples have stirred in his calm heart, which is connected to me. I'm not elated; instead, I feel a bit lost. A voice echoes, "He is a police officer. You are a masseuse, incompatible, impossible!"

To avoid unnecessary worries, I stopped overthinking. If he wants to pick me up, I'll accept the ride. There's nothing wrong with that.

Sometimes, I want to tease him, brushing my chest against his back and hugging him with both arms, feeling his flustered reaction. Unfortunately, the journey home is too short, only five minutes. If only it could be fifty minutes. But women are greedy; even if there were fifty minutes, we would still hope for five hours, five days, or even fifty years! Thinking of this Ge Weiming, I can't help but smile. He has indeed become my designated chauffeur. A handsome guy, a police officer, escorting a masseuse home late at night—perhaps it's an unprecedented situation? Well, as long as he is willing and it's free, I'm happy to let him drive me! Sitting on the back seat of his motorcycle, it feels pretty nice, much more comfortable than when I used to sit on the back of my brother's bicycle when I was young.

At night, Ge Weiming came to pick me up again. At the entrance of our rented place, we ran into Sister Wu and Xiao Hong, who had just finished work. They saw me with a man, and Sister Wu said, "Xiao Jing, you have a friend now? Why don't you introduce him?" Xiao Hong also said, "Why let him stand at the door? Isn't that impolite? Hurry up and invite him in!" Ge Weiming didn't know how to explain and just looked at me, feeling awkward, and said, "No, we're not..." Sister Wu pulled him and said, "Hey, handsome guy, don't say no. Come in and sit for a while!" I said, "It's getting late, and Mr. Ge, the police officer, still needs to go home. Let's not make it difficult for him." Sister Wu was taken aback momentarily and said, "Xiao Jing, what's going on? You two?" Xiao Hong was startled, "Xiao Jing, are you going in too?" Xiao Hong thought I had been detained and this police officer had released me. I laughed, "Let me introduce him. This is my savior, the handsome and mighty Police Officer Ge! And two, one is Sister Wu, my good sister; the other is Xiao Hong, my good friend. We all live together."

Sister Wu and Xiao Hong looked at me, puzzled, as if in a daze. I briefly explained the unexpected incident that day, and Sister Wu and Xiao Hong were shocked, mouths agape. "Ah? Is that what happened? Then what should we do? What about when we come back? We also need someone to protect us! Who do we turn to if there are more bad people or something happens?" Ge Weiming comforted, "Please rest assured, our department is addressing this matter, and we will dispatch patrol officers to the old street." Sister Wu laughed, "Officer Ge is biased. You can escort Xiao Jing home from work. Why can't you escort us? Is it because Xiao Jing is young and beautiful?" Ge Weiming explained, "Work arrangements are up to the department, not me personally." Sister Wu persisted, "If you can escort Xiao Jing home from work, why can't you escort us? Are you having ulterior motives towards Xiao Jing?" Ge Weiming fell silent. I laughed, "Sister Wu, please don't trouble him. He is a good person. Let him go home early. He has to work tomorrow." Sister Wu laughed, "That's right, you already have something special between you?" Xiao Hong chimed in, "Is it a mutual understanding?"

After Ge Weiming left, Sister Wu asked me, "Tell me the truth. What is the extent of your relationship?" I said, "We don't have any relationship, purely a police-civilian relationship, let alone any extent." Sister Wu said, "Really? I see he seems to protect you." I said, "What has he protected? He escorts me home from work. It's not like he'll make me marry him, right?" Sister Wu smiled, "I was just about to say that. Your body isn't that valuable. Why not strike while the iron is hot and win him over?" I laughed, "Sister Wu, are you trying to be a matchmaker? As for me and him, there's nothing between us yet, so let's not jump to conclusions." Xiao Hong said he has a good character. If there's a chance, Xiao Jing, you'll be blessed!" Who doesn't want a true man to be their partner and live happily together? Massage is just the profession I currently rely on to make a living, but my heart and emotions, like those of other girls, also have ideals and dreams. I hope that one day I can have a sweet love!

Sister Wu advised me, "For those of us in this line of work, it's rare to meet a good man. Xiao Jing, you should seize the opportunity and not let him slip away from you!" Xiao Hong added enthusiastically, "Yes, regardless of whether he's a police officer or anyone else, who says a masseuse can't marry a police officer? As long as there is genuine love, even fairies marry cowherds!" I laughed, "What are you all talking about? He hasn't expressed anything to me, so let's not get ahead of ourselves!" Sister Wu said, "As the saying goes, when a man pursues a woman, they may be separated by mountains, but when a woman pursues a man, they may only be separated by a thin veil. If you're interested in him, why not take the initiative? He's so handsome and a police officer, truly a rare and excellent match. Don't let someone else snatch him away, or you'll regret it!" Xiao Hong said, "Sister Wu is right. If you can't speak up, we can do it for you. Let's test the waters and see what he thinks. We hope you can have a good partner, so we can also share some of the glory!" I had made up my mind. I said, "Alright, I'll try it and see if he is interested in me." Xiao Hong said, "Wishing you great success, may you succeed quickly!" I smiled, "I'll do my best."

I continued chatting with Xiao Hong while lying on the bed. We could talk about anything, private matters and secrets. Initially, I only wanted a job to support myself. Even doing some side jobs was, to a certain extent. Youth is our resource, but if it's exploited recklessly, it will be depleted, and people will age faster. Xiao Hong and Sister Wu wanted to make some money while they could. Xiao Hong was relatively good as she could come back to sleep, but Sister Wu had more socializing to do. She not only went out with customers but sometimes brought them here. I firmly refuse to bring customers home to spend the night because it's unsafe. If their wives discover them in the future, trouble will come knocking on our door. Although we can move, we develop a sense of attachment after living here for a long time. This place is relatively peaceful, and I like living here.

Ah Chun and Ah Fang went to Suzhou, and Sister Xu returned. After Sister Xu returned, she came to the club to find me and discuss Aran's situation. She said, "What should we do? Aran's parents don't have the money for her treatment. We can't just stand by and watch her die. Can we ask a journalist to write an article and appeal to the public for assistance?" I said, "Perhaps it's feasible. People might donate money, but the critical issue is that Aran's chances of recovery are extremely slim. No matter how much money we have, we cannot save her life!" Sister Xu said, "At this point, we can only leave it to fate. Let's accompany her on her journey if we can't hold her back." I said, "As long as Aran is alive, we will find a way to treat her." With tears, Sister Xu said, "Xiao Jing, I didn't misjudge you. You are a kind-hearted and good girl! Aran is lucky to have a friend like you!" I said, "We are good sisters. When she's in trouble, I lend a helping hand. It's only natural."

The moonlight was bright, like mercury pouring down. A Mei and I came out after work, and A-Mei said, "Look, your chauffeur is here to pick you up again!" I knew it was Ge Weiming and smiled at A-Mei, saying, "There's no way to avoid it. I can't quit." I walked towards Ge Weiming, who was approaching, and he smiled and said, "I heard you call me your chauffeur. Is that true?" I smiled and replied, "What do you think?" He said, "Get on." Holding onto his waist, I climbed on and said tenderly, "Would you like to take me home?"

Chapter 22

Enchanting Spring Night

Would a man remain indifferent if a beautiful girl asked, "Would you take me home?" Would he remain unmoved? When a woman takes the initiative to seduce a man, it may be a bit shameful, but it becomes insignificant compared to the possible happiness. Ge Weiming seemed to have misheard and stopped the car, asking, "Xiao Jing, what did you just say?" I replied, "It's still early, and I don't want to go home yet. Can you take me somewhere for a stroll? Anywhere is fine!" Ge Weiming didn't expect me to say that and hesitated, "All the shops are closed now. Where should we go?" I said, "I'm a little hungry. Let's get some late-night snacks." He said, "Restaurants are closed now, and street stalls are unhygienic." I took the opportunity and said, "Then let's go to your place. Do you have any food at home?" Seeing the surprised expression on his face, I wasn't sure if he felt troubled or pleasantly surprised.

As a junior police officer, Ge Weiming might have strong skills in catching thieves, but I am no less capable of playing mind games. I intentionally sent him flirtatious glances. Could he resist? Ge Weiming said, "Alright, it's late. Let's go to my place and have something to eat." I felt a surge of joy in my heart. This was the first step to success, giving me a glimmer of hope! I couldn't guarantee that I would capture him as my captive, but his resistance to the advances of a beautiful woman seemed weak. Even if I couldn't easily conquer him, I could at least make him retreat! They say that women mature two to three years earlier than men. Despite my young age, I had ample social experience. While I might not be adept at love and romance, I had become skilled at seducing men.

His home was located in a villa district in the southern part of the town. The houses in that row were gorgeous, each with a large courtyard. I had been here for some time and knew that property prices had skyrocketed. Even an ordinary residential unit would cost several hundred thousand yuan, but his family owned a villa. They were genuinely hiding their wealth! His family was well-off. Could I be so lucky? It felt like Cinderella meeting the prince. I would be fully confident if he were from an ordinary family like mine. It didn't matter if he was a police officer or not, as long as he treated me well, I would make a move on him! However, the disparity between his family and mine was too great. I was just an ordinary girl from a mountain city. Could I be friends with a wealthy young man from Jiangnan? I felt uneasy.

Ge Weiming opened the gate and parked the motorcycle, softly saying, "Come in." I followed him into the courtyard, and I could smell the fragrance of flowers in the moonlight. There were potted plants in the yard and two peach trees with branches full of blossoms, looking particularly beautiful in the moonlight. This was a three-story villa with a spacious interior and many rooms. Ge Weiming led me to the dining room and said, "Please have a seat. Let me see if there's anything to eat." I nodded. In truth, I just wanted to test him and see if he was willing to take me home. My claim of being hungry was just an excuse. I wasn't used to eating late at night. Eating supper could easily lead to weight gain for girls, which would be counterproductive if I tried to lose weight later.

He searched the kitchen for a while and returned to say, "I'm sorry, there's not much to eat. How about I make you a bowl of instant noodles?" Without thinking, I blurted out, "Sure, I love eating instant noodles!" That was true. When I was at home, I loved the egg noodles my mom made for me, adding some chili peppers to make them spicy and fragrant, which would greatly whet my appetite and leave me wanting more! Ge Weiming inadvertently brought back memories of home. He smiled and said, "Cooking instant noodles is my specialty. Just wait a moment. I'll make it for you." Watching his back as he prepared the noodles, I found it both unfamiliar and familiar. If a man is willing to make noodles for you, does it mean it's a sign of love?

Listening to the clinking of bowls in the kitchen, two bowls of fragrant noodles were brought to the table in just a few minutes. I wasn't starving, but the aroma in front of me awakened my appetite. I took a small sip of the soup and couldn't help but laugh, "So flavorful! The taste is delicious!" Then I picked up the chopsticks and hungrily started eating. At home, I only had a meal with spice, but since coming to Jiangnan, I have adapted to the local preference for lighter flavors. Ge Weiming was also eating, and he smiled and said, "Looks like you're starving. I didn't ask you when I sent you home the other day." I mumbled in agreement, eating half a bowl of noodles before saying, "Why didn't you ask me?" I saw him shyly smiling and replied, "We didn't have much time. I arrived at your doorstep before thinking of what to say." I chuckled secretly and said, "What preparation is needed to speak? Just say what you want to say."

After finishing the noodles, I wanted to delay the time and chat casually with him. If I found that he wasn't interested in me, then I would gracefully retreat. I would seize the opportunity if I discovered that he had feelings for me. I said, "Weimin, you pick me up after work every night. I don't know how to thank you." He smiled and said, "What's there to thank for? It's not tiring at all, just a few minutes." I said, "Don't you need to spend time with your girlfriend? Won't she get jealous?" To know oneself and the enemy is the key to victory. Before I could employ my "feminine wiles" on him, I needed to ensure he was single. I knew deep down that despite being a police officer, he was, first and foremost, a man. Men have weaknesses, such as cherishing and protecting delicate women. They yield to tenderness rather than force. As a masseuse, our trump card against men is using our softness to overcome their strength. Under our gentle assault, how many can retreat unscathed?

Ge Weiming shook his head and said, "Don't make fun of me. I've never been in a relationship." I pretended to be surprised, "Really? With your good qualities, are your standards too high?" He smiled wryly and said, "After high school, I enlisted in the army. After being discharged, I started working at the police station. I didn't have a chance to meet the girls. Sometimes, my parents would arrange blind dates for me, but I couldn't accept them. How can the lifelong matter of two people be decided so easily? It's being irresponsible to one's love and marriage." I laughed, "Blind dates are popular these days, both in the city and the countryside. I wanted to go on a blind date, but unfortunately, no one wanted me." Ge Weiming said, "You also want to go on a blind date?" I smiled, "Can't I? Do you think there's something wrong with me?" He quickly denied it and said, "You're great. Although your job isn't the best, you're a good person." Hearing his words, I felt delighted.

We chatted casually about various topics, and unconsciously, time passed quickly. I estimated that it was already past 2 am. He didn't urge me to leave, so I lingered to see how he would react. He told me fascinating stories from his work and how they caught thieves and robbers. I asked, "Do you feel scared when you're fighting against criminals?" Unexpectedly, he burst into laughter and said, "Why would I be afraid of them? Evil can't suppress justice. All the bad guys are afraid when they see the police. Sometimes, they may fight back fiercely when they are desperate, but the law is impartial, and they cannot escape!" When discussing work, he became spirited and exuded a sense of righteousness. It was completely different from his restrained behavior in front of girls.

We sat for a long time and talked a lot. Seeing his hesitating expression, I understood he felt awkward telling me to leave. I thought he wouldn't let me go alone even if I wanted to leave. He would accompany me. It was my first time at his place, and I didn't want to reveal any intention of staying the night. That would make him look down on me. It was late, so I pretended to be very tired, yawned, and said, "I'm sorry, I'm feeling drowsy. I've stayed at your place for too long, and I should go back." As I said that, I stood up, but Ge Weiming stopped me and said, "Xiao Jing, it's so late you..." I swayed my body a few times, and he hurriedly supported me, concerned, "It's too late; just rest at my place for a while." I half-pushed, half-accepted, and said, "Sleep at your place? That would be embarrassing." He whispered, "It's okay. There's an empty room upstairs at my place."

A single man and a single woman, alone in a room. It would be a disservice to us and this beautiful moment if nothing happened. Moreover, once a woman's desires are awakened and experienced, there is a need for such intimacy. As long as there is an opportunity, it is easy to ignite the flames buried in the depths of the heart. I admit I am a masseuse and have slept with many men for money, but I still have integrity. I won't treat myself like trash. I will give my body and emotions to someone who truly loves me. Facing this man who was so close and within reach, the dam of my desires inevitably overflowed!

I heard his heavy breathing as I embraced his head and pulled him towards me. His head was buried in my chest, resembling a baby nursing at his mother's breast. He seemed like a naive child, but his clumsiness wasn't laughable. Instead, it made me feel pity and cherish him. I could sense that he was still an inexperienced man! He was a man worthy of my respect and admiration! He had found my moist lips and began to explore them incessantly, which ignited a firestorm of emotions within me! I thought about all the customers I had encountered. Even if I were beautiful and slept beneath them, they rarely kissed me. Perhaps they thought I was dirty, but in reality, I found them to be messy!

He found his way to my wetness on the moonlit bed in the darkness. My excitement and emotions filled my chest, every inch of my young and hungry skin! I was deeply intoxicated! "When golden wind and jade dew meet, it surpasses the countless encounters in the mortal realm!" I thought this incredible moment of love had finally come, albeit a bit late!

Chapter 23

Tinder and Blaze

❝Being alone elsewhere, I feel like a stranger. Every time a festival comes, I miss my family even more." A few days ago was Qingming Festival, and my mood was somewhat low and restless. From the beginning until now, this diary has been about me reminiscing. For some people, memories of the past may be sweet, but for me, most of them are gray and unable to bring me happiness. These past few days, I have been strongly yearning for Ah Lan, because she left us forever on the eve of Qingming in 2004. Looking back, I still feel deep sorrow, and tears flow uncontrollably!

We come from different places but engage in the same profession. The smiles we put on are all for the sake of basic survival. I'm not seeking sympathy from everyone. Among us sisters, some are lazy, but the vast majority are forced by poverty. My family's situation is pretty good because my brother and I are working and earning money. We can even provide some financial support and lighten the burden at home. But some sisters go out to work alone, not only to find a way for themselves but also to carry the hopes of their entire family and bear the burden of supporting them! Some families are in mountainous areas, where parents have little income besides farming. They also have siblings going to school, so imagine how tough their lives are. The poorer the place, the harder it is to afford education. Coming out here without an education and without qualifications, it's incredibly difficult to find a job. But the entertainment venues are always hiring, and some even provide meals and accommodation. Can you blame us for being tempted?

The work we do outside is kept secret from our families. Not just me, but also Ah Lan, Fang, and others. None of us would reveal our identities as massage girls to our families. It's not that we have no shame, but it's a result of circumstances and the lack of anyone to control us in this place far from home. It's easy for us to let loose. If our families knew what we were doing, they would never forgive us. They would never allow their daughters to lose face even if we were poor! Sometimes, I look down on myself. Why didn't I choose a different job instead of getting involved in something degrading? But we also like to dress up and be fancy. Buying fashionable clothing or a cosmetics bottle costs tens or even hundreds of yuan. But where would the money come from? Although it's a bit degrading, the work we do is no less tiring than working in a factory. But it brings in cash quickly, much more than a regular job. It provides us with a source of income, making our lives better. It's still better than having empty pockets and a worried face.

At Ge Weiming's house, I employed a little strategy and trapped him in my tenderness. After accumulating energy for over twenty years, he found the opportunity to unleash his potential. Apart from being brave on the battlefield, men also exhibit their heroism with women. Ge Weiming was inexperienced, but he shed his shyness under my influence and indulged himself with me. The exhilarating feeling made me shout with joy! It must still be cool outside in the early spring morning, but inside the room, it was as hot as summer. At that moment, we completely forgot about each other's identities; all that existed was physical intertwining. Although it was our first time being intimate, we acted like passionate lovers, burning with youthful passion!

To reach this stage so quickly with Ge Weiming was partly planned and partly unexpected. Looking back, I am primarily responsible for us getting to this point because I seduced him first. Whatever happened between us, it wasn't excessive, right? After all, we interacted, and he picked me up a few times. We had a mutual liking for each other. The dynamics between men and women may not differ much, but the connotations are entirely different. My interactions with customers are merely transactions, finishing the job and parting ways without any obligations. But with Ge Weiming, there were budding emotions. It wasn't just an impulse; it naturally evolved. I admit I pursued him actively, with emotions being a secondary factor. Mainly, I had my future in mind. I hoped to find a partner, stay in this place, and live worry-free. That way, I could leave the sauna city and embrace a better tomorrow. Unexpectedly, everything fell into place, and Ge Weiming and I slept together.

Perhaps our voices were too loud, forgetting to consider that only the living room separated his parents' bedroom from ours. At 7 a.m., while we were still sound asleep, a woman's voice outside the door called, "Weiming, it's time to wake up! You'll be late for work!" He jolted awake and quickly pulled his hand from under my head, saying, "My mom is calling me. Oh no, I have to be at work by 7:30, there's no time!" He hurriedly got up, dressed hastily, and remembered I was still lying in his bed. He said, "Xiao Jing, you should get up too. I'll take you back home first." I stretched lazily and got up, searching for my scattered clothes on the floor. In someone else's house, it's more casual than being in my place, where I can wash my face and brush my teeth in my underwear. Here, I had to maintain a respectable appearance, or I would be criticized.

Ge Weiming's room had a bathroom. After freshening up, just as we opened the bedroom door, Ge Weiming said, "Mom, why are you standing outside?" I followed behind him and was also taken aback. I didn't expect his mother to be waiting by the door. Ge's mom said, "I was waiting for you. What time is it already? Why did you oversleep?" She saw me in one glance, and her expression changed slightly. She asked her son, "Weiming, you brought someone home to sleep without telling your mother? Who is this?" I greeted her affectionately, "Hello, Auntie! I'm Xiaojing." Ge's mother uttered an "Oh" and said to her son, "You have a girlfriend now?" Ge Weiming blushed and looked at me, saying, "Uh, yeah, we just met." Ge's mother muttered, "Just met and already sleeping together, how improper." I wondered if she was referring to her son or me.

As we descended the stairs and walked to the restaurant where I had eaten noodles the night before, I suddenly noticed a familiar face sitting at a table, eating porridge. He happened to look up when I saw him, and I couldn't help but freeze! Can you guess who it was? After officially starting work, he was my first customer, the one I gave a massage to, who quietly gave me a 100 yuan tip! I never dreamed that he would be Ge Weiming's father. Ge Weiming saw my expression and asked, "Xiaojing, do you know my dad?" To avoid embarrassment and unnecessary suspicion from Ge Weiming and his mother, I lied, "Oh, no, I just feel like your uncle looks very familiar, like a relative from my hometown." I saw Ge's father sigh in relief, and I smiled too. Ge's father warmly said, "Come over and have some porridge. The rice porridge from the south is very fragrant." I had never tasted rice porridge from this region before. I usually don't eat breakfast; if I do, it's usually buns or noodles.

I didn't hesitate to sit down. I thought since Ge Weiming and I wanted to be in a relationship, there was no need to be too reserved. Ge's mother served us the porridge, and I enjoyed it with relish. It was light and fragrant, with the aroma of rice. Their pickled vegetables were also delicious; I ate them with great satisfaction. Ge's mother asked me, "Where is your hometown?" I said, "Chongqing." Ge's mother said, "It's a mountainous area, right? Quite far." Ge's father said, "Chongqing is a direct-controlled municipality now, a key city in western development, developing quite rapidly." I smiled and said, "It's much better than before, but compared to here, we still have a long way to go." Ge's mother saw that I had finished the porridge and asked, "Do you want more?" I smiled and said, "No, I usually don't eat breakfast. The porridge was great, so I had a bowl." Ge's father said, "You should eat something in the morning to have energy for the day." Ge's mother asked, "Where do you work?" Ge Weiming was afraid that his parents would object to our relationship if they knew about my profession, so he quickly interrupted and said, "Mom, you're overstepping your bounds. Checking someone's background is the job of our household registration police." Ge's mother glared at her son and said, "Hurry up and finish eating, I want to chat with Xiaojing for a bit." Ge Weiming said, "Next time, let her rest. It's not good to bombard her with questions the first time we meet." He rarely considered my feelings. He's a good guy, and I should hold onto him.

After spending the night at Ge Weiming's house, he treated me even better. He would pick me up after work at night and sometimes come to my rented place during the day. If Sister Wu and Xiao Hong happened to be out, he would also try to seize the opportunity for a quick encounter.

I am curious to know how men lived before having women in their lives. I spent several days enjoying the bright and beautiful moments with Ge Weiming. I wonder if this is love. I became intoxicated with this man's happiness and learned to indulge in fantasies. Even when giving a massage to a client, my mind would be filled with thoughts of Ge Weiming. I almost forgot that Ah Lan was still in the hospital these days. If it weren't for the return of Chun and Fang to Nanxun, I would have completely lost myself in playing with Ge Weiming.

Recently, I have been sending money home or calling home very few times. One day, my brother called me and asked what was going on. He wondered if things weren't going well at work. I said, "No, everything is going well." My brother said, "Then why don't you call Mom and Dad? They miss you." I said, "I've been busy lately. Brother, aren't you getting married on May Day? I'll take leave and come home." My brother laughed and said, "We changed our plans. We want to save some money, go on a honeymoon trip, and broaden our horizons. We're thinking of going to Hangzhou and Suzhou and visiting you too." I said, "A honeymoon trip is nice, but I'm happy for you. It would be even better to have the wedding at home and let Mom, Dad, and the relatives celebrate. It would be more lively that way." My brother said, "That's a good idea, but what do we do if we don't have money? Xiaojing, do you have any money? Can you lend me some?" I said, "I don't have any money with me." My brother said, "Mom said you haven't sent money home lately. I thought you were saving up for your dowry." I said, "It's too early for that, but recently, I've started seeing someone here who happens to be a local policeman." My brother exclaimed with joy,

"That's great!"

Chapter 24

The Taste of Love

I didn't gain anything. Otherwise, I would be doing something other than my old job today, staying up late to write a diary instead of comfortably being a young lady nursing a baby. Who can predict the future? Wasn't I once filled with naive dreams? Sometimes, it's not that we are giving up on ourselves or don't want to escape from that environment, but rather that we have no other options!

Women want to earn money comfortably, while men want to spend money comfortably. This supply and demand has been a prominent feature of feudal society for thousands of years. I greatly admire Chairman Mao. He was the founding leader of New China, and regardless of his achievements, since he passed away before I was born, I respect that during his rule in New China, he managed to eradicate the ugly phenomenon of prostitution. That is indeed the work of a great man. Besides him, who else has been able to do so throughout history?

The sauna city I'm in has a reputation. People from all walks of life come here. Who doesn't know about Sea Paradise? For men, who wouldn't want to go to Sea Paradise for a bath? And perhaps find a girl? If you wish to do something legitimate, we have that here too. If you want something more exciting, we have a lot to offer. Compared to those shabby roadside shops, we have a higher class. We proudly massage girls at Sea Paradise, wearing our work badges on our chests, attracting attention. Do the shady shops dare to do the same? We, as masseuses, may not be on par with the hostesses in star hotels, but we don't rely on our looks to make a living. We earn money based on our skills.

A few days ago, there was a large-scale crackdown on entertainment venues in the Huzhou area, and many roadside shops and beauty salons that provided sexual services were closed down. However, Sea Paradise Sauna City remained unscathed. I saw on the news that those hair washing and foot massage shops didn't have the tools for hair washing, hairdressing, or foot massages. Instead, they directly provided sexual massages and services. From the footage, I could see a larLady Gessage room divided by plywood into many small rooms, with some girls engaging in inappropriate activities with customers, caught in the act. I felt a bit sympathetic toward them, but I also felt some resentment. Their actions tarnished the reputation of massage girls and painted our legitimate profession with an ambiguous brush. They are what we commonly refer to as "wild chickens," right? Then what does that make us? Are we "three-legged chickens" or "grass chickens"? Who compared us women to chickens? What about the men? If we are the fragile eggs, aren't they the despicable flies that don't spare even seamless ones?

I visited Ah Lan at a hospital in Suzhou. At first glance, I almost didn't recognize her because she was wearing a hat, and her face had become plump, erasing her previous beauty. If she hadn't called out my name, "Ah jing," making her voice sound familiar, I would have thought I went to the wrong ward. Ah Lan had completely changed. It wasn't that she was overweight; she was swollen. Her eyes no longer sparkled; they appeared dim, like a dull light bulb. During our conversation, I learned that she was aware of her fate and that her remaining days were limited. Ah Lan said, "I'm not afraid of death, but I still have regrets." I said, "I understand. Our lives have just begun, but... Ah Lan, we are close friends. Tell me if you have any wishes, and we will all help you." Ah Lan's eyes welled up with tears as she said, "I can no longer repay my parents' care, and I feel guilty for the money and efforts you all have spent on me. I can't repay your kindness in this lifetime. And... there's one more thing, I haven't tasted the flavor of love in this lifetime, and I feel a bit unwilling!" I was speechless, and every word Ah Lan spoke was filled with her deep affection and attachment. But why did fate have to be so cruel, snatching away a young girl's beautiful life? I had wanted to tell Ah Lan about my love life, to bring her some joy, but I was afraid it would only make her more sorrowful, so I held back.

Ah Lan required regular dialysis treatment once a week. Her whole body's blood was filtered like combing through tangled hair, refreshing her spirit and giving her more confidence. I asked Dr. Shen about the possibility of a kidney transplant for Ah Lan. He said, "Doctors have limitations, and the current medical technology cannot cure all diseases. The hope of curing Ah Lan's condition is almost zero. We can only provide conservative treatment to prolong her life as much as possible." Hearing this, the glimmer of hope in my eyes faded, and I helplessly said, "Ah, Ah Lan is truly unlucky."

I returned to Nanxun with Ge Weiming's company, and my life suddenly became lively. Yes, I'm only 20 years old, still at an age of carefree innocence. It's just that I entered society's current so early, which has worn away my purity and dreams. This has taught me the importance and necessity of seizing happiness in the present. Ge Weiming and I haven't officially defined our relationship yet, and for now, I don't want to give up my self-supporting job. However, I no longer provide services like oil massages or chest massages, which are on the edge of sexual services. Massage is my means of making a living, not my career. The salary is enough for my expenses. I can no longer accept other men. In my heart, there is only Ge Weiming. With him, I am content.

As the saying goes, "The master leads the way, and the cultivation is self-improvement." Although I'm five years younger than Ge Weiming, I might know more about the affairs between men and women. When we explore together, we often reach the pinnacle of pleasure simultaneously. He understands I'm not a virgin, but he doesn't seem to mind. He said, "As long as you treat me well, I don't care about your past. I like you and am willing to accept you completely!" I was happy to hear him say that. Men are usually highly selfish, and they can freely play with other women outside, but they can't tolerate having a girlfriend who is not pure. However, Ge Weiming seems to be tolerant. When we are together, he never shows any displeasure. Instead, he says, "It's a pity I didn't meet you earlier. I could have protected you if I had known you when you first arrived." I smiled and said, "Those two bad guys facilitated something good between us. You probably wouldn't even know my last name if they hadn't bullied me." Ge Weiming laughed and said, "Now I know you like the back of my hand. You have a mole in a certain spot, and I know it well."

Indeed, I have a small mole there, and it was Ge Weiming who discovered this new continent. Once, he said he wanted to see what secrets women hold that can captivate men so much. As a result, he actually found it—the faint mole. He said, "According to international conventions, for newly discovered islands, the one who discovers it has the right to develop and use it exclusively. In other words, I now own the exclusive rights to this territory. I have the right to exercise sovereignty at any time, and it is sacred and inviolable." At first, he seemed serious and not very talkative, but now I find he has a great sense of humor and loves to joke around in bed. That year, China successfully launched the Shenzhou 5 spacecraft, and during foreplay, he would say it was the "pre-launch phase." When we started, he would say we were "successfully entering orbit and undergoing intense debugging." And when it was over, he would say, "Now the launch is complete, everything went smoothly." When he calmed down, he would say, "Return module safely landed"... His jokes added a lot of fun to our intimate moments.

Just as my relationship with Ge Weiming was flourishing, tragedy struck Ah Lan! It happened on April 3rd, two days before the Qingming Festival, and the weather was still so clear. I thought they said, "Rain falls during the Qingming season," but there were no signs of rain. I had just started my shift at work when I received a phone call from Sister Xu. The sobbing in her voice gave me a sense of foreboding. Sister Xu spoke intermittently on the phone, saying, "Xiaojing, Ah Lan... she's not doing well!" I was shocked and quickly asked, "Is Ah Lan being treated? I'll take a leave and come right away!" After crying, Sister Xu choked and said, "She's gone..." I felt a chilling sensation throughout my body as if the cold air of an iceberg enveloped my heart. Despite expecting this day to come, I still couldn't accept such a tragic event happening so suddenly!

Chapter 25

Love in Suzhou City

I called Ah Chun and Ah Fang and quickly hailed a taxi to Suzhou. However, our sister Ah Lan had already closed her eyes forever. Due to her illness, her appearance changed, but we would remember her beauty. Her face was peaceful, without any signs of pain or struggle. Sister Xu told me Ah Lan's last words were only three: "I'm sorry..." Ah Fang and Ah Chun cried, and Sister Xu's eyes were red. We were all very saddened, and tears streamed down my face uncontrollably as I covered my face and cried.

I didn't find Ah Lan's parents. Sister Xu said, "Her mother fainted and is receiving an IV in another ward, and her father is taking care of her." To witness your child pass away while being unable to do anything, it's such a heartbreaking and helpless situation. What should we do about Ah Lan's funeral? Should we have it at the funeral home in Suzhou or take her body back to her hometown in Yancheng? Sister Xu said, "Let's temporarily store her in the hospital's morgue tonight and discuss it with

Ah Lan's parents tomorrow. But I think it's better to handle it here. Her parents are not in good health and are deeply saddened. It's better to take care of Ah Lan's funeral sooner so that they can find peace and bring her ashes back home." I said, "They say fallen leaves return to their roots, but can her soul accompany her parents back home?" Sister Xu said, "She will go back. Even though she doesn't want to leave us, after all, that is her hometown. She was a respectful girl; she won't wander like a lonely ghost outside."

Sister Xu also said, "There is still some money left in the account. The hospital said they would refund us. We can use it for the funeral arrangements." I said, "I don't know anything about this. Do we need to notify her relatives if we handle it here?" Sister Xu said, "I'm not sure either. We can go and ask Ah Lan's parents tomorrow." That night, Sister Xu and I stayed overnight at the hospital and visited Ah Lan's mother. Her mother looked even weaker as if she had aged ten years overnight. Ah Lan's father was honest and silent, his face filled with wrinkles of hardship and helplessness. Sister Xu and I sat with them for a while and chatted. Sister Xu said, "Auntie, about Ah Lan's arrangements, are you planning to take her back or have the cremation done here in Suzhou?" Ah Lan's mother moved her lips a few times and said, "We want to take her back, but we don't have many relatives left, and we are not in good health..." Sister Xu said, "Auntie, please rest assured. Let us handle this. We will make sure Ah Lan rests in peace." Ah Lan's mother's eyes became moist, and she said, "I see it all. You are all good girls, so kind to my daughter! I don't know how to repay you." Sister Xu said, "Auntie, no need to thank us. Ah Lan was my dear sister, and her life was too tough. It's only right for us to do something for her."

In the morning, Sister Xu and I made arrangements with the funeral home. When we returned to the hospital, we were surprised that more than twenty of our sisters from Sea Paradise Sauna City had gathered in front of the outpatient building. The mid-shift and night-shift sisters were all present, apart from those on the day shift. I knew they had come to pay their respects to Ah Lan. It was our final farewell. They surrounded me and asked with concern, "Where is Ah Lan? Is she still in the hospital?" Sister Xu was also surprised and said, "Why did all of you come?" I said, "She is in the morgue. We'll go to the funeral home together." I like reading Gu Long's martial arts novels, such as Chu Liuxiang, Lu Xiaofeng, and Li Xunhuan. Gu Long once said, "Whether a person is successful in life can be determined by their state at the time of death. If it is filled with loneliness and despair, then they have failed. If someone accompanies and mourns for them, then they have succeeded." I thought Ah Lan was a success. Although her life was short, we, her sisters, never forgot her!

I don't know who leaked the news to the media, but when Ah Lan's body was brought out of the morgue, TV cameras suddenly were in the hospital corridor, wanting to interview us. Sister Xu pushed me forward to take the interview. I had never experienced such a situation before and was quite nervous. I couldn't remember exactly what I said. Still, I vaguely recall the reporter asking about my relationship with Ah Lan, what illness Ah Lan had, and how we helped her seek medical treatment. I knew the news had to reflect the truth and couldn't lie, so I answered honestly. Later, I found out that Dr. Shen had called the reporters from "Social Fax" at the television station, saying that there was a touching story in the hospital, and invited them to film it.

The reporters also interviewed Ah Lan's attending physician, a few nurses, and Ah Lan's parents. Ah Lan's mother wept uncontrollably in front of the camera, expressing her gratitude towards us. It was a touching scene; even people from other wards expressed their regret and respect for us massage girls. They said, "It's scarce to see such deep sisterhood among massage girls. It's truly moving! When you think about it, some neighbors can't get along even in our society. It's not right!" When the twenty-plus of us sisters bid Ah Lan farewell at the funeral home, the cameras no longer asked any questions.

A wisp of smoke, a handful of ashes—all that remained of Ah Lan. Seeing her frail mother and elderly father, my heart ached. How would they live from now on? I told Ah Lan's mother, "Although Ah Lan is gone, I am still here, and so are our sisters. We are all your daughters! If you have any difficulties, please tell us. We will be by your side!" I told all the sisters, "I know most of us don't have much money, but for Ah Lan's sake, let's contribute a little more so that Ah Lan's parents can live their remaining years in peace and continue with their medical treatment!" Everyone responded and contributed a few hundred yuan each. Even the reporters and photographers from the TV station each gave 500 yuan, expressing their support.

When leaving the hospital, Sister Xu told me that the hospital had refunded 90,000 yuan that was unused. I knew that 70,000 yuan of it was from Sister Xu returning the money for the house. I said, "Sister Xu, take back the 70,000 yuan. Leave 50,000 yuan for yourself, and the rest can go to Ah Lan's parents." Sister Xu said, "Then I'll keep 50,000 yuan, and the remaining amount will go to Ah Lan's parents. We are still young and can earn money, but they are getting old and have no income in the countryside." I handed over the urn containing the ashes, several bundles of orchids that Ah Lan loved, a passbook with 40,000 yuan (I later called Ah Lan's father to tell him the password), and the more than 7,000 yuan we had donated to Ah Lan's mother. She knelt on the ground, holding the urn and the orchids, kowtowing to us with tears streaming down her face, unable to say a word.

We saw off Ah Lan's parents onto a long-distance bus, and our group boarded a direct bus from Suzhou to Nanxun. It happened to be Qingming Festival that day, with bright sunshine and no rain, but our hearts were filled with tears. Sending off a life, we all felt heavy-hearted. We were all still young, around 20 years old. The youngest was 17-year-old A Rong, who had just finished junior high school and started working here. The oldest was 28-year-old A Zhen, who already had a husband and child. To make a living, she left her husband to tend to the fields, take care of the elderly and children, and come to work alone. Each one of us here is like a book filled with tear-stained pages. We are not seeking sympathy. If we could find satisfactory jobs in our hometowns, why would we come so far to work? Moreover, the work we are currently engaged in is only temporary, relying on our youth rather than a long-term solution.

After the news aired on "Social Fax," our business became even more prosperous. The flow of customers who came to Sea Paradise Sauna City for baths and massages doubled compared to usual! Some even said, "We came here specifically for the massage girls. They are amazing! It's so rare to see genuine affection like this!" Although the customers who came that day only wanted pure massage services, the day's revenue still broke historical records. The ten-plus service staff on the night shift were bustling, and we barely had time for dinner.

The crowd continued to surge in the following days, and the customers' attitude towards us massage girls changed. They no longer looked down on us but showed us appropriate respect, and the tips we received increased. In just a few days, reporters from Huzhou TV came to interview us again and Mr. Sun, the boss. With a beaming smile, Mr. Sun said, "We at Sea Paradise Sauna City are proud to have these kind-hearted massage therapists! We welcome friends from all walks of life to visit our comfortable and superior environment at Sea Paradise!" Mr. Sun was a true businessman, never straying from his line of work, even on a free advertisement within the program. The business has been perfect lately. Mr. Sun said that Mr. Sun had taken care of it, and this month we would each receive a bonus of 500 yuan. Money was not the main thing; the absolute joy came from the honor and respect we received!

After the program aired on Huzhou TV, it sparked another wave of public attention. Sea Paradise and us massage girls became the focus of social news. People everywhere were discussing us, saying they had never expected a group of massage therapists to have such great compassion and righteousness. We became well-known, and more eyes were now watching us. Initially, everything went smoothly for us, but because of your actions, the business became difficult!"

The situation was better than Tian had anticipated. Starting from the evening of the following day, our business became exceptionally bustling, and the number of customers coming to Sea Paradise Sauna City for baths and massages doubled. Some even said, "We came here specifically for the massage girls. They are amazing! What a rare display of genuine emotions!" Although the customers who came that day only requested pure massage services, our daily revenue reached a new record. The ten-plus service staff on the night shift were busy beyond measure, and we barely had time for dinner.

The crowd continued to surge in the next few days, and the customers' attitude towards us massage girls underwent a complete transformation. They no longer looked down on us but showed us appropriate respect, and the tips we received increased. Within a few days, reporters from Huzhou TV came to interview us again, this time also interviewing

Manager Tian. With a beaming smile, Manager Tian said, "We at Sea Paradise Sauna City are proud to have such kind-hearted massage therapists! We welcome friends from all walks of life to visit our comfortable and superior environment at Sea Paradise!" Manager Tian was a true businessman, always sticking to his line of work, even during free advertisements within a program. The business had been perfect lately. Manager Tian said that Mr. Sun had taken care of it, and each of us would receive a bonus of 500 yuan this month. Money was not the main thing; the absolute joy came from the honor and respect we received!

After the program aired on Huzhou TV, it sparked another wave of public attention. Sea Paradise and us massage girls became the focus of social news. People everywhere were discussing us, saying they had never expected a group of massage therapists to have such great compassion and righteousness. We became well-known, and more eyes were now watching us. Sister Wu, Wu Fang, and Xiao Hong expressed their "jealousy" towards me. They said, "Xiao Jing, you've become famous as a massage girl. We've been here for years but remained unknown!" I laughed and said, "Fame can be both good and bad for a person like me, and I'm not sure yet which it will be."

Ge Wei Ming continued to pick me up, sometimes dropping me off at home, sometimes bringing me to his place. The sadness left by Ah Lan's passing couldn't suppress the fiery passion of love. Something was missing when I didn't see him for a day. I was only 20 years old and still below the legal marriage age. In two years, I would become a native of Jiangnan and Ge Wei Ming's wife. The thought made my heart blossom with joy.

As I got out of bed and quietly walked downstairs to the living room, I heard what seemed to be an argument coming from the dining room. I stopped and listened for a moment and began to understand that Ge Wei Ming's parents were arguing. Weren't they always getting along well? Why were they suddenly arguing? It was related to me because they mentioned my name. I couldn't help but feel curious and wanted to know what they were arguing about. I heard Ge's mother say, "Okay, so you already knew she was a massage girl! Then why did you let her stay at home? Do you want her to be our daughter-in-law?"

Chapter 26

The Best Masseuse

I needed clarification on what Lady Ge meant. Could I not become a part of the Ge family? I didn't know where I went wrong, causing such rejection from her. Yes, I am a massage therapist and have lost myself before, but haven't I changed for the better now? In life, who hasn't made mistakes? Since becoming friends with Ge Weiming, I have been wholeheartedly devoted to him and haven't been with other men like that. Ge Weiming has also said that he doesn't care about my past! Judging from Lady Ge's tone, she is unwilling to accept me. Weren't things fine just a few days ago? Why did she suddenly change her mind? Could it be that she heard some gossip?

I heard Ge Baba say, "What's wrong with being a massage therapist? That's just Xiao Jing's job. She has been to our home more than once, and you know what kind of person she is. Now everyone outside is praising her, aren't they?" Lady Ge said, "It's precisely because people are talking about her that I can't stand it even more! If people discover that my Weiming married a massage therapist, won't they ridicule us? Will our Ge family still have face walking on the street?" Ge Bo angrily said, "You still stuck with feudal thinking in this day and age? I don't think she brings shame to us. Instead, I think your mindset is inferior to hers!" Lady Ge was furious and said, "Alright! How can you compare me to her? She's an outsider, a massage therapist. What's so good about her? Did you find a treasure? I don't care!" Ge Baba said, "How can you say that? No matter what she does, at the very least, you should respect her!" Lady Ge snorted and said, "I don't have your high ideological consciousness. She's an outsider, and I tolerated her. I didn't expect her to be a prostitute, working in that place. Can she be a good girl? Weiming must be blind!"

Ge Baba said, "Why are you becoming more unreasonable as you speak? She's not a prostitute; she only works at the sauna city doing massages. What does that have to do with being a prostitute?" Lady Ge said, "I think it's the same thing. She always touches men, and it won't lead to anything good! Lao Ge, haven't you heard? The first time she stayed at our house, she slept with Weiming and yelled and shouted brazenly. Are you deaf? Didn't you hear?" Ge Bo said, "That doesn't prove anything. Young people, they're inevitably a bit casual." If someone looks down on me, no matter who it is, I would also look down on them! Since Lady Ge despises me, why should I stay here? Fine, I'll leave immediately!

I entered the dining room, and Lady Ge was surprised to see me suddenly appear. Ge Baba smiled and said, "Xiao Jing, awake already?" Lady Ge also realized and greeted, "Xiao Jing, come, have some porridge." Looking at Lady Ge acting as if nothing happened, I felt a bit sad. Why do people have snobbish eyes and enjoy gossiping behind others' backs? I said, "I won't eat, I'm going back." Lady Ge said, "Eat before you leave. The dishes and porridge I cooked today are delicious."

I wasn't happy, and I didn't care if it was delicious. I said, "I'm leaving. I made plans to go shopping for clothes with friends." I turned around and started walking out. I heard Lady Ge say from behind, "I hope she didn't hear us arguing." Ge Baba said, "You're too meddlesome. Let our son handle his matters. Why are you worrying about it?"

Late at night, when I finished work, Ge Weiming didn't come to pick me up, which surprised me. Didn't he constantly say he liked me? Didn't he promise to come pick me up rain or shine? Why wasn't he here tonight? He didn't even call me? He really couldn't withstand any tests! My temper has changed dramatically since coming to this small town in Jiangnan, but I was still stubborn. If he didn't come to pick me up or even call me, I would ignore him. Who was afraid of who? That night, without considering anything, even if there were evildoers on the road, I walked back to my place alone. No matter how hard I tried that night, I couldn't fall asleep. Why? Was Ge Weiming, just like any other man, unreliable? Didn't he like me, either? They say, "A woman's heart is as deep as the ocean," but I didn't think it was that complicated. Why was this man's heart so hard to understand? Even if he listened to me about love matters, shouldn't I have a say? Did I still have to obey the "parents' orders"?

For three consecutive nights, Ge Weiming didn't show up. I didn't want to go to his workplace to find him, and I didn't want to go to his house either. If he didn't care about me, I must have misjudged him! I thought to myself, "Ge Weiming, you're ruthless! You're not coming to find me. Can't I live without you? Let me tell you, I can live on my own. I don't need to rely on anyone!" I was dedicated to my work at the sauna city, and my reputation was good. But this night, I felt uneasy. While massaging a customer, my thoughts were elsewhere, and I applied too much pressure when it should have been light and too little pressure when it should have been strong, which irritated the customer. When it was time for him to pay, he complained loudly, "What gold medal masseuse? It's all nonsense!"

The floor supervisor, Ah Mei, heard the customer's complaints and came over to ask me, "Ah jing, do you have something on your mind?" I said, "It's nothing. I didn't do well." I stopped the customer who was about to leave the lobby and said, "Sir, please wait a moment!" He turned around and grumbled, "What's the matter?" I took a hundred yuan and handed it to him, sincerely saying, "Sir, I'm sorry! I didn't do a good job with your massage just now. Please forgive me! This is a refund of your service fee. You're welcome to come again next time!" He took the money, looked at me, and smiled, "That's more like it!"

Ah Mei came to me with a smile and said, "Ah jing, you're getting better and better. The quality of service you provide to customers is truly admirable!" I said, "It's because I didn't do my job well. I should take responsibility. Customers trust us and come here for massages. If they go back and tell their friends that the massages here are terrible, won't that affect our future business?" Ah Mei smiled and said, "Ah jing, you think long-term. Compared to you, I fall far behind." I said, "Don't say that. We are sisters, we are family. Let's help and learn from each other." Ah Fang came over and winked at me, saying, "Ah jing, did you have a breakup? I haven't seen your dedicated chauffeur these past two days." I said, "It's better if he doesn't come. I can have some peace." Ah Fang laughed and said, "Saying one thing but meaning another? If he doesn't come for a few days, it's not quiet, it's just lonely, right?" I said, "If he thinks I can't live without him, then he's wrong! I'll be single for the rest of my life, so what?" Ah Fang hugged and laughed, persuading me, "Don't be angry. It's normal for lovers to have their ups and downs. Maybe tomorrow will be a sunny day, and Ge Mingjing will come to pick you up again."

As it turned out, Ah Fang was right. When I finished work that night, that familiar motorcycle was parked in front of me. Ge Weiming took off his helmet and said, "Xiaojing, get on!" I ignored him and walked straight ahead. Ge Weiming got off the motorcycle and caught up with me, saying, "Xiaojing! Don't be angry, okay? Come home with me!" I didn't respond kindly, "Go home with you? Your mother doesn't like me, so why would I go back?" Ge Weiming looked startled momentarily, then grabbed my hand and said, "Did my mother say that to you? Did she say she doesn't like you?" I pushed away his hand and said, "I heard it myself. Your father and mother argued because of me. I don't want to be the one who ruins your family!" Ge Weiming said, "Xiaojing, don't worry. My mother may not like you, but I like you!" I said, "Don't say one thing and mean another! Do you like me? Then why couldn't I see you for the past few days? Aren't you afraid that I'll be mistreated again?" Ge Weiming said, "Listen to me, I also have my reasons!" I said, "I don't believe you. What reasons could you have?" Ge Weiming sighed and said, "To be honest with you, my mother went to my superiors at work. They put pressure on me and told me to stop associating with you. If I don't comply, they'll transfer me elsewhere. But I like being a police officer, so I've hesitated these past few days." I half-believed him and said, "Then why did you come today? Have you decided not to be a police officer?" Ge Weiming said thoughtfully, "I've thought it through. Being a police officer is important, but you are more important! So, I came." My heart softened, and I smiled, "Aren't you afraid that your mother will be angry with you? She won't spare you!" Ge Weiming laughed, "Love is free, and my mother can't interfere with my happiness!"

That night, we booked a room at a small hotel and spent a sweet night together, with a feeling of a reunion after a short separation. We lingered for a long time, seemingly tireless. Unfortunately, Ge Weiming had a family, and I had a place to stay, but there was a home I couldn't return to. I shared a room with Xiaohong and Wufang, so it wasn't convenient to bring him over. And he was worried about his mother's rejection of me and didn't want to put me in a difficult position, so he didn't bring me home for the time being. Ge Weiming said, "If we get married, and you don't want to live with my mother, we can buy a house and move out." I smiled, "Buy a house? I don't have money. Do you have money?" Ge Weiming said, "I haven't been working for long. Where would I get the money? But my family has money, and I can ask my dad." I laughed, "Who has the final say in your family?" He scratched his head and said, "My father has the final say, but my mother controls the money." I chuckled, "So if you buy a house, don't you still have to go through your mother?" Ge Weiming said, "Wait for a couple of years, wait until I have the money, and then we'll get married!" I snuggled up in his embrace and fell asleep sweetly.

When I was full of anticipation for the future, little did I know that Ge Weiming's two-year agreement promise would be broken in less than two weeks! Promises are so fragile under scrutiny that it fades away quickly like a woman's lipstick. What does it mean to like someone? What does it mean to love someone? If he truly loved me, would he succumb to rumors and gossip? Men are more selfish than women, often thinking of themselves, and women usually suffer the consequences! Especially girls like us, we have nowhere to complain. Love, for us, is nothing but a mirage, a way to fill our hunger, a weapon that men use to exploit our bodies and emotions!

Labor Day was approaching in a few more days. That afternoon, Ge Weiming came to my place. Sister Wu and Xiao Hong deliberately kept their distance, leaving us some space to be together. I knew that Sister Wu and Xiao Hong wished me to find happiness and become an example for all the massage girls. The power of a sample is infinite. My joy can inspire others and give my sisters less self-abandonment and more courage to pursue happiness. As massage therapists, we may appear glamorous, but in reality, we are "good on the outside, broken on the inside." Who knows the grievances, pain, inferiority, and self-blame we endure? We are like snails, with a shell that is not firm, accommodating a tender heart that can't withstand people's trampling and destruction.

After a stormy conversation with Ge Weiming, we lay on the bed and chatted casually. I smiled and said, "This place is so run-down. The bed is shaky. You have to be careful, or Xiao Hong will blame me." Ge Weiming laughed and said, "If that happens, I'll buy her a new bed." I said, "Are you planning to take me out on May Day?" Ge Weiming said, "Sure, we have a week off. Suzhou and Hangzhou, whichever you choose." I said, "Let's go to Suzhou. I feel a sense of familiarity there. Ah Lang was hospitalized there before, and I've been a few times. The people there are very friendly, even the journalists helped us." Ge Weiming said, "Speaking of Ah Lang, there is also a negative side. Since you appeared on TV, too many people are talking about you. Our colleague Lao Zhao told others that the girl on TV, Xiao Jing, is my girlfriend. It almost made me unable to lift my head."

I was slightly surprised, "Made you unable to lift your head? So you also look down on me and my job?" Ge Weiming denied, "I'm not looking down on you. I don't oppose you being a massage therapist. I want you to be more low-key. The more people know, the more unfavorable it is for us. After all, rumors can be frightening!" I looked at him, "So you're afraid? Afraid of what others say behind our backs? You can tell me if you don't want me to work there. Your family has money, so you can support me!" Ge Weiming said, "That's not what I mean. I'm saying that some people say very unpleasant things behind your back, and it makes me uncomfortable to hear." I said, "What are they saying? Do you believe them?" Ge Weiming said, "I don't mind what others say, but some people say that you and the other girls are high-class prostitutes, that doing massages is just a cover, and you actually accompany men. Can I feel good hearing that?" I angrily said, "Who is maliciously gossiping? You're a police officer. Wouldn't you have shut us down long ago if we did something illegal? Do we need people to say it?" Ge Weiming said, "People have different opinions, and there will always be gossip. I can't go and silence them! Xiao Jing, I wanted to discuss with you whether you want to change your job. So as not to affect our image together." I sat up abruptly and said, "Ge Weiming, have I affected your image? What are you saying? Do you even know who I am and how I treat you?" Ge Weiming awkwardly said, "But you have done it in the past. I heard someone say you received a hundred thousand yuan from a boss. Is there any truth to it?" I was angry and anxious, "Who is spreading rumors? Who is making mischief?"

Chapter 27

Brief Romance

I understood it now—they all looked down on us, looked down on massage therapists. In their minds, we were synonymous with sleaze. Even the man in front of me, Gao Weiming, pretended not to care, but deep down, he still did. We were massage therapists, not famous mistresses or kept women. However, some women portrayed themselves as ladies secretly engaging in affairs, dubbing themselves "confidantes." But wasn't it just a veil to hide and excuse their infidelity? After all, wasn't "one-night stand" just a euphemism for "one-night sex"?

In this era, do arranged marriages still exist? Do we still see "beating Mandarin ducks" (forced separation of a married couple)? The truth is these situations persist, even in the prosperous Jiangnan region. True "free love" is rare and often hindered by external factors, with parents being the most challenging obstacle. History has witnessed countless love stories sacrificed at this threshold, just like the tale of Liang Shanbo and Zhu Yingtai. Today, I found myself facing the same situation. Would I be lucky enough to overcome it?

Gao Weiming's words left me puzzled. How did he know about my relationship with Zhang? This was rare knowledge. Only Sister Wu, Xiao Hong, Wu Fang, Ah Lan, Ah Chun, and Ah Fang knew my story. So where did Gao Weiming get this information? Could he have investigated me in secret? If that's the case, then he's gone too far! I detest being doubted by others. If you have any opinions about me, speak to my face. Tell me what's wrong or needs improvement, and I won't get angry or upset. I'll "improve where needed and strive for excellence." But please, don't scheme behind my back. That's a cowardly act!

I was about to ask Gao Weiming when I heard someone shouting outside the courtyard gate, "Weiming! Weiming! Are you in there?" The voice sounded familiar—it was Gao Weiming's mother! How did she find this place? My confusion deepened. I said, "Your mother is here. How did she know about this?" Gao Weiming looked innocent and replied, "She goes wherever she pleases. How would I know?"

We both went to open the gate, and there stood Gao's mother, wearing an angry expression. As soon as she saw her son, she scolded him sternly, "Weiming, why are you fooling around again? Didn't I tell you not to be with her? It'll ruin your future!" Gao Weiming said, "Mom, I like her!" His mother glanced at me and continued, "There are plenty of good women out there. Why must you choose a massage girl?" I felt uncomfortable hearing her call me a massage girl. I asked, "Auntie, what's wrong with being a massage therapist? We earn a living with our skills. Please don't insult us." Gao's mother looked at me and said, "Little Jing, I'm not here to argue with you. I want my son to come home, and I hope you'll have some self-awareness and stop hanging around him. Aren't you fascinated with Weiming? Your involvement will hinder his future! Think about him!"

What a joke! I like him, and I should consider his future. But has he considered mine? I said, "He's the one who comes to me. I didn't seek him out. Auntie, what's wrong with us being together? Why do you want to stop us?" Gao's mother replied, "What's good about it? I don't want Weiming to be laughed at, saying he couldn't find a wife, so he had to settle for a massage girl!" Gao Weiming interrupted, "Mom, how can you say that in front of Jing? I voluntarily chose to be with her. Please don't stop us. We'll treat you and Dad well." His mother said, "People have hidden motives. Who knows what's in her heart? Do you think she's the only woman you have in mind? How can you, a police officer, like a massage girl? It could be better for your image! The chief said that if you persist, he'll dismiss you. He doesn't want your personal life to affect the image of the entire police force! Weiming, you're not young anymore. Think about everything carefully. Is it worth it to risk your future for a massage girl?

I felt a strong sense of discomfort after hearing Mrs. Ge's words. I said, "Auntie, I am not yet a part of your Ge family. Please show me some respect. I don't believe that I'm unworthy of Ge Weiming. In this day and age, it's not just about social status or family background. As long as there is love between two people, it's like a prince and Cinderella, and they can still lead a happy life." Mrs. Ge sneered, "That's a fairy tale, not reality! Xiaojing, Weiming is infatuated with you, but don't think you can jet your way. Your profession, being a policewoman, is that suitable for marriage?"

"I..." I was getting frustrated. With her looking down on me like this, could I even become a part of the Ge family? I became a massage therapist out of necessity, and while people have different roles in society, everyone should be treated equally. Why was she discriminating against me? I said, "Auntie, please let Ge Weiming say something. If he doesn't like me and doesn't want to be with me, I promise that from now on, I won't approach him anymore, as if I never knew him. Ge Weiming, please express your stance."

It seemed like Mrs. Ge feared I would take away something precious to her. She stared intently at her son and said, "Weiming, say something. Either come back home with me right now or stay with her. Don't ever come back home!" Ge Weiming was torn between his mother's demands. He hesitated and said, "Mom, please don't force me. Can I have some time to think?" Mrs. Ge said, "What's there to think about? Do you know what kind of person she is? Do you still want such a woman?" I said, "Auntie, what kind of person am I? What did I do wrong?" Mrs. Ge said, "Didn't you sleep with other men and take 100,000 yuan from them? With such behavior, how can Weiming truly love you?" I didn't know where she heard about this, and I found it difficult to defend myself.

Ge Weiming said, "Mom, Xiaojing did what she did to save Ah Lan. The news about the massage therapists' heroic act was covered on television. Why are you still blaming her?" Mrs. Ge said, "Could any foolish man donate 100,000 yuan to a stranger like a massage therapist? Is that possible? The lies she fabricated might have fooled the reporters, but they can't fool me!" I truly felt helpless. Mrs. Ge's baseless suspicions shattered the most fundamental trust and respect between people. In a family like this, did I want to marry into it? It was time for me to wake up.

I was infuriated and yelled at Gao Weiming and his mother, "Get out!

Both of you, get out! I never want to see you again!" Gao Weiming tried to reason, "Xiaojing, what's wrong? Don't be angry!" His mother shouted at him, "Weiming, aren't you leaving? Why are you still standing here? Can you tolerate her aggressive behavior?" Did she dare to call me aggressive? This only made me angrier as I retorted, "Yes, I'm aggressive. So what? I don't depend on you for a living, and I'm doing just fine! Gao Weiming, you're pathetic! You said you loved me? But can you protect me? Even your mother is bullying me, and you stand by idly. Can I trust you? I see it now. You're all materialistic and selfish! Now go, both of you! Gao Weiming, I don't want to burden you. Just go!"

Two women fighting over a man, is it even worth it? One is his mother, and the other can be considered his girlfriend, but I have yet to lose my mind to the point of no return. Even if Gao Weiming truly likes me, he won't abandon his family and future to stand by my side! I like that saying: "Indecision leads to trouble." Since there's no hope, let disappointment come a little earlier!

Gao's mother wore a victorious smile on her face and said, "Weiming, did you hear that? She told you to leave. Why are you still here?" Gao Weiming turned to me and said, "Xiaojing, do you not care about me? Do you want me to leave?" I didn't understand what love was. I didn't know Gao Weiming's true feelings or if he cherished me. But I couldn't feel the nourishment of love; it felt more like a mutual need. Love is not just about taking but also about giving. Could we, as massage therapists are looked down upon to the extent that we don't deserve love? In that instant, I lost all passion and interest in him. I felt indifferent. I said, "Yes, you can leave. I'm not right for you. Go and find a love that suits you!" It might be more accurate to say finding a woman that suits him. We, women, are the same; finding a suitable man is more practical and meaningful than searching for so-called love.

Gao's mother pulled her son and said, "What are you dilly-dallying for? Women are everywhere. Why do you have to choose her? Let's go, son, wake up!" Gao Weiming looked at me and said, "Xiaojing, are you being so heartless to me? Wait for me, I'll convince my mother, and I'll come to find you!" Did he call me heartless? I wondered who was genuinely heartless here.

Gao Weiming left, and I wondered how his mother found this place. Then I realized they were locals, and there was nowhere they wouldn't be familiar with. They even managed to learn about my secret with Zhang. What else could I hide from them? Gao's mother's attitude made me understand that, in the eyes of others, we are just lowly individuals. Even if we have done good deeds, their prejudices won't change. I felt exhausted and disillusioned. Being carefree like Wu Fang, living life on my terms, would bring me closer to happiness.

A week after breaking up with Gao Weiming, I was indifferent. You look down on me, and I look down on you! However, after a month, I began to regret it. Did I make a mistake in handling this situation? Gao Weiming was a decent man, and I let him go just like that. Wasn't it a bit regrettable? Could I become more tolerant and not bother with his mother's behavior? Ah Chun and Ah Fang advised me not to act impulsively; it would only harm me. They said we must learn to swallow our pride in life. But I couldn't bear Gao's mother's biased look and attitude. She had a deep prejudice against me. Even if I married Gao Weiming, could I find happiness? Thinking about these things now seems redundant. There is no cure for regret; even if there were, I wouldn't easily compromise. I'm still young, and the road ahead is long. Who's to say I won't meet a man who truly loves me? Gao Weiming hasn't come to reconcile with me, so why should I bother myself?

Within a month, I lost my good friend Ah Lan and my boyfriend. I felt a bit down. While others were cheerful during the Labor Day holiday, I felt low. Nothing brought me joy. In this moment of confusion, I thought of Zhang. How is he doing? He helped me and Ah Lan so much, and I haven't even thanked him. Now Gao's mother has somehow found out about my connection with Zhang. It's nothing for me, but I don't want to bring trouble to him. That would be unfair to him. I felt a bit bored these days and wanted to go out to clear my mind, but I didn't have any close friends or relatives. I thought about calling Zhang, but it didn't feel appropriate during the holidays. He should be with his family, and I didn't want to disturb him.

In the past few days, Wu Fang unexpectedly returned, and I saw her constantly making phone calls that couldn't get through, sighing on the side. When Wu Fang was away, Xiao Hong quietly told me, "Wu Fang's boyfriend is now getting close to Sister Wu. It seems like they have a good relationship. Maybe that man thinks Wu Fang has nothing to offer and wants to break up with her, focusing on winning Sister Wu's favor. They've gone on a trip to Suzhou these days." I was stunned. I never expected things to turn out this way. Sister Wu is something else. Why would she compete with her sister for a man? If Wu Fang finds out, the sisters will have a massive fight! Xiao Hong warned me, "Don't tell Wu Fang about this. If she finds out her sister stole her boyfriend, who knows what crazy things she might do?" I have my concerns now and couldn't be bothered by their petty drama. I can only sigh; I'm afraid Sister Wu and Wu Fang will fall flat on their faces because of a man!

On the Labor Day holiday, while everyone else was off, we sauna center employees still had to work as usual. When the sisters protested,

Manager Tian confidently said, "Labor Day means laboring. Others misunderstood." It was a weak argument, but what can we do when we are under someone else's roof? I decided to forget about Gao Weiming; his love for me was not steadfast, which disappointed me. Work could make my life fulfilling. Besides being a "massage therapist," I also became a "counselor." My relationship with the floor supervisor, Ah Mei, was good. In the massage hall on the second floor, I had relatively more freedom, and nobody bothered me. Since the time I appeared on TV, bringing economic benefits to Haitian Tang, Manager Tian raised my salary to three thousand. My life gradually improved.

On the afternoon of May 3rd, Ah Chun, Ah Fang, and I were out shopping. The weather had warmed up, and we bought a few shirts, laughing and heading back to the sauna center. Suddenly, my phone rang, and it was my brother's number. He said, "Xiaojing, I and your sister-in-law are on our honeymoon. We arrived in Hangzhou yesterday and will stay here today. We plan to see you tomorrow and go to Suzhou the day after." I was stunned, not knowing how to respond. My brother was coming to see me, which could be a problem. He would disapprove if he knew I was working as a massage therapist. I learned how hot-tempered he could be, and there was a chance he might beat me up and drag me back home. If my family found out, my parents would be furious! They will be arriving tomorrow. What should I do?

Chapter 28

White lies

The May sunshine had brought the early summer heat, and the festive atmosphere made the hustle and bustle of the Jiangnan town even more apparent. This town was a place where talented individuals thrived. During the Song, Ming, and Qing dynasties, it produced 41 scholars who passed the imperial examination. In the Ming Dynasty, a saying went, "Within nine miles, three were high-ranking officials, and within ten miles, two were high-level officials." Indeed, talent abounded here. The town's beauty and literary atmosphere dampened my fiery Chongqing temperament by about seventy to eighty percent. As the ancients said, "A graceful and virtuous lady is the ideal partner for a gentleman." People who first met me thought I was a gentle Jiangnan woman.

Venturing out to work was impulsive. If it weren't for Sister Wu's help in finding me a job, I wouldn't have necessarily found work, let alone become a masseuse. I still didn't know where the road ahead would lead me. Where was my home? I had once thought that once I mastered the art of massage, I would start my training center like Sister Xu, working for myself and no longer taking orders from others. However, creating a training center required capital, and I didn't have money. Despite having received over a hundred thousand yuan, I wasn't greedy. My thoughts were focused on getting treatment for Ah Lan because nothing was more precious than life.

My life was like a river, with ripples but no raging waves. There's a saying, "A single drop of water can reflect the sun!" You can see the shadows of many masseuses through my experiences. Our lives are not as good as you imagine or as bad as you think. Everyone's destiny is different, and I hope that the path I have traveled can serve as a "lesson learned" for you. May it help you take fewer detours and stay on the right path rather than envy me. No matter how bad life gets, hope is always ahead, and we should not look down on ourselves. Regardless of the rumors and gossip, we accept them. We may deceive men for money, but we should not harm their families or innocent women. As the saying goes, "Why should women make things difficult for other women?"

Ah Chun noticed that I looked a little nervous and asked with concern, "Whose call was it?" I replied to Ah Chun, "It's my brother." Then I told my brother, "If it's inconvenient for you, you don't have to come. I'm doing just fine." My brother said anxiously, "The weather is terrible! We finally arrived and got drenched! Xiaojing, where are you? Come to the station and pick us up!" I said, "Brother, you guys find shelter from the rain. I'll be right there."

We needed to devise a plan to deceive my brother to avoid exposing any flaws. After all, he was only staying for one day, so there would surely be a way to get through it. The three of us sisters discussed and brainstormed, and as they say, "Three heads are better than one," we could always come up with a solution. A-Chun said, "A-Jing, we can't let your brother know you work in the sauna city." I said, "Exactly if he finds out where I work, it would be trouble." A-Fang suggested, "Take your brother to your rented apartment. It's just for one day, and we can keep it a secret." I shook my head and said, "That won't work. My brother knows Sister Wu, and the truth will come out as soon as they start talking." A-Fang proposed, "Then settle your brother and sister-in-law in a hotel, and you can take a day off to accompany them. Go out, chat, have a meal, and buy some things. It'll be a nice day." I said, "That's the only option. But what do I tell my brother if he asks about my job?" A-Chun laughed and said, "That's simple. Just mention any factory name. Will he go and investigate?" I said, "Alright, tomorrow, you all need to cooperate with me in this act." A-Fang and A-Chun stretched out their hands, and A-Fang said, "Show us the red envelope!" A-Chun said, "I want a bonus!" I chuckled and said, "We haven't even started yet, and you're already asking for performance fees?"

The following day, it unexpectedly rained, with thunder accompanying it. The rain poured down, washing the small town clean and diluting the festive atmosphere in an instant. Thank goodness, I hoped for even heavier rain to dispel the idea of my brother coming to visit. However, things went differently than planned. At eleven o'clock, my brother called anxiously and said, "This damn weather! We finally arrived, drenched like a bunch of wet chickens! A-Jing, where are you? Hurry and come to the station to pick us up!" I replied, "Brother, you should find shelter from the rain. I'll come right away."

I grabbed an umbrella and arrived at the station, where I saw my brother standing under the eaves, eagerly waiting. Standing beside him was a girl in her twenties. I approached them and said, "Brother, you've arrived!" My brother smiled happily, looked at me for a while, and said, "Xiaojing, I almost didn't recognize you after two years." I laughed and said, "What can I do? I'm still your little sister." My brother said, "In my eyes, you're still the little girl with pigtails. You've caught me off guard with this new look. Oh, this is your sister-in-law, Fangfang." My brother had grown taller and darker since the last time I saw him, and I had grown up and become independent. I no longer followed behind him like I did as a child.

I warmly greeted Fangfang, "Hello, sister-in-law!" Fangfang smiled and said, "Your brother often praises you, and now that I've seen you, it's true, you're beautiful, much prettier than your brother." I laughed and said, "Sister-in-law, you're beautiful too. My brother has good taste!" Fangfang laughed and said, "Xiaojing, you have such a sweet mouth." I said, "You guys must be tired from the journey. Let's go have a meal first." My brother said, "Just find a simple restaurant, as long as it can fill our stomachs." I smiled and said, "Brother, that's not right. You're on your honeymoon, not experiencing hardships. How can you settle for something simple? Good food, good fun, and a good mood should be the purpose of your honeymoon! Don't worry, and I'll cover the expenses here." My brother laughed and said, "Xiaojing, you've grown up. You can talk now?" I laughed and said, "If I couldn't talk by this age, wouldn't I be mute?" Fangfang laughed and said, "Look at you two, bickering as soon as you meet."

We arrived at the "Jiangnan Spring" restaurant, and I called Ah Chun and Ah Fang, asking them to join my supporting cast. In no time, they arrived, and I introduced them to my brother and sister-in-law, saying, "These are my good friends Ah Chun and Ah Fang. We're a terrific trio!" My brother said, "That's great. When you're away from home, it's good to have a few friends to look out for each other." I ordered dishes totaling 150 yuan, a few bottles of orange juice, and a bottle of white wine. I knew my brother liked to drink, and we Chongqing people loved hot pot and drinking and playing mahjong. My brother said, "This wine is too expensive. Just get something ordinary." I smiled and said, "A drop of water repays a gushing spring. Brother, consider this wine as my gratitude. You always gave me your leftover ice popsicles when we were young." Fangfang smiled, "You wanted to eat his leftover ice popsicles?" Ah Chun said, "I can understand. When we were kids, as long as there was something to eat, hygiene was the last thing on our minds."

We, the siblings, had endless topics to discuss, and with the addition of Ah Chun and Ah Fang, the atmosphere was lively. It was raining outside, so we stayed longer in the restaurant. My brother said, "Xiaojing, where do you work? Mom said you earn over 2,000 yuan a month. Is the salary here really that high?" I said, "I work at an electronics factory and am a team leader, so my salary is a bit higher." My brother asked, "Do you live at the factory?" Fangfang jumped in and said, "Yes, we live at the factory. We share a dormitory." I said, "Knowing my brother and sister-in-law were coming, I took a day off. I wanted to accompany you and show you around, but unfortunately, the weather is bad, and it's raining." Ah Chun said, "Aijing is very busy. In our company, taking a day off means losing the full attendance bonus for the month." My brother said, "Xiaojing, we won't delay your work. We came to see you today, and we'll go to Suzhou tomorrow." Fangfang said, "Xiaojing, we're sorry. I advised your brother not to come, but he insisted. He said he hadn't seen his sister in years and was worried about you."

I went to the grocery store next to the hotel and bought several umbrellas for my brother and sister-in-law. Ah Chun and Ah Fang said,

"Xiaojing, we won't accompany you anymore. We won't be the third wheel. We'll take care of getting you a day off." My brother asked in surprise, "Is Xiaojing working the night shift? Didn't she already take a day off?" Seeing the situation wasn't good, I almost slipped up, but I quickly said, "The company is busy now, and as a team leader, I often have to work overtime. I won't go tonight, so I have to ask my supervisor for another day off, or else they'll deduct my pay." Fangfang said, "Nowadays, working is like this. We have to work overtime all the time. In Guangdong, it's the same. If you don't work overtime, it's not enough, and team leaders have to work even later."

The rainy town appeared exceptionally serene. The scenic spots, historical buildings, and cultural landscapes captivated my brother and sister-in-law, leaving them amazed. I said, "Strolling through the ancient town in the rain adds a touch of charm." My brother remarked, "This place is great—prosperous and full of ancient charm. A-Jing, you've come to the right place." Fang Fang said, "The reputation of the ancient towns in the Jiangnan region is well-deserved! I truly envy you in this peaceful and beautiful place where you work, A-Jing!" I chuckled inwardly. If my brother and sister-in-law knew my real job, they probably wouldn't be envious but would curse me instead.

I said, "Indeed, it's beautiful. As soon as you step into the old street, any anger in your heart dissipates, and all that remains is poetic and picturesque scenery. I like it here." My brother laughed, saying, "Then find a local and settle here. Our family can also have distant relatives in Jiangnan." His words struck a chord, and I felt a tinge of sadness. That damn Ge Weiming, we were so close to being together, but now it's all gone like smoke. I said, "I want to marry here, but no one seems interested. They all consider me an outsider." My brother said, "What's wrong with being an outsider? Being an outsider is also a unique characteristic of China! With your looks, how could you possibly not find a good husband's family? It's their loss." I had told my brother about dating a local during a previous phone call, but he probably needed to remember. Fang Fang said, "A-Jing, you're still young. Don't rush it. Wait a few more years." I smiled and said, "I'm not in a hurry. I want to work for a few more years and save money." Love and marriage require fate. Only when you meet the right person at the right time and place can it bear fruit? I had thought Ge Weiming was my true soulmate, but what happened? He retreated, succumbing to the influence of societal opinions. What could I say? What if he has money? What if he's educated? It doesn't change the fact that he lacks understanding and consideration.

As we walked on the street, some people recognized me. Some smiled at me, while others whispered behind my back. My brother asked, "A-Jing, what are they talking about? Something about Ah Lan and TV? It seems like they all know you?" I made up an excuse and said, "Oh, it's a colleague named Ah Lan from my workplace. She recently fell ill, and all the employees in our company donated money for her. It even made it to the news on TV. They probably recognized me from seeing me on TV." My brother said, "So that's the story. I thought they were badmouthing you." I replied, "I haven't done anything wrong. I'm not afraid of what people say, whether it's good or bad." My brother said, "You should get along well with your colleagues when you're outside. Don't let them look down on us Chongqing people." I laughed and said, "Of course, I'll bring honor to our hometown!"

After dinner, I booked two rooms at the hotel in town—one for my brother and sister-in-law and one for myself. I didn't return to my rented place and continued the charade with my brother and sister-in-law. Seeing them so affectionate, I sincerely wished them happiness. I said,

"Brother, you're finally married. Now our parents can rest assured. As your younger sister, I wish you happiness and hope you have children soon! You must treat your wife gently, as the clever baby will rely on your efforts!" My brother glared at me and laughed, "What does a child like you understand? No shame!" Little did my brother know I wasn't a little girl anymore. When it came to matters of love and relationships, I couldn't claim expertise, but I was no longer as innocent as he imagined.

The small hotel had poor facilities, and the rooms didn't have attached bathrooms, so I had to use the public restroom outside to relieve myself. The soundproofing of the rooms was terrible, and my brother and sister-in-law occupied the next-door space. I could hear that familiar sound, faint yet clear, making me blush. When I exited the restroom and passed by my brother's room, I listened to my sister-in-law's earth-shattering scream! I knew it was her singing voice expressing pleasure! My heart couldn't help but feel a bit heated.

Chapter 29

Sisters Rival for Boyfriend

I always wanted to be a good girl, both in my actions and in my heart, hoping to escape the shadows brought by my profession. I remembered filial piety towards my parents, love for the weak, and genuine friendship. However, it could be wishful thinking. No matter how hard I tried, I was still a lowly masseuse in the eyes of the world. I was just an ugly duckling, not a swan or a good girl. I knew myself well and could only say that my heart was not evil, but my willpower was not strong enough, and my abilities were limited. I couldn't disregard the temptations of reality. I was just a tiny woman, an outsider, a masseuse, trying to make people accept me and carve out my own place. There was still a long way to go.

I bought a dress for Fang Fang and a shirt for my brother. I also bought them some local specialties. When I sent them off at the train station, my brother hugged me and said, "Xiao Jing, call home more often when you have time. Mom misses you." I replied, "I will. It's just that work keeps me busy, and I don't have time to return. Please give my regards to Mom and Dad!" My brother said, "As long as you're safe out there, it doesn't matter if you earn less money. Xiao Jing, you're not young anymore. If you meet someone suitable outside, you can have a relationship. A young woman should get married, after all. If you don't go astray, your life will improve." Fang Fang said, "Take care of yourself here. It's nice here, and I want to stay a few more days." I smiled and said, "Sister-in-law, it's perfect for a honeymoon. Visit a few more places and let my brother spend a little." As my brother got on the train, he laughed and said, "I don't have money. I can only save. Sister, if you can sponsor us, we can stay a few more days." I chuckled and replied, "I can barely take care of myself. I hope my brother can look after his little sister more."

After my brother and sister-in-law left, my life returned to tranquility. Most of my female colleagues who worked with me had boyfriends, although their relationships were not necessarily genuine. Some did it out of loneliness, while others needed men to serve as protectors. Some had loose morals and changed boyfriends every few days, more diligent than changing clothes. There was one named A Tao who had three boyfriends in a month, as active as a grasshopper. Those who couldn't keep up ended up being played by men. Although I also desired men, seeking their comfort and protection, I was selective. I couldn't be bothered to deal with men over and over again. Besides, some men were not easy to handle. It was easy to invite trouble, and it could ruin one's life. I wouldn't say I liked brief encounters. I preferred something long-lasting, so I wouldn't end up like Ge Weiming, deceived, and left with a heavy heart.

At night, a client came for a massage. He introduced himself as Mr. Sun Zhengfu, the owner of an advertising company in Suzhou. He came to

Huzhou to discuss business and decided to go and experience the skills of a masseuse at Sea Paradise due to its reputation. I smiled and said, "What skills do we have? We're just earning a living." Mr. Sun replied, "No matter your profession, it has its own image. Everything has two sides. In officials, there are both honest and corrupt ones; in business, there are both ethical and unscrupulous merchants; among ordinary people, there are both law-abiding citizens and troublemakers; and in being a person, there are both good and bad. Although the massage industry is mixed with both good and bad, the image you portray is beautiful, kind, and admirable. Over time, it can change people's prejudices against masseuses. It's about how you do your job, not just the job itself. Massage is your profession, but how you do it and what you make of it is up to you."

Mr. Sun's words enlightened me. I couldn't help but feel enlightened. Could we masseuses also represent a positive image? It was something new, something I had never heard before. Sister Xu hadn't mentioned such things to me either. There were always different perspectives and people beyond our understanding. Mr. Sun was indeed in the advertising business, knowledgeable and eloquent. I said, "We have been working hard, but people still don't accept us. They call us seductresses and the like." Mr. Sun replied, "That is because of your environment. Like dyeing cloth in different vats, the color will vary. No matter how hard you work, the effect will be minimal. To change this situation, you must strive for a different environment, and the result could be completely different." I didn't quite understand and asked, "Can changing the environment make such a huge difference? No matter how much I change, I'll still be a masseuse, right?"

Seeing my skepticism, Mr. Sun continued, "I just experienced your massage. Although your skills are not outstanding and cannot be compared to traditional Chinese massage, you are excellent in terms of leisure massage. I don't know how you are treated here, but if you were in Suzhou, your massage skills would be intermediate. If you worked at a higher-end bathhouse, you would earn a minimum monthly salary of 5,000 yuan. An averaLady Gesseuse could earn two to three thousand yuan a month." I asked, "Is there that much?" Mr. Sun replied, "A monthly salary of 5,000 yuan is not much. That is the income of a legitimate masseuse. If you engage in illicit activities, your income can be much higher. However, in my opinion, income is secondary. The important thing is that your professional honor will be elevated because you will become a respected masseuse!" I was moved and said, "Mr. Sun, are you telling the truth?" Mr. Sun said, "Miss Jing if you are interested in developing in Suzhou, I can help you make connections." I smiled and said, "Thank you for your kind offer, Mr. Sun. But for now, I haven't considered changing jobs. I'm doing fine here, and I have feelings for this place." Mr. Sun laughed, saying, "I didn't ask you to switch jobs immediately. Water flows downhill, and people seek higher ground. By changing the environment, you might discover a whole new world."

Mr. Sun left me his business card, saying that I could contact him anytime if I ever wanted to change my environment. His words stirred something within me. We worked so hard as masseuses. Who wouldn't want to earn a little more money? However, changing to a new environment made me uncertain. I had become familiar with this place. I had Sister Wu, Xiao Hong, and the sisters I worked with. Everyone treated me well, and for the sake of earning more money, I couldn't bear to leave. As for Mr. Sun's identity, I only found out later. I had initially thought he owned an advertising company, but he was a headhunter. He discovered talent, and potential stars, and convinced them to switch to a brighter path. Then, he eloquently recommended them to related companies and earned a commission or fee as a middleman.

Mr. Sun's words gave me some inspiration. They made me feel that I didn't belong exclusively to Sea Paradise. I could venture out and seek opportunities elsewhere. Although I had new thoughts, I continued to live my life step by step. I approached my work thoughtfully and meticulously but wouldn't flirt with customers. For those with ulterior motives, I acted deaf or laughed it off. It wasn't that I pretended to be virtuous, but those men had such poor taste that I didn't want to give them face. Besides, I wasn't interested in casual encounters. I preferred something more lasting so as not to end up like Ge Weiming, deceived and hurt.

One morning, I was still half asleep when startled by a loud argument. Opening my drowsy eyes, I recognized the voices—the Wu sisters fighting. They hadn't returned all night, so why were they arguing this morning? I was about to get up and mediate when Xiao Hong held me back and said, "A fair judge cannot resolve family matters. Just sleep and mind your own business." Since I came to Nanxun, I have been sharing a bed with Xiao Hong, and we were like sisters. I had heard of same-sex love and how two girls could develop feelings for each other, but it was a joke! Men and women, apart from emotional factors, could complement each other physically. But what could women do with other women, no matter how intimate they were? That's why I didn't like lesbian movies. In technical school, I watched a film called "Happy Together." Leslie Cheung starred in it, but I couldn't bear to continue after watching the beginning. I couldn't understand how men could love each other so passionately.

I was shocked to witness the brutal confrontation between Sister Wu and Wu Fang, who were sisters. They didn't hold back, hurling insults like "slut," "shameless bitch," and "disgraceful" at each other. It was truly unexpected. Several days later, I learned from Xiao Hong what had led to their argument. It turned out that Wu Fang had been secretly trailing her boyfriend. Like a spy, she lurked in the underground passage beneath his dormitory. One late night, Wu Fang unexpectedly discovered her sister and boyfriend returning together, laughing and talking. Wu Fang watched as they went upstairs, turned the lights on and off, and it infuriated her. She couldn't believe that her sister had intervened and ruined her relationship with her boyfriend. She couldn't swallow this humiliation and couldn't forgive her sister.

Wu Fang's relationship with her so-called boyfriend was not based on genuine feelings. It was merely a pretense and mutual exploitation. Seeing her sister "replace" her, Wu Fang reached her breaking point and angrily rushed upstairs to catch them in the act. The outcome was predictable—the sisters quarreled while the man slipped away. Their intense argument disturbed the residents in the building, and they were kicked out. However, they continued arguing back, their faces red and voices loud. Wu Fang thought her sister was outrageous, and Sister Wu believed her sister was disobedient. In short, they fought to their heart's content.

Their relationship as sisters became strained. Although they didn't become enemies, they were like strangers. Wu Fang continued to stay out all night, and Sister Wu secretly communicated with that man. One day, Wu Fang told me that she wanted to leave this place. She hated this place, hated her sister, and hated that shameless man! However, she had spent all her money on that man, and it was too late for regrets. In today's society, it's easier to get by with money. Unfortunately, she had no choice but to continue doing "delivery jobs" to save up some money and then leave quickly. I sympathized with her, but I couldn't help her.

After experiencing this, I hoped she would learn a lesson, understand that people's hearts are not kind, and learn to protect herself. Sometimes, people bring their fate upon themselves and have to drink the bitter wine they brewed.

The two subsequent events dealt a heavy blow to me and ultimately made me determined to leave Sea Paradise and Nanxun. The first event occurred on May 28th—my ex-boyfriend, Ge Weiming, got married! In the town, there is a custom on a couple's wedding day where they walk through the old street and cross several bridges, but I'm unsure of its symbolism. Ge Weiming's marriage caused a crisis of trust in men for me. Men's words are unreliable. His marriage cast a shadow over my soul. On my way to work, seeing their intimate figures together, I felt a pang of sourness. If it weren't for Lady Ge's opposition and Ge Weiming's untrustworthiness, I should have been the one standing beside him, not some other girl. But I knew that rather than reminiscing and being jealous of what was lost, it was better to let go and let him be.

The other incident was absurd. I couldn't determine if that person had a grudge against me or was purposely trying to set me up. In any case, I didn't understand why someone would trap me when I had no grievances with anyone. That day, a customer specifically requested me for a massage. While massaging his back, a wristwatch somehow fell from the bed's edge. At first, I didn't pay much attention and picked up the watch from the floor. However, the customer took a look, examined it, and started shouting at the manager, claiming that I had broken it and demanded compensation! I thought to myself, "It's just a wristwatch. How many people still wear watches these days? Besides, it's not worth much, maybe just a hundred yuan. I'll accept the compensation!" Little did I know that things would take time to be resolved!

Chapter 30

Beautiful Beginning

I didn't expect everything to go smoothly in life. Along the journey, there are always storms accompanying us. As massage therapists living at the bottom of society, we are constantly subject to the mockery of fate because our power is weak, and we are powerless against insults from others! Workers have unions, businessmen have associations, and consumers have consumer associations, but what do we have? Who truly understands us, protects us, and supports us? Our bosses are only concerned about making money for themselves. Where is the umbrella that can shield us from the wind and rain?

Manager Tian hurriedly arrived, accompanied by Ame. The customer claimed that the wristwatch was a precious 18,000 yuan Rolex. The diamond on the watch had fallen off, and he said he had intended to give it to a business acquaintance. He couldn't give it away and demanded total compensation; otherwise, he would take the matter to court! I was stunned. I had never experienced such a situation before and never imagined that a mere wristwatch could be so expensive. 18,000 yuan, what does that mean? It was the sum of my six months' salary. With eating, drinking, or spending, it would be enough to buy him a wristwatch. At that moment, I felt he was trying to extort money. How did the watch fall? If he wore it on his wrist, how did it end up on the floor? How did I not notice it when massaging him if it was placed by the bedside? I had a faint feeling that this was a trap premeditated by the customer.

Manager Tian was also suspicious and couldn't understand the customer's intentions. Could someone in the industry be jealous and deliberately causing trouble? Manager Tian suggested that the sauna center cover the repair cost. The customer insisted on total compensation and a formal apology. Helpless, Manager Tian had no choice but to call the police. Shortly after, a few police officers arrived, inquired about the situation, and called experts to authenticate the watch. It was confirmed to be a genuine Rolex, but no one could explain how the diamond had fallen off. The customer presented the purchase receipt, proving that he had bought it just the day before for 18,000 yuan. According to the Consumer Rights Protection Law, the operating entity is liable for any property loss consumers suffer at the place of business. The customer accused me of accidentally dropping the watch, and the masseuse and the operating entity should share the responsibility. After police mediation, Manager Tian had to compensate the customer for the total amount.

Due to the customer's commotion, business on the second floor was disrupted. Customers and staff gathered to watch, some wearing expressions of schadenfreude. Behind everyone's back, some people gossip about them. In Sauna City, I had always valued harmony, but there were still people who didn't like me, envious of my higher salary.

After discussing with Ah Fang and Ah Chun, we came up with three possibilities for this incident: either the owner of Sauna City had offended someone outside, so they sent troublemakers; or one of the sisters had conspired with an outsider to stage this act, wanting to embarrass me; or someone wanted to use this method to drive me out of Sea Paradise and make it impossible for me to stay here.

Manager Tian angrily said, "Xiao Jing, this incident was caused by you. You have to take responsibility for today's losses! We'll compensate for the watch at 18,000 yuan, and the floor has also lost significant business. Damaging a customer's property and having it spread will reflect badly on us. How could you be so careless?" I said, "I find this whole situation inexplicable. How could this happen?" Manager Tian said, "Considering your usual performance, I'll let you compensate 15,000 yuan, and we'll consider the matter closed." I handed over my hard-earned savings for several months and paid the compensation, leaving myself with just over 400 yuan. I had initially planned to send money home, but once again, it fell through. I became a needy person once more. The loss of funds was secondary; what bothered me more was feeling helpless and cheated for no reason!

Coincidentally, Wu Fang had a massive fight with her sister and wanted to leave. As for me, losing money in such a bizarre way made me want to get out and breathe fresh air. I thought of Mr. Sun's words. Why not try Suzhou? One night, Wu Fang and I were feeling dejected. I said, "This place is not bad, but we haven't gained anything here. Wu Fang, how about we find a new place to work?" Wu Fang replied, "I want to, but I don't have a penny. I can't leave even if I want to!" I said, "I know someone who can help us find jobs. He said wages are higher in Suzhou. Wu Fang, you know beauty and hairdressing; with those skills, you'll always have food on the table." Wu Fang said, "Beauty and hairdressing work is exhausting. I'd rather not do it. I prefer the way things are now. It's more relaxed, and I have money." I said, "It's not good to think like that. You're ruining your health. Why not do a massage like me? It's better than working in a factory, isn't it?" Wu Fang casually replied, "Women only have a few years of youth. It's better to seize the opportunity and make some money!" Wu Fang was obsessed with that kind of thinking, and no amount of persuasion worked. I said, "I'll resign soon and go to Suzhou. If you want to come with me, we can go together. I'll make sure you won't go hungry." Wu Fang agreed, "Okay, I'll follow your lead."

The next day, I submitted my resignation to Sea Paradise. Manager Tian was surprised, "You've been doing well here. I promised you that you would be promoted to team leader next month and receive a raise." I smiled and said, "The sea is boundless. Birds can fly freely in the sky. I want to see the outside world. It's not about money." Manager Tian consulted Mr. Sun, and he said to me, "Xiao Jing, if you agree to stay, Mr. Sun is willing to refund you 2,000 yuan of the compensation you pay every month. How about staying?" Manager Tian needed to understand my personality. As long as I had decided, I would fight for it. And if I wanted to give up, even if it was given to me, I wouldn't want it! Luckily, Sea Paradise didn't give me a hard time and terminated my employment contract. Wu Fang also resigned smoothly.

Wu Fang and I set off for Suzhou with around 500 yuan in our pockets. I called Mr. Sun Zhengfu, and he was delighted to hear from me. Shortly after, he drove over in his car and brought us to his advertising company. He asked us to fill out personal resumes and smiled, saying, "I'll arrange your jobs tomorrow. Normally, there would be a registration fee, but I'll waive it. However, there is an agreement you need to fill out." I became cautious. The contract at Sea Paradise had scared me, and I was afraid there might be some trap. So I carefully read through it. There was nothing unusual except for a clause stating that starting from the third month of employment, the advertising company would deduct a 10% commission from our salaries, to be deducted by the employer upon salary payment. I thought this condition wasn't excessive and asked, "Do you know the specific monthly salary?" Mr. Sun said, "There will be a one-month probationary period. Based on your massage skills, your monthly salary will be at least 3,000 yuan. I haven't seen the skills of Miss Wu, but it won't be lower than 2,000 yuan. If you perform well, your income can increase." Wu Fang and I smiled at each other and said, "Thank you, Mr. Sun!"

Although Mr. Sun mentioned a monthly salary of 3,000 yuan, less than the 5,000 yuan he had mentioned in Nanxun, we were satisfied with this income as newcomers. In the evening, Mr. Sun treated us to a meal. After we were full, he took us to a hotel and jokingly said, "This hotel is cheaper, 100 yuan per night. If you stay at Zhu Hui Hotel or Friendship Hotel, a regular room will cost 800 yuan per night." I laughed and said, "So expensive? Just staying one night without taking anything with us costs 800 yuan?" Mr. Sun jokingly replied, "When a man is with a woman, he still leaves something behind even if he doesn't take anything. Don't you still have to pay for that?" I was surprised. Mr. Sun was always polite, and I didn't expect such remarks from a man. They all had ulterior motives!

The hotel had many rooms, but the facilities were a bit old, and the lock made me feel insecure. However, the room had a bathroom where we could take hot showers. In the past, when I visited clients at hotels, I encountered electronic locks that would open when a magnetic card was inserted, which was convenient and secure. Wu Fang went to shower first, and there was no need to be discreet between sisters. She came out of the bathroom naked, and I noticed her dense hair covered her private area ultimately while mine was sparse. I had seen sisters who were utterly bare down there. Curiosity exists not only between the opposite sexes but also among the same sex. We wondered if there were any differences between us.

I visited Suzhou not long ago, and my current mood differed from back then. At that time, my mind was heavy, focusing solely on accompanying Ah Lan for treatment, and I had no thoughts about anything outside the hospital. Now, we would live in this city, immerse ourselves in this new world, and become part of the flow of people here. Suzhou would change from being unfamiliar to familiar, from blurry to transparent. Could I open a new chapter from my hometown Chongqing to Nanxun town, and now to beautiful Suzhou? I did not know the future, but I wasn't afraid. No matter what lay ahead, I believed there would always be a solution.

Suzhou and Hangzhou in the Jiangnan region had always been known as places of elegance and wealth and for producing beautiful women. As I walked the streets of Suzhou, I noticed the figures and temperament of the girls, which were pleasing to the eye. However, I didn't come across any stunningly beautiful women. Later, after spending more time in Suzhou, I realized that local girls in Suzhou rarely wore makeup or only applied light makeup. They embraced their natural beauty, while those who were beautiful and heavily made-up were usually from other places. In Suzhou, the girls from outside felt inferior, fearing being ridiculed in an area known for producing beauty. I should have paid more attention to dressing up. I knew I wasn't a lady, so casual attire was sufficient. In truth, every place has its beauty, and even in mountainous areas, you can find a golden phoenix soaring.

Mr. Sun took us for an interview, which was more like assessing our appearance. We arrived at Ganjiang Road and entered an upscale Oriental Bathhouse. Mr. Sun told us to wait in the lobby. After a while, a lady approached us and said, "Are you here for the job interview? Please follow me." Wu Fang and I followed her into a luxuriously decorated office. Mr. Sun and a man who looked like the boss were talking. When they saw us enter, Mr. Sun said, "These are the two beautiful girls from Chongqing with excellent massage skills. Mr. Gao, how about it? Isn't Sun's judgment accurate?"

The boss, whose surname was Gao, nodded and asked, "How long have you been doing this?" I truthfully replied, "One year." Wu Fang said, "Same as Xiao Jing." Mr. Gao looked at us, then through the information Mr. Sun had given him. His gaze suddenly stopped, and he turned toward me, expressing a pleasant surprise. He said, "So, you're Xiao Jing? The admirable massage therapist from the Passionate Suzhou program?" I didn't expect Mr. Gao to know me, and I couldn't help but feel happy and a bit embarrassed. I replied, "Yes, I'm Xiao Jing." Mr. Gao asked, "So, why did you resign and come to Suzhou?" I said, "We wanted a change of environment. I hope Mr. Gao will take care of us." Mr. Gao's face lit up, and he smiled, saying, "Great, welcome!" He turned to Mr. Sun and said, "Sun, my friend, you know how to do things! Thank you so much for introducing Miss Xiao to me!" Mr. Sun said, "Well, I'm just a matchmaker!" Wu Fang and I were surprised and were about to stand up. Mr. Gao chuckled and said, "Don't misunderstand. He's not a real matchmaker. He's an intermediary for talent referrals." Wu Fang and I were relieved and couldn't help but laugh.

Chapter 31

Temptation of Summer

Mr. Gao, the boss, asked us to find a place to rent first, as the bathhouse didn't have dormitories. We were unfamiliar with the area and needed to figure out where to rent a house. There were many rental listings online, but also many scams. Going to a real estate agency would take time, and besides, we only had 500 yuan, which was our combined savings. How could we survive until the next month's salary with such little money? In desperation, I thought of Mr. Sun and had no choice but to ask for his help to alleviate our financial crisis. I told Mr. Sun at the advertising company, "We don't have money. Could you lend us a thousand yuan? We'll pay you back when we receive our salary." Mr. Sun was surprised and asked, "How did you end up with no money? Did someone steal it from you? Or were you deceived by a swindler?"

I replied, "We're temporarily out of money. I sent most of what I earned back home before. Please help us out for now, alright?" Mr. Sun smiled and said, "Of course, but how will you repay me?" What? Do I have to repay the loan? Will there be interest charges? He's too shrewd, isn't he? I was stunned and didn't say anything. Mr. Sun chuckled, "Don't be nervous, I was just joking. If you're really in need, a thousand yuan is too little. Let's make it three thousand yuan, and if it's not enough, let me know." He took a stack of money from a drawer and handed it to me. Surprised, I asked, "Are you lending us three thousand yuan?" Wu Fang jokingly said, "Mr. Sun, aren't you afraid we'll take the money and run?" Mr. Sun laughed and said, "It's only three thousand yuan. Would you do that? Even if it were thirty thousand yuan, I wouldn't worry. Firstly, I trust Miss Xiao's character, and secondly, I have your identification information recorded. Don't worry, hehe." I smiled and said, "Thank you for your trust, Mr. Sun. We also plan to settle down in Suzhou. Even if you wanted us to leave, we wouldn't."

Mr. Sun helped us find a house a bit further away from the bathhouse, in Meihua New Village near Beihuan Road. It was a relatively new two-bedroom, one-living-room apartment costing 1,200 yuan monthly. Wu Fang and I shook our heads; spending so much on rent in a month and other miscellaneous expenses would leave us with only three thousand yuan for our living expenses. Mr. Sun smiled and said, "There are many outsiders in Suzhou now, and houses are like hot cakes. You have to grab one before someone else does. Just make do with this place for now, and you can upgrade later." We didn't find the house undesirable, but we felt the rent was too high!

I said, "Why is it 1,200 yuan? In our hometown, it's only 400 yuan." Mr. Sun said, "Your hometown is a small town, while this is a city. The market conditions are different. If you go to the countryside, you might not find anyone willing to rent for 200 yuan. It's all about the location." I said, "With these expenses, we'll be using up all our earnings for our living expenses. How will we have any extra money?" Mr. Sun said, "A person is like a spring. Only with pressure can you bounce back. In the past, you had to earn more to spend more. Now, you have to spend more to earn more. The concept has changed. Think about it, and there's a whip cracking behind you. Can you not increase your horsepower and move forward?" Mr. Sun's theory made sense and was refreshing. Sometimes, it's true that pressure can give birth to motivation.

The room was equipped with all the necessary living supplies: beds, tables, chairs, TV, washing machine, gas stove, electric rice cooker, dishes, basins, and so on. It was ready for us to move in. I cleaned the place, and Wu Fang and I went out to familiarize ourselves with the surroundings. We also went to a nearby convenience store to buy daily necessities such as pillows, thin blankets, towels, toothpaste, etc. This place was our temporary home, but we didn't know how long we would stay. After moving in, we realized the rental environment here was complicated. More than 70% of the houses in the community were rented to outsiders, and it was an older community without property management, posing some security risks. There were also many thieves and sex workers around.

We started working. Wu Fang and I worked in the massage rooms, and there weren't many customers, so the work was relatively easy. My salary was 3,000 yuan, while Wu Fang's was 2,500 yuan. Mr. Gao said that he would consider a raise after one month. I understood that businessmen prioritize profits, and Mr. Gao wanted to assess our abilities. I had confidence in my massage skills, but Wu Fang needed to improve. She had limited knowledge, and during her time in Nanxun, she had a carefree attitude and was always fooling around with men. Now that she was in Suzhou with me, we were like sisters, and I felt obliged to help her. During breaks at work, I would teach Wu Fang some massage techniques and patiently demonstrate the movements.

She made progress.

On our first day at work, we met a girl named Lin Xiaoshu from Xinxiang, Henan. People at the bathhouse called her "Xiaoshu," which sounded like "fiction." She was only 18 years old, younger than Wu Fang and me, and quite clever. Although we were new, she called us "Jingjie" and "Fangjie" very affectionately, and we couldn't refuse her warm gestures. We quickly became acquainted. However, we didn't expect that she had ulterior motives for getting close to us. When we finished work, she said, "Jingjie, my rented house expires in two days, and the landlord has rented it out to someone else. I have to move, but I've been looking for a place to stay for days and couldn't find anything. Could I stay with you temporarily in your rented house?" We were all struggling outsiders, trying to make a living, and since we were colleagues, how could we disregard her difficulties?

Initially, Wu Fang and I each had rooms, but when Xiaoshu came, Wu Fang moved into my room, freeing up a space for Xiaoshu. We treated Xiaoshu like a younger sister, so we accommodated her. However, we didn't expect that she would eventually take advantage of us, which gave me a deeper understanding of the fable "The Farmer and the Snake." Most people I encountered were good people, and I had a weak sense of caution. I thought that if I treated others with sincerity, they would also be friendly to me, but I didn't realize that there were ungrateful people in the world. Being too kind to others only led to our losses.

After a week at Oriental Bathhouse, my strengths gradually became apparent. I was meticulous and attentive, always wearing a smile on my face. I handled my work efficiently, and my massage techniques left customers feeling refreshed and highly satisfied. They said they had never been so pleased with their experience at Oriental Bathhouse! The positive customer feedback reached Mr. Gao's ears, and he was delighted. He called me over and asked me to become the head of the massage department, replacing the previous leader. I hurriedly tried to dissuade him, saying, "Mr. Gao, you're too kind. I'm still on probation, and I can't accept such an arrangement from you. Besides, I don't want to be a leader. I'd rather continue as a massage therapist." Mr. Gao seemed puzzled and said, "I'm promoting you. When employing people, we shouldn't be limited by conventions. What are you afraid of? I'll support you!" I replied, "You're the boss, and you may not fully understand the feelings of us employees. If I were promoted to a leadership position when I arrived, others might have opinions and exclude me. I would become isolated and lose my footing. I should work together with everyone as a massage therapist."

Although I declined Mr. Gao's kind offer, everyone knew he valued me highly. They were polite and friendly on the surface, but behind my back, they gossiped, claiming that I was Mr. Gao's mistress. Some even vividly described how they allegedly saw Mr. Gao and me flirting in the office. I was angry and helpless about these baseless accusations. Thinking back to my days in Nanxun, although the work was hard and the pay wasn't high, the relationship between my sisters and me was harmonious. Unexpectedly, it was a bit cold here. I did better than them and had more competence, but they still had grievances against me. I comforted myself, "As long as I am righteous, I don't need to fear unfounded accusations. People's hearts are flesh, and I believe that with time, they will come to understand and accept me as a good friend."

The distance from Guanjian Road to Beihuan Road was considerable. During the day, it was fine as there were buses for transportation, but it became troublesome during night shifts. After midnight, there were no more buses, and taking a taxi cost more than ten yuan per trip. We had not received our salaries, so we had to spend carefully. Wu Fang and I went to the local secondhand market and bought two bicycles for 100 yuan. I laughed and said to Wu Fang, "These are our dedicated vehicles now." Wu Fang rolled her eyes and said, "One day, I will have a small car!" I chuckled and said, "Life is difficult, so let's not dream too big." Riding bicycles were quite good — convenient, exercise, and environmentally friendly. No need for fuel. Why not enjoy it? I noticed that Xiaoshu was picked up and dropped off by a man on a motorcycle when she went to and from work. I thought he might be her boyfriend, so I asked her, but she said he was just a fellow villager.

After staying in Meihua New Village for a while, we often saw some women standing near bus shelters, trees, or alley entrances, dressed provocatively and flirting with passing men whenever we returned home at night. We knew what they were doing and couldn't help but look down on such showy behavior. Wu Fang sneered and said, "Is that all they do? Selling themselves like cheap goods!" Some men shamelessly called out to us as we rode our bikes past them, saying things like, "Beautiful ladies, stop! How about 50 yuan? 100 yuan?" Wu Fang and I would speed up and leave them behind. Sometimes, Wu Fang couldn't take it and would dismiss a vulgar remark, saying, "Want some action? Go find your mother!" This would infuriate those men, and they would try to catch up and fight with her, but we would quickly ride away.

The probation period ended, and Wu Fang and I passed successfully. I declined Mr. Gao's offer to raise my salary to avoid creating distance with our colleagues. I said, "I came here to earn money, but not just for the sake of money. It's also about accumulating experience and broadening my horizons, which will benefit me in the long run." Mr. Gao praised me and said, "You're an extraordinary massage therapist.

Work hard, and I won't treat you unfairly!" In the first month, Mr. Gao privately gave me a bonus of 500 yuan, and I accepted it with gratitude. I wasn't after just a measly 500 yuan; it was because I was now tight on cash. We had to pay next month's rent and repay the money to Mr. Sun, leaving us with very little.

Summer is beautiful, sexy, and full of temptation. There's a river in the middle of Guanjian Road, with grasslands on both sides, where young men and women often hide among the trees for intimacy. Although young, I'm considered a "veteran" and understand that people can easily be impulsive in summer. Oriental Bathhouse operated relatively legitimately, without providing explicit services, but business was booming—massage therapists dressed in cool attire, which was refreshing. I always believed leaving a bit to the imagination is more attractive than completely exposing it.

Chapter 32

Fragrant Night of Spring

The job of a massage therapist is to provide massages, and it does not involve erotic content. Those who divert massage therapists from their professional path are unscrupulous businessmen and wealthy individuals seeking pleasure. For those who do not understand, various speculations assume that a massage therapist's work is unsavory. That's genuinely unjust. When I joined the Oriental Bathhouse, I performed massages there. No "oil massage" or similar services were offered, let alone special ones. The opposite-sex massages here are relatively healthy. The massage itself has therapeutic benefits, and from a psychological perspective, opposite-sex massages can have subtle therapeutic effects. If a male massage therapist massages a man or a female therapist massages a woman, it remains solely a surface-level physical experience without any emotional fluctuations.

That summer, camisole tops were trendy. They showcased one's figure while providing a cool and comfortable outfit. Mr. Gao, being creative, designed a unique uniform for us staff members. It consisted of a bellyband and tailored shorts made from indigo-dyed fabric. The uniforms looked youthful, elegant, and exquisite, receiving unanimous praise from the staff members. Everyone loved them and said that the uniforms could rival designer clothing. Mr. Gao smiled and said, "Don't judge me because I run a bathhouse. Ten years ago, I worked as a cutter in a clothing factory. My appreciation for clothing is no less than yours." Xiaoshu said, "The uniforms designed by Mr. Gao could even participate in a fashion competition!" Mr. Gao laughed and replied, "You all look beautiful, and the guests feel comfortable too."

The second floor of the Oriental Bathhouse was dedicated to male guests, while the third floor catered to female guests. Both floors featured comfortable indoor swimming pools, with adjacent small rooms for showers, changing rooms, resting areas, and massage rooms. There were more than twenty female massage therapists in the massage department, including myself and two others who could be considered professional massage therapists. Male massage therapists were also available for male customers who preferred massages from the same gender. Female customers were more conservative and desired to be serviced by female massage therapists, except for a few progressive women who requested massages from male therapists. In the resting area, there were recliners and beverages and snacks available. The massage rooms here were not completely enclosed but semi-transparent, resembling offices in large companies. Each room had a massage bed and a dressing table with massage oils and essences. Soft conversations were allowed, but loud noises were prohibited. I was satisfied with the working atmosphere here because of the improved treatment and because I received more respect.

The VIP rooms were separate, similar to private compartments, where customers could receive massages, rest, and entertain guests. The decoration was exquisite, but there were only a few rooms, usually accommodating distinguished individuals such as managers of foreign companies, leaders of government departments, and private business owners. The bathhouse didn't oppose staff members' relationships with customers outside of work. After work, we could go wherever we wanted and do whatever pleased. However, staff members were prohibited from engaging in inappropriate behavior with customers within the bathhouse premises. Such conduct would not only result in dismissal but also fines. I appreciated this regulated lifestyle. Most sisters working at the bathhouse had boyfriends, while Wu Fang and I remained single. Some of the sisters joked, "You two are always together. Are you lesbians?"

During our night shifts, we had free time during the day, so we went to visit the gardens in Suzhou, including Canglang Pavilion, Lion Grove Garden, Humble Administrator's Garden, Master of the Nets Garden, and Tiger Hill. We had already visited them all, and their exquisite beauty was beyond description. Chongqing is a mountainous city, while Suzhou is known for its waterways. There are so many differences between the two. Chongqing girls are fiery and passionate, while Suzhou girls are delicate and refined. Their appearances are distinct. During our two months in Suzhou, Wu Fang was obedient, and we lived together without going out to play. Xiaoshu stayed temporarily with us, but we minded our business and didn't inquire much about her affairs. She spent a long time in the room with that motorcycle guy before coming out. The man seemed a bit rough and didn't appear to be an honest office worker. He seemed like someone involved in shady activities.

After three months, we finally breathed a sigh of relief, saving a few thousand yuan. Next month, I plan to send some money back home. I knew that my parents longed for news from me, not money. After arriving in Suzhou, I called home and informed my parents that I had left Nanxun, separated from Sister Wu, and found a new job in Suzhou. Everything was going well. I didn't mention sending money; my mother didn't bring it up either. She only told me to take care of myself and not to be too frugal with food and clothing. Family and parents hold a warm place in the hearts of us wanderers. When I first left home last year, I missed my family terribly and was concerned about everything at home. As time went by, I became accustomed to the life of working and gradually calmed down.

One night, Wu Fang said, "Jingjie, we've been in Suzhou for three months. Don't you feel like something is missing?" Isn't life here quite good? I didn't understand and asked, "What do you mean by 'missing'?" Money? We'll have to earn it slowly!" Wu Fang smiled and said, "Humans are made up of men and women. What we're missing is men! Jingjie, I'm not a child anymore. I want to find a boyfriend. You don't object, do you?" I looked at her and said, "Have you forgotten the pain of being deceived by a man? You ended up penniless and in a miserable state. Why are you thinking about finding a man again?" Wu Fang stretched and yawned, saying, "Men can't do without women, and women can't do without men. Life becomes so dull without the other half!" I laughed and said, "Just bear with it for now. Playing around won't lead to anything substantial. Find a serious partner, and then you can do whatever you want!" Wu Fang said, "I'm not a nun. I can't eat vegetarian food every day. Can you handle it? I can't! Let me satisfy my appetite with some meat dishes."

I'm not Wu Fang's biological sister, so I can't control her too much. Even if Sister Wu were here, she couldn't hold her either. I knew that Wu Fang had an itch in her heart for a long time, which wasn't surprising.

Can a cat that has once stolen fish stay disciplined? Honestly, I had also thought about it and felt lonely. But they are considering our current situation, which man is worth loving? Despite the guests speaking highly of us, they are outsiders. If their girlfriends were female massage therapists, they would hesitate as well. Besides, good men are scarce nowadays. The young ones are unreliable, and the slightly older ones are often already "committed." We can only meet each other when it's too late. If we become third parties, we would be inviting trouble, and it's unnecessary.

Wu Fang said, "Jingjie, you're smarter than me, but why don't you understand? We're young now, and youth is our capital. We shouldn't waste it! Who will still interest us if we wait until we're old and undesirable?" I chuckled and replied, "Wu Fang, are you lecturing me? Youth is our capital, but we shouldn't squander it. What if we get sick? How can we get married then? You'll ruin the rest of your life!" Wu Fang shrugged and said, "Investments always come with risks. Of course, we have risks too. They can play with women, and I want to play with them in return! Let them suffer losses!" What was Wu Fang thinking? Can she be so casual about it? I regretted bringing her here. If something happened to her in the future, Sister Wu and her family would hold me accountable!

In the end, Wu Fang took that step. She was pretty scheming and printed a box of perfume business cards. She would hand out those cards to male guests who seemed somewhat distinguished, with her contact number published on them. Those guests were experienced and aware of Wu Fang's intentions to seduce them, but they couldn't resist the temptation and secretly contacted her. "The grass is always greener on the other side." In their subconscious minds, who wouldn't want to try something new? Although Wu Fang wasn't charming, her youthful figure was enough to excite those restless men, making them lose their senses. Wu Fang maintained private contact with the guests, and I needed to find out where she went. If one day she was abducted, I wouldn't have any clue.

Work was going well, and Mr. Gao wanted to give me a raise. I said, "Let's keep the salary at 3,000 yuan. If Mr. Gao wants to give me more money, you can give it to me as a bonus. It won't show on the salary slip, and no one will envy me for having a higher salary." Mr. Gao smiled and said, "To be honest, with your massage skills and service attitude, even 5,000 yuan wouldn't be too much. However, the other two massage therapists we hired at the bathhouse earn 3,500 yuan. If I give you a higher salary, they might feel dissatisfied. So how about 3,800 yuan?" I smiled and said, "Okay, on International Women's Day, it's 3,800 yuan. I'm delighted, but I want the net income after taxes." Mr. Gao laughed and said, "Don't worry, I'll take care of the tax deductions. I run a legitimate business and don't try to evade taxes."

Mr. Gao's casual remark about not evading taxes touched a nerve and made me realize my vulnerabilities. It had been a long time since anyone had exploited my vulnerabilities, and at that moment, I felt a bit embarrassed and flustered. Ah, women are emotional creatures. Sometimes, we can be overly sensitive, and a single word, a glance, or a gesture can set our hearts racing. I quickly regained my composure and said, "Mr. Gao, I wanted to say Sun Boss deducts 10% from our earnings. Can you help me pay that off? I'll take home 3,800 yuan." Mr. Gao smiled and said, "Sure, no problem. Xiao Jing, what about Wu Fang? Who came with you? It seems like her skills are not as good as yours. For the sake of your face, I can raise her salary to 3,000 yuan. But I heard from the staff members that she's doing side jobs. Is that true?"

I expected him to be less well-informed. He already knew about Wu Fang's private interactions with guests. I didn't hide anything and said, "That's her matter, and I shouldn't say too much about it. Besides, the bathhouse doesn't seem to interfere with our personal lives. Is Wu Fang's behavior violating the rules and regulations of the bathhouse?" Mr. Gao said, "I won't interfere with her personal life, that's for sure. But she can't just focus on attracting customers and neglect her job responsibilities. If everyone acted like her, how could the bathhouse continue to operate? People might not come to the bathhouse anymore and look for her directly! Xiao Jing, it would be best to remind her to be more careful. If things continue like this, it will affect the reputation of the bathhouse!" Hearing Mr. Gao say this, he had some grievances against Wu Fang. Although the situation wasn't serious, Wu Fang had gone too far. Interacting privately with guests is one thing, but she should prioritize her job responsibilities. Mr. Gao treated us fairly, and we shouldn't undermine his position. I wanted to advise her to be more restrained.

Recently, Wu Fang's whereabouts were unpredictable. Her carefree attitude from our time in Nanxun had resurfaced. When she got off work, she would make a phone call or send a message, arranging to meet someone and hastily rushing off for the appointment. Sometimes she would return late at night and in the early morning. I couldn't understand what she aimed for by indulging in such youthful pursuits. Did she need money? Our current salary was enough. Earning 3,000 yuan per month was already good, considering many university graduates were still unemployed. Did she need men? She could find a boyfriend and didn't have to accept anyone who came along. I remember a saying from a book: "When young, people sacrifice their health for money; when old, they spend money for their health." In the end, the money still flows away. Focusing on one's health, being steadfast, and living more freely is better.

We had three days off each month, and on one of my days off, I sent 5,000 yuan back home. Many things were happening, and I didn't have any savings. Now, I could finally breathe a sigh of relief. Filial piety comes first among all virtues, and indulgence in sensual pleasures is the root of all evils. I have dabbled in virtues and vices and can't determine if I'm good or bad. I'm not very respectful since I'm not by my parents' side and can't take care of them. I've also disgraced them. I feel uneasy, but I still remember my parents' nurturing and will repay them well. I once was trapped in the mud and still hovered around its edges. I'm cautious, fearing I might slip and fall again one day. I am a contradictory woman.

In the evening, I had fried rice for dinner at home and was about to wash the dishes when I heard a knock on the door. I was a bit puzzled because Wu Fang and Xiaoshu had keys, and we had already paid the electricity and water bills. Who could be visiting at this hour? I cautiously opened the door, a crack, and saw a man standing outside with a helmet in his hand. He asked, "Is Xiaoshu at home?" I recognized him. He was the guy who rode a motorcycle to pick up Xiaoshu. I said, "She's not here." He said, "Really? Her phone is unreachable. I went out on business in the afternoon and didn't have time to come back to pick her up. Could she be upset and doesn't want to see me? Can I come in and check?" I saw that he seemed skeptical, but since he was Xiaoshu's acquaintance and not a stranger, I relaxed my guard and opened the door.

He glanced at me and said, "Thank you!" As he entered, I caught a whiff of a scent that was a bit like sweat but also different. I am clean; if a man smells sweaty, it makes me uncomfortable. However, he emitted a rough and rugged aura, which inexplicably gave me a slight liking. The men I had encountered at the bathhouse had all taken showers, and they were clean and fresh, with no other odors besides the scent of soap. I had gotten used to it and found it too monotonous. The man in front of me was about 1.7 meters tall, with thick eyebrows and big eyes, exuding a somewhat masculine vibe.

Xiaoshu's room was empty, and the bedding was scattered and untidy on the bed. I said, "I didn't lie to you. She hasn't come back." However, he showed no intention of leaving and said, "Can I stay here and wait for her? You can do your own thing, and I'll stay in her room without bothering you." I hesitated a bit, but strangely, I didn't insist on asking him to leave. I washed the dishes and watched TV until 9 p.m., but neither Wu Fang nor Xiaoshu returned. I was ready to rest, but I habitually showered before bed to feel more comfortable. I grabbed a change of clothes and passed by the living room, noticing that Xiaoshu's door was closed. I wondered what the man was doing inside. I anxiously and uneasily slipped into the bathroom, closed the door, took off my clothes, and stood under the showerhead, listening to the rushing water sound...

Chapter 33

In the Men's River

Women have strange psychology; they are cautious around men, yet they crave a man's infatuation with them. While I was taking a bath, although the bathroom door was closed, an unfamiliar man was in the house, making me uneasy. He was still in Xiaoshu's room, and his secretive presence made it difficult to figure out his intentions. I suspected he had ulterior motives and thought, "Whatever your plans are, don't bother me."

I used a towel to wash my body, and the water flowed like a stream, dancing and spreading all over me. The curves of a woman's body harmonize with the flowing water, creating a fantastic scene. Bathing is meant to be a relaxing activity, but fearing someone might be peeping, I felt somewhat restrained and hurriedly finished after a few minutes. I put on my nightgown and listened intently, ensuring no one was outside the door. I quietly opened the bathroom door. No one was there, and I checked to see if the man had left Xiaoshu's room. Would it be safe for me to sleep alone in my room if he hadn't? Although I had seen Xiaoshu getting along well with him, she insisted they were just fellow villagers, not friends. It was amusing.

As I was about to close my door, suddenly, a pair of solid arms hugged me from behind, and the man's grip was tight, rendering me unable to move. His hands held my arms and chest firmly, and he pressed his hand against my chest. Startled, I shouted, "Who is it?" In a low voice, he replied, "It's me." Recognizing him as Xiaoshu's fellow villager, I said, "Let go of me! What do you want?" He replied, "Don't scream, and I'll let go." I nodded, and he indeed released his grip. Feeling a little nervous, I asked, "Why haven't you left yet? Why did you come into my room? Go away!" He chuckled, "You're much prettier than Xiaoshu!" I didn't like men with a sneaky appearance, and since he was untrustworthy, how could I be interested in him?

He continued, "Don't be afraid. Let's chat for a while." I said, "What do we have to talk about? It's late, and I want to sleep. Please leave! If you want to talk to Xiaoshu, go to her room!" I might have indulged him a little if he were a courteous man. After all, we were adults, and whatever might happen wouldn't matter much. But since he had ulterior motives, I couldn't accept him. I didn't want him to linger and make me uncomfortable. He said, "I got bored waiting, so I thought we could chat. I promise to leave in a little while." Since he didn't move further, I relaxed and asked, "What do you want to talk about?" He sat by the bed and said, "Don't rush. We can get to know each other better. You are Xiaoshu's good friend and also my friend." I calmly replied, "We're just colleagues, not good friends." He said, "Let me introduce myself. I'm Gu Hongwei, from the same village as Xiaoshu. Our parents both work in the coal mine. A couple of years ago, I came out with Xiaoshu. She works, and I ride a motorcycle to pick up customers." I was somewhat surprised, so he quickly explained, "I'm the one who drives customers, not the one soliciting them."

He mentioned his parents working in the coal mine caught my attention. I knew the hardships of poverty; my family was also not well-off. Transportation could have been more convenient in some remote areas, and making more than a small income in a year was challenging. Going to work was also exhausting. Coal mine accidents were often reported, and every year there were several incidents of miners being trapped underground for days before being rescued, which was heartbreaking. The coal mine owners earned money unscrupulously, disregarding the workers' lives. Compared to that, our job as massage therapists was much safer and more accessible. Some people found work outside their hometown smoothly, while others faced difficulties and even walked a crooked path.

After all, we weren't familiar, and there wasn't much to discuss. I leaned against the bed and watched TV. Facing the fan, I combed my wet hair, and the cool breeze seeped into my nightgown, causing it to billow. Even though it was autumn, the late summer's lingering heat was still evident, and the weather was still hot. I casually said, "How is your relationship with Xiaoshu? Did you come to see her for something today?" He replied, "We are fellow villagers and have a good relationship. I pick her up and drop her off from work, and sometimes she visits me." I understood that when fellow villagers were away from home, they would support and take care of each other, and even if they lived together, it didn't necessarily mean they were in a romantic relationship; it might just be a pure mutual need. Nowadays, people are more open-minded, and everything is negotiable. If two people don't get along, they can break up. There's nothing extraordinary about it. If I had a male fellow villager here, at the very least, we could get together, chat in our hometown dialect, and reminisce about old times.

I finished combing my hair and turned to glance at him, only to find him staring intently at me. I should ask him to leave quickly; otherwise, I won't be able to rest, and if Xiaoshu comes back and sees this, she might misunderstand me. Women are more jealous than men, and when they go crazy, they can be ruthless. If he weren't Xiaoshu's fellow villager and a stranger in my room, I may be absent-minded and have a vague desire. I don't believe in saints or chaste women; women are not made of ice or iron; they have emotions and needs. However, I have yet to encounter a man who could capture my heart, and with sufficient external forces, I won't be swayed. Nevertheless, I won't be like Wu Fang; I want to live in the sunshine, not chaos.

I sent him away, saying firmly, "I'm sorry. Please go back. I need to sleep!" He said, "It's still early. Can we chat a bit longer? I promise I'll leave soon." He didn't make any further advances, and I relaxed a bit. I said, "What do you want to talk about?" He walked over and sat by the bed, saying, "Don't worry. Let's get acquainted. After all, you're Xiaoshu's good friend, and now you're my friend too." I calmly replied, "We are colleagues, not good friends." He said, "Let me introduce myself. I'm Gu Hongwei, from the same village as Xiaoshu. Both our parents work in the coal mine. A couple of years ago, Xiaoshu and I came out together. She works while I drive customers around." Seeing my surprise, he quickly clarified, "I provide motorcycle transport for customers, not the kind of services you're thinking of."

As I closed the door behind him with a loud bang, I finally breathed a sigh of relief. I felt a cool sensation on my body; cold sweat had formed due to the nervousness. That night, I slept uneasily, feeling half-awake; I couldn't tell if I had fallen asleep. I heard some noises outside the door in the middle of the night. In the dim darkness, every movement of the curtains made me uneasy. I didn't want to get involved in any trouble; I didn't want any association with this man. Some people bring good luck to my life, like Sister Xu, Mr. Zhang, and Mr. Gao; others only bring trouble, like Gu Hongwei, who gave me a sense of foreboding.

Wu Fang returned in the morning, and I worriedly said, "You keep spending the night outside; be careful not to get into trouble!" She waved her hand dismissively, saying, "Jing, you worry too much. With my wit, how could I get into trouble? Last night, the boss was too stingy; he only gave me three hundred yuan for spending the night with him. What a miser!" Her words reminded me of Mr. Gao's warning, and I said, "Fang Fang, you need to be careful. Mr. Gao has noticed that you're secretly contacting customers during work hours. It's not good." Wu Fang impatiently replied, "So what? I can just quit. A boss will support me with sixty thousand yuan a year!" I said, "Don't be delusional; they're trying to deceive you! You might end up being sold and not even realize it!" Wu Fang said, "I'm not that stupid. Don't worry about me. I'm exhausted; I'm going to sleep. Jing, please get in touch with Xiao Li for me and ask her to cover my shift. I'll cover her evening shift." I sighed, afraid she would slide further down the wrong path.

Mr. Gao values me highly, and the business at the Eastern Bathhouse is steadily growing. I have established a good reputation at the bathhouse, and Mr. Gao has provided me with a private massage room, raising my value. Each massage session costs a minimum of 150 yuan, and a full-body massage costs 300 yuan. This is purely for massage, without any additional services. With such high prices, only wealthy people can afford it, and many people come to make reservations. The rich are troubled by how to spend money, while the poor worry about how to earn it. Mr. Gao said, "Schools have their campus beauties, film companies have their leading actresses and TV stations have their golden microphones.

Similarly, our Eastern Bathhouse needs an image spokesperson, and Xiao Jing, you are the best choice! Mr. Sun has a good eye, and you have earned a good reputation for Eastern Bathhouse." I smiled, "Mr. Sun is the matchmaker, and here, at Mr. Gao's place, is my husband's family."

Xiao Shu has been acting mysteriously lately. She returns around two or three in the morning, and when asked what she is doing, she says she went out to have fun. Where could she be having fun at such a late hour? Is she going to bars? If she wants to go to bars, then fine, but why won't she tell the truth? We don't lock the rooms inside the house; there's nothing valuable. We keep our money in the bank, and the cards have PIN codes, so it's challenging to get any money even if someone steals them. But I noticed Xiao Shu's room is always locked. It's strange; what does she need to keep so secret? Her fellow villager with the surname Gu visits her regularly, and they stay out late, only coming back in the early morning. Once they're back, they hide in the room and sleep until noon. I'm suspicious of what they might plot, but I haven't asked Xiao Shu about it, pretending not to know.

One night, Xiao Shu was bathing, and I was in the living room having some water when I unexpectedly found her purple bag on the sofa. Xiao Shu had just gone in to take a bath, and would be a while before coming out. I became curious about what was inside her bag, not out of malicious intent to invade her privacy, but just wanting to see what she had. I gently opened the zipper and found a makeup mirror, condoms, lipstick, a passbook, and a small bottle of tranquilizers. Tranquilizers are prescription drugs that can't be bought directly from a pharmacy. Even with a doctor's prescription, you can only get a few pills, so how did she end up with a whole bottle of them? I checked the passbook and was stunned by the deposit records! There were over a dozen entries, each worth several thousand yuan, some even in US dollars and Japanese yen! Impressive, she managed to get involved with foreigners and earn foreign currency! I had doubts, but I didn't overthink about it. I returned the passbook to the bag and returned it to its original place.

I know Mr. Fang, a friend of Mr. Gao's, a local from Suzhou, 35 years old, with a printing factory and a Mercedes car. I was introduced to him by Mr. Gao initially, but later, Mr. Fang started coming on his own, almost every day, to get a massage. We got to know each other well. He used to work at a bank but voluntarily gave up that stable job and started a printing business with a friend. The company wasn't doing well initially, and the partner withdrew his investment, but Mr. Fang persevered, and soon things started to improve. He made a lot of money, and his business kept growing yearly. Mr. Fang mentioned that he was married and had a son in elementary school. His wife had a difficult temperament, and their marriage caused him some distress, but he never considered getting a divorce. He also said that he was happy to have met me. While enjoying the massage, he felt relaxed, like opening a window in a closed room and breathing in fresh air. I might not be as good as he described, but I also enjoyed our conversations. He opened up to me, trusting me as a friend, and I felt grateful for that. He was a successful man with a kind heart. Why do good men always belong to someone else?

A good woman is like a bright pearl, and a good man is like a precious gem. However, people always seem to meet at the wrong time—either too early, too late, or not in the same direction. The reason I admire Mr. Fang is not only because of his refined manners but also because of his sense of responsibility. Although he, like other men, complains about his unhappy marriage in front of women, he clearly states that he doesn't want to divorce. This shows he doesn't intend to deceive me intentionally and is much more sincere than those who promise to divorce immediately. I understand one thing very clearly: when a man readily abandons his ex-wife, he might do the same to you. He quickly gets bored and changes his feelings frequently. His promises are not to be trusted, and maybe while you're still not fully committed, he already has another woman by his side. I've been hurt before, so I'm cautious regarding matters of the heart.

Mr. Fang is Mr. Gao's friend, and based on that, I accepted his advances relatively quickly. "Birds of a feather flock together," and I know what kind of person Mr. Gao is, so Mr. Fang can't be too different. Mr. Fang hinted that he sought a lover who understood and liked him but didn't interfere with his life. I understood he had feelings for me, but I hesitated whether to become his lover. Being a lover is easy, but being someone's cherished one is more complex. There might be little financial return, and I know that Mr. Fang and I don't have a future together. It's not about whether he divorces; I don't have romantic feelings for him, just a fondness. I don't want to become a decorative vase; I need a man who loves me with sincerity and righteousness. That's the harbor I'm looking for. If he's just a "waiting shelter," do I need to take refuge there? Should I stick to the "better to be alone than in bad company" principle? I'm torn.

In late autumn, Suzhou hosts the annual Tianping Red Maple Festival. I visited the famous Tianping Red Maple with Mr. Fang. The colorful and enchanting red maple leaves immersed us in the beauty of the mountains and forests. The vibrant colors of life moved me, a young girl, and I felt the urge to be passionate and accessible, with no need to hold back. Thinking of Wu Fang's carefree lifestyle and how she quickly makes money from men, I condemn and secretly envy her. I'm not inferior to her in physical appearance, but my life is as calm as water, with no waves. I understand that poverty is not an excuse to sell one's body, but in the face of society, the dignity I strive to uphold is as thin as a piece of paper. One strong push and a big hole might be revealed.

Mr. Fang invited me to dinner and later to have tea at a café. We chatted casually and also talked about some personal matters, feeling comfortable with each other. He was the second man to make me feel close since I started working here. The first was, of course, General Zhang. I shared my work experience and life as a masseuse, which fascinated Mr. Fang. I didn't mention the private services, but he knew about them. Can anyone in that environment avoid getting stained by the mud? When I talked about my time in Nanxun, especially the events surrounding Ah Lan's passing, I was so sad that I almost cried, and Mr. Fang sighed in sympathy. He hadn't seen the TV show "Emotions in Suzhou," so my recounting those events touched him even more deeply.

Mr. Fang shared about his first love, a beautiful girl from middle school. He wrote her several love letters, but later, she didn't get into high school and had to work on the farm while he got accepted to Suzhou Middle School. She felt the pressure and probably thought she wasn't good enough for him, so she took the initiative to end their relationship. The letters he wrote to her went unanswered, and she avoided him when he went to see her. When he got his university acceptance letter and wanted to share the good news with her, he found out that she was already in a relationship with a soldier, and they were engaged. The law protected military marriages, so there was nothing he could do but give up on her, which marked the end of his first love. After graduating from college, he worked at a bank, and a female colleague extended an olive branch to him. At the time, he had just started working and didn't have much social experience, so he moved in with a colleague, and they started living together. Soon, they got married, and their son was born.

However, his wife's temper became more challenging to handle. She would quarrel with him over trivial matters at work, causing him to feel embarrassed. Feeling suffocated, he decided to go against his family's objections and resigned to start his own business, opening a small printing factory that laid the foundation for his current success.

Around eleven in the evening, I said I needed to go home. Mr. Fang walked me to the entrance of my rented place. I didn't invite him to come up; it was too late, and inviting him up might imply something more intimate. Even if something happened between us, I didn't want to rush things. If he does treat me well, I wouldn't mind being his lover, leaning on his shoulder for support, and longing for warm affection. I can control my life, be close or give up. I don't want Mr. Fang's influence to result in more favors from Mr. Gao; I want him to accompany me during my time in Suzhou, giving me more confidence to face reality.

Mr. Fang stood by the car, not leaving immediately but watching me go upstairs. When I reached the front door on the second floor, I noticed something unusual—the door lock had been pried open! Had I been robbed? Were Wu Fang and Xiao Shu not at home? My heart pounded loudly, and after calming down a bit, I pushed open the door and found the interior in chaos. The sofa in the living room had been moved, and the gates of the two rooms were wide open. I listened for any sounds inside. Worried that a thief might be hiding, I hesitated about entering. I cautiously peeked through the corridor window downstairs and saw Mr. Fang bending down to get into his car. I rushed over in a flurry, like a lost child running into a mother's embrace, shouting, "Mr. Fang, wait for me!"

Chapter 34

Money Corrupts

No matter how capable a woman is, at critical moments, she still hopes that a man can come forward, support her, and make decisions for her. Although I can't entirely agree with the notion that "women are inherently weak," men are like mountains, and women are like water. Whether it's a waterfall or a stream, water thrives in the mountain's embrace, showing its charm and beauty. The hill, in turn, is enriched by the lingering water, and masculinity gives birth to tenderness.

As I rushed towards Mr. Fang, he probably noticed me from the rearview mirror and quickly exited the car. I ran up to him without much thought and instinctively hugged him, saying incoherently, "It's stolen! My house has been robbed! Brother Fang, what should I do?" This was the first time I called him "Brother Fang." In the past, I always politely addressed him as Mr. Fang, deliberately keeping a distance from him. I was afraid that getting too close would make me lose control. Remarkable men have a magnetic power over women, and leaning against a man's chest feels secure. In his embrace, I forgot the anxiety of my robbed room.

Mr. Fang asked, "Xiaojing, what happened? Was there a thief in your house?" I left his embrace and replied, "My room was forced open. I wonder if the thief is still inside?" Mr. Fang suggested, "Then call the police at 110." I took out my phone and was about to dial when I saw a motorcycle stopping downstairs, and the people on it were none other than Xiao Shu and her fellow villager. Why were they coming back so late? Xiao Shu spotted me and exclaimed in surprise, "Sister Xiaojing, why are you here downstairs?" She noticed Mr. Fang and jokingly said, "Oh, Sister Jing, you're doing well, attaching yourself to a big boss?" I knew she misunderstood, thinking I was having a secret rendezvous with a client to earn extra money, but I didn't explain. I said, "Xiao Shu, you came back just in time. My place was robbed, and I was about to report it!" Xiao Shu was shocked and a bit nervous, "Is there a thief? Let's go check. If nothing is missing, we don't need to report it!" Her fellow villager said, "Let's go upstairs and check first. It's better not to report it if possible. The process is troublesome, and they might be unable to find anything."

Our reasoning was sound, and since we were a group, we decided to go upstairs together to inspect the situation. The house had little valuable stuff, just clothes and the old TV. I carried my money and ID but wanted to know if Xiao Shu left her money at home. I said, "Let's go up together, be cautious, and if the thief hasn't left, we'll block the door and report to the police as soon as possible!" Mr. Fang said, "I have a steel rod in my car that I usually carry for self-defense. Let me go get it." As expected, he went to the driver's seat and retrieved a 50-centimeter-long steel rod. Mr. Fang led the way, and we all went upstairs.

We entered the apartment and searched around; there was no one inside. Mr. Fang and I arrived at my room, finding it chaotic, with drawers, pillows, and straw mats scattered on the floor. I noticed Wu Fang's passbook. I remembered she had hidden it inside the pillowcase, and now the thief discovered it too. These thieves were quite skillful; however, they didn't take it. The passbook had a password, and if they attempted to withdraw money, they would be unsuccessful and expose themselves, caught on camera. Therefore, thieves usually target only cash and valuable items. They must have been disappointed; it seemed they stomped many dirty footprints on my bedding!

Fortunately, nothing seemed missing, and the thieves had long gone. I breathed a sigh of relief and went to the adjacent room where Xiao Shu stayed with her fellow villager. I wanted to ask them if they lost anything. They talked in low voices and looked nervous when they saw us coming in. I asked, "Did you lose anything?" Xiao Shu replied, "Nothing is missing, but they ransacked everything." I said, "That's good. The lock on the outside door is broken. We can only replace it tomorrow. What should we do tonight?" Gu Hongwei suggested, "Xiao Shu can stay at my place, and you two..." I interrupted, "I'll tidy up a bit."

I returned to my room and started arranging things, and Mr. Fang helped. After a while, everything was neatly arranged, except the straw mats, bedding, and pillows were all dirtied by those despicable thieves. How could I sleep without washing them? Mr. Fang said, "There's nothing valuable here. Let's sleep outside tonight and buy new ones tomorrow before sleeping inside again." I hesitated and didn't say anything. If I agreed to sleep outside, Mr. Fang would arrange a room for me, but would he stay with me or ask me to stay alone in the hotel? If he asked, should I agree? Mr. Fang said, "Stop hesitating. Come with me." When a man is decisive, it often leads a woman to follow him involuntarily, revealing her dependence on men.

We didn't speak in the car. I was no longer an innocent girl, fully aware of what would happen next. Mr. Fang was neither a naive young man nor a saint. He understood the plot of the story better than I did. The best chance for a romantic relationship between a man and a woman lies in timing, opportunity, and the individuals involved. The presence of thieves unintentionally provided us with a chance. We always had a good relationship, but it had yet to progress. Now, finding a safe place to be together seemed quite natural. I hadn't fallen in love with Mr. Fang, but I didn't dislike him either. Even if we were to have a more intimate relationship, it could be described as mutual affection. I couldn't resist the care of men; men ultimately sway women.

On the other side of the North Ring Road was an overpass and a larLady Gerket, with the Su Jiahang Expressway running close to the New Village. I rented a place there, and it was said to be slated for demolition soon, but nothing had happened yet. The area had a complex population, with frequent fights and brawls. It was also a gathering place for many drifters and stealing and pickpocketing were common occurrences. I usually dressed casually, like a working-class person, so no one would suspect I was a masseuse. Both masseuses and prostitutes were vulnerable groups and quickly taken advantage of, so I had to learn to protect myself. Some girls would dress up with heavy makeup, looking alluring and unmistakably like prostitutes. They associated with gangsters and conspired to deceive people for money, even having to pay protection fees. Many of these girls were manipulated by someone behind the scenes.

Mr. Fang knew that my current living situation wasn't safe. He had advised me to move to a different place, maybe to the city center, where work would be more convenient. Finding a suitable location was difficult, and the rent was high. Earning money was challenging, and I hoped to save for my future. I didn't want to be too particular about food, housing, and clothing; I just wanted to get by. Mr. Fang said, "Xiao Jing, consider moving elsewhere. Thieves have already targeted your current place and might strike again." I replied, "Don't scare me. They didn't steal anything this time. Why would they come back in the future?" Mr. Fang said, "How about I help you rent another place?" I shook my head, knowing what that would imply. If I moved into a place he rented for me, wouldn't that make me his kept woman? I didn't want to take that step. Even if I were to be in a romantic relationship, I wanted to have my freedom. Being supported by someone else meant losing much of that freedom, including pursuing love. What if I met a good man? I wouldn't be able to chase him.

We went to a hotel, and Mr. Fang registered, taking me to the room. At this moment, what did I have to hold back? Regardless of love, I had the right to pursue happiness. We understood each other without speaking. When we entered the room, Mr. Fang hugged me tightly, exciting me. He caressed me from my hair to my chest and thighs, awakening my half-asleep desires. His hands roamed on my back; our chests pressed together, and I felt my whole body heating up. Youth may be beautiful, but without the moistening of a man, it lacks a certain charm. Since there are men and women worldwide, why should there be too many constraints?

We didn't shower and fell onto the bed. We rolled together, stripping off each other's clothes, as if this moment had been long awaited. I embraced him, embraced his thrusts, and embraced his invasion, feeling pleasure being gradually stirred. While he oppressed me, I hugged him more deeply until he couldn't hold back and let out a wolf-like howl, collapsing weakly on top of me. My body felt like a string that had ended, tight, and gradually relaxed. I hadn't reached the peak, but I still felt a sense of satisfaction all over my body. Mr. Fang, also known as

Brother Fang, was the first man I had intimate relations with since coming to Suzhou. A critical factor for a man's attraction to a woman is his liking for her body. A woman's attraction to a man involves many aspects; only then is she willing to show herself to him. If a man likes you but doesn't desire you, it's friendship, definitely not love.

The next day, I started work in the afternoon. I slept in the hotel until noon; my body felt lazy, but my heart was warm. Mr. Fang wasn't a client; he didn't give me money but attentive care. In the morning, he urged me to get up and wash, made me eat the milk and bread he bought, and only then allowed me to continue sleeping. He said, "Skipping breakfast is bad for your stomach and can make you gain weight." I retorted, "If I eat and sleep, I'll gain weight easily." He laughed and said, "A little weight gain is not a problem; as long as you're healthy, it's good." He had something to attend to, so I stayed alone in the room. The morning sun was warm, and the room was filled with sunlight through the curtains, exuding a soft and friendly atmosphere. I curled up in the blankets and laughed for no reason.

In the afternoon, Mr. Fang accompanied me to visit Tiger Hill. Su Dongpo said, "It's regretful if you come to Suzhou and don't visit Tiger Hill!" Tiger Hill was originally called Haichong Mountain, and in ancient times, it was a vast expanse of water. Over time, it accumulated silt and gradually emerged as a hill. Why was it called Tiger Hill? Legend has it that during the Spring and Autumn period, King Helü of Wu was buried here, and a white tiger lurked in front of his tomb, thus giving the hill its name. There was a huge stone used for testing swords, and according to legend, Gan Jiang and Mo Ye, master swordsmiths of Wu, forged 3,000 blades hidden in the tomb of King Helü. When Emperor Qin Shihuang unified China, he came here to test one of the swords, splitting a massive rock with it. So, on the sword-testing stone, we see today, the sword makes a split mark. Tiger Hill also has many other scenic spots, such as Erxianting and Qianrenshi, where it's said a Buddhist monk once preached. There's also the "Sword Pool," a small pool with shallow water filled with tens of thousands of coins thrown in by tourists. When we visited, Tiger Hill held a "Golden Autumn Flower Festival," where osmanthus, chrysanthemums, peonies, and other flowers competed for attention, creating a beautiful sight. There were also many singing performances, including Suzhou Pingtan and ethnic dance performances, dazzling the visitors.

I asked, "Don't you need to go home to eat and sleep? Doesn't your wife care?" Mr. Fang said, "She used to be very strict, but I got busier with work and socializing, and I went home less often. She's probably gotten used to it and doesn't bother me anymore." I laughed, saying, "What socializing? They're all lies! Men become bad when they have money!" Mr. Fang chuckled, "Bad people exist both with and without money. Good people also exist both with and without money. It's not absolute. You can get bored after being married for many years and seeing each other's faces every day. Going outside to relax and avoid her nagging is better." I asked, "Will you get tired of me too?" Mr. Fang smiled, "How could I? I care about you too much!"

One morning, I was sleeping when Wu Fang received a call and had to go out again. Wu Fang was a bit careless at work, and the boss had already talked to her about it. I also advised her to focus on her job at the bathhouse and not get involved in other messy things. With a monthly salary of 3,000 yuan, where else could she find such a high-paying job? Wu Fang said, "Working eight hours daily, now that business is good, I don't even have time to drink water. It's so tiring. What's so good about that? Xiaojing, you talk lightly. You're doing well. You get a higher salary, and Mr. Gao treats you well. Everyone says you receive red envelopes and are Mr. Gao's mistress. How can I compare to you?"

Chapter 35

A succession of Accidents

There's a saying, "Domestic flowers are not as fragrant as wild ones." Domesticated ones can't compare to the deliciousness of wild creatures like turtles and crabs. Pond-raised ones are less tasty than the wild ones. The same goes for ginseng; artificially cultivated ginseng may resemble the real thing, but can its nutritional value match that of wild ginseng? Men enjoy seeking excitement outside while disregarding their wives. After all, wives might not lack tenderness or beauty; it's just the men's curiosity at play. Although I had an ambiguous relationship with Mr. Fang, I was unsure about what he saw in me. Did he want me to bear a daughter for him, or was it just a joke? I didn't care about the outcome as long as he treated me well. "Having once possessed is enough, why does it need to last forever?" Isn't that the way things are nowadays?

The profits of the bathhouse came from bathing, massages, and private rooms. Bathing relied on quantity, the more customers, the higher the income. However, massages were the primary source of profit. Massage profits were from more than just the service fee and the essential oils. The prices of massages varied not based on the different techniques but on the quality of the essential oils used. Some oils cost only a few yuan per bottle, while others could cost hundreds or thousands, just like shampoo; the price difference was due to the quality of the shampoo. The income of massage therapists was based on hourly rates, but the essential oils were the real gold mine. If a bottle of oil costs 20 yuan, the price charged to customers is usually around 100 yuan. If the oil costs 100 yuan, the customer must pay 1000 yuan. This high-profit margin wasn't unique to our bathhouse; it was the norm in the massage industry. And that's just for legitimate massages; some establishments operated under the guise of massage while engaging in sexual services, and their profits were unknown.

Mr. Gao was a creative man who created his special essential oil that received high customer praise. In Suzhou, the famous Biluochun tea was on par with West Lake Longjing tea. It was said that Biluochun tea was once a national gift sent by Premier Zhou to foreign guests. Tea leaves were meant for brewing, but Mr. Gao used them for massages. He ground the tea leaves into powder and soaked them in essential oil. When we massaged the customers, the oil was evenly spread, filling the room with the pleasant fragrance of tea leaves. This aroma was much more appealing than regular essential oils, and the fine particles of tea leaves enhanced the massage experience, leaving the skin more vibrant. After using it for a while, the customers responded positively and loved this green, eco-friendly, nutritious, and innovative massage oil.

That day, Mr. Gao called me into his office to show me an article in a magazine. I was puzzled, "Why is he showing me a book? Isn't he neglecting his duties as a boss?" The article was a travelogue written by a female tourist about her trip to Bali, mainly focusing on her enjoyable massage experience. She described how a male masseur provided meticulous and considerate service that relaxed her deeply and enlightened her. There was a passage that Mr. Gao marked with a pen, which praised the masseur's professionalism and dedication, creating an immersive experience for her. The female tourist cherished this trip and particularly enjoyed the massage experience.

Such a gender-neutral approach to massages might be complex for Chinese people to accept, not to mention that finding masseurs with exceptional skills and professional ethics in China was highly challenging. In short, this combination of oil massages and sexual services was hard to implement in China. I returned the book to the table and asked, "After reading it, what are your instructions, Mr. Gao?" He smiled and asked, "What are your thoughts?" I replied, "Finding such skilled masseurs is challenging, and I'm afraid female customers might not have the courage to try this kind of massage." Mr. Gao chuckled, "You mean we can't imitate it? There's also an article about it online, and the response has been very enthusiastic. Female customers hope to experience this service in China too. Since the customers like it, why not cater to their preferences?" I said, "Suzhou is a bit conservative. It's challenging to promote such services. It's like sunbathing; it might be common abroad, but who would dare to try it here?"

Mr. Gao said, "You make a valid point, but there's a business opportunity here. It's better to act sooner rather than later. That's why I want to give it a try. However, we'll only do the oil massages for now, not the deep tissue massages. Xiao Jing, do you have confidence in this?" I replied, "It's just oil massages. What's so difficult about that? However, is it appropriate to offer this service at a bathhouse? Won't it ruin the image of your well-established business?" Mr. Gao laughed, "It's easy for those who know how and difficult for those who don't.

Xiao Jing, you know quite a lot." I said, "Mr. Gao, will you compromise like this? The line between oil massages and sexual services is blurred, aren't you worried?" Mr. Gao smiled, "I know my boundaries. What we do doesn't involve illegal activities or breaking the law. Offering professional surface massages for both men and women is reasonable and legal." Can rules and regulations manage these kinds of situations? People will always try to push boundaries. Once oil massages become available, who knows what might happen? After all, not all men are gentlemen, and not all women are ladies.

Mr. Gao was a businessman who knew that men's money was easy to earn in the massage industry, and women's money was too. People's living conditions improved, so they didn't mind spending on beauty and health. He also knew that doing something similar to what they had in Bali would be difficult and might need to be better received publicly. It might attract media attention, cause a commotion, and even lead to the bathhouse closing down. He printed some exquisite promotional materials and asked us to distribute them to customers first to see their feedback. At the same time, he wanted me to train a few employees to recommend the oil massages to customers on a small scale. Many beauty salons and hair-washing shops had secretly offered similar massages to capitalize on the high profits. Still, their hygiene and safety standards could have been better, and the staff needed more professionalism, which made customers interested but hesitant to try. Since we introduced this service at the bathhouse, customers were delighted.

Experience comes from constant accumulation, and I learned many new things at work. Regarding massages, my knowledge was only superficial, while Ah Ying, one of the massage therapists, had studied authentic traditional Chinese massage. She was well-versed in hundreds of acupuncture points on the human body and could locate them with her eyes closed. She brought a human body chart and explained the relevant knowledge of the acupuncture points to me in detail, helping me see the light and grasp many essentials of traditional Chinese massage. Although Ah Ying excelled in theoretical knowledge and had excellent massage techniques, she needed to improve at communicating with customers during the massages. The atmosphere during her massages felt a bit stuffy, and customers enjoyed it less. On the other hand, I would massage and chat with the customers, and they appreciated this relaxed interaction. As a result, I gained a reputation among customers and held a respected position among the staff at the bathhouse.

Xiaoshu occupied my rental room, and I was furious, but I didn't want to make enemies with her or publicly confront her. Although she started working at Dongfang Bathhouse before me, her position was lower than mine, so I had the authority to manage her. However, I didn't seek personal revenge and didn't make things difficult for her. She wasn't my friend nor my enemy; I didn't want to have much to do with her. We each minded our own business, and there was no need for further interaction. If we happened to cross paths, I would smile and move on. I let her have the rental room at Meihua New Village, and she would pay the rent herself in the future. Wu Fang and I lived in a residential community, which was more convenient and safer than before. The community had security guards, electronic gates at the stairs, and our room was equipped with a theft-proof door. It would be difficult for thieves to break in again.

In the spring of 2005, one day in mid-April, we were busy at work when suddenly, several police officers walked in. We were panicked, thinking they were there for a surprise inspection. However, they directly took

Xiaoshu, who was massaging a customer, away. We all felt puzzled, and I thought she might have been caught engaging in prostitution by the police. We didn't ask him about the situation until the end of our shift when Mr. Gao arrived at the bathhouse. Mr. Gao said, "She committed a crime, and it's serious, but I don't know the specifics." That night, when I watched the news on TV, I learned from the "Social Truth" program about the details of Xiaoshu's arrest.

It turned out that Xiaoshu had a conversation with a Taiwanese businessman last night. After accompanying the businessman to his hotel, she tricked him into drinking a beverage laced with sleeping pills. When the Taiwanese businessman was tired and about to fall asleep, Xiaoshu and several of her accomplices stole all of his belongings, including a laptop, passport, thousands of US dollars, several bankbooks containing a large sum of money, and some important documents. During the theft, the Taiwanese businessman didn't drink much of the laced beverage, so he didn't fall into a deep sleep. They accidentally woke him up while rummaging through the room, and as he tried to ask questions, one of Xiaoshu's accomplices hit him on the head, causing him to bleed. After committing the crime, Xiaoshu calmly returned to her place to sleep. Her three accomplices took some of the stolen items, called a taxi, and fled toward Shanghai.

The security staff discovered suspicious individuals entering and leaving the Taiwanese businessman's room on the surveillance footage. They immediately checked the room and found the Taiwanese businessman lying on the floor with the space in disarray. Realizing the Taiwanese businessman had been robbed under anesthesia, they promptly called the police. The 110 police quickly set up a blockade, and fortunately, not much time had passed since the incident. At the Jinjihu toll station on the Suzhou-Shanghai Airport Road, the armed police were waiting.

Taxis leaving the city at night had to go through registration procedures. When the cab carrying the suspects approached, the police routinely stopped it for inspection. They noticed three people in the taxi looking nervous and acting suspiciously. Several police officers quickly surrounded the vehicle, and when the suspects saw the situation wasn't in their favor, two of them opened the car door and tried to escape. The police chased after them, and a scuffle broke out between the officers and the suspects.

A thrilling scene unfolded: Another suspect in the taxi, seeing his accomplice caught, jumped out of the car and immediately took action. He held a handgun and pointed it at one of the police officers. Sensing the danger, a brave soldier from the armed police rushed towards the armed suspect, and with a loud bang, the suspect's gun fired. The bullet passed through the gap in the soldier's armpit, but undeterred, the soldier struggled with the suspect, pressing the weapon down to prevent him from shooting and harming innocent people. Several other backup police officers arrived, swiftly arrested all three suspects, handcuffed them, and put them in police cars.

Due to the presence of a "Social Truth" reporter who followed the police cars to the scene of the interception, the shocking footage not only incited public hatred towards the criminals but also filled people with great respect for the bravery of the police officers who disregarded their safety. When I saw this news, I remembered finding sedative pills and foreign currency in Xiaoshu's bag. It turned out that she had been involved in heinous activities with her accomplices all along. No wonder they always acted suspiciously and hid in the room for long periods. I assumed they were having intimate moments in the room, but they were plotting anesthesia robberies. They deserved the punishment! What surprised me even more was that they had a gun. I had lived with such criminals under the same roof for several months. In retrospect, I couldn't help but feel a bit scared!

Chapter 36

An Anesthesia Robbery

As the saying goes, "Domestic flowers are not as fragrant as wildflowers." Domesticated ones like turtles or crabs may not be as delicious as their wild counterparts. The ones raised in ponds can't compare to the taste of those from the wild. Take ginseng, for example. Cultivated ones may resemble ginseng in shape, but can they match the nutrition of wild ginseng? Men often seek excitement and adventure outside while neglecting their wives. However, their wives might be just as gentle and beautiful, but men's curiosity takes over. Though I have a complicated relationship with Mr. Fang, I am unclear about what he sees in me. He mentioned wanting me to have a daughter for him, but is it a joke or an earnest request? As long as he treats me well, I don't need to demand any specific outcome. "Having had something is better than having it forever." Isn't this the way it goes these days?

The profit in the bathhouse comes from baths, massages, and private rooms. The profit from baths relies on quantity - the more people, the more income. On the other hand, massages bring substantial earnings from the service fee and the use of essential oils. The prices of massages don't vary based on different techniques but rather on the grades of essential oils used. Some oils cost a few dozen yuan per bottle, while others can reach hundreds or thousands. Just like hair salons, where washing hair costs differently based on the quality of the shampoo used. Masseurs are paid by the hour, but essential oils yield huge profits, and it's an art to manage them. If a bottle of essential oil costs 20 yuan, it can be sold to customers for around 100 yuan. If it costs 100 yuan, customers will have to pay 1000 yuan. Such high-profit margins are not unique to our bathhouse; it's the same in the entire massage industry. This is still in the realm of legitimate massage, while those who engage in illicit activities use massage as a cover; their profits are incalculable. However, this is a legitimate profession, not something to be ashamed of. I earn my living with my skills.

Mr. Gao is an innovative person, and he created a unique type of essential oil that receives excellent customer feedback. Suzhou is famous for its green tea, Biluochun, which is as renowned as Longjing tea from West Lake. It's said that Biluochun tea was once a national gift presented by Premier Zhou to foreign dignitaries. Generally used for brewing tea, Mr. Gao started using it for massages. He ground the tea leaves into powder and soaked them in essential oil. When we massage our clients, we evenly apply the oil, and the room fills with the refreshing aroma of tea. The fragrance of this oil is much more pleasant than regular essential oils, and the delicate tea particles offer a delightful experience when massaged onto the skin, making it more supple and radiant. After using this oil for some time, our customers responded very positively. They loved this green, eco-friendly, and innovative essential oil massage.

That day, Mr. Gao called me into his office and showed me an article from a magazine. I was puzzled, "Why is he showing me a book? Isn't he deviating from his business?" The report was a travel journal written by a female tourist about her trip to Bali, particularly her enjoyable massage experience. She described a male masseur who provided meticulous and considerate service, making her feel completely relaxed and utterly enchanted. She even mentioned the professional skills and dedication of the male masseur, creating an immersive experience for her readers. The female tourist cherished this trip and especially her unforgettable massage experience.

Foreign countries are relatively open, and Chinese people may not readily accept this mixed-gender massage that combines essential oils internally and externally. Moreover, finding massage therapists with exceptional skills and professional qualities in China is extremely difficult. In short, it ingeniously combines oil massage and special services, but achieving the same effect in China is impossible. I put the magazine back on the table and asked, "After reading it, do you have any instructions, Mr. Gao?" Mr. Gao smiled and said, "Good, what are your thoughts?" I replied, "Such skilled massage therapists are hard to find, and I'm afraid our female compatriots may not have the courage to try this kind of massage." Mr. Gao chuckled, "Are you saying we can't imitate it? There's a lively response to this article online, and female customers hope to experience this service in China. Since the customers like it, why not cater to their preferences?" I said, "Suzhou is a bit conservative; promoting this widely is challenging. It's like sunbathing, which is no big deal abroad, but who would dare to try it here?"

Mr. Gao said, "Your analysis makes sense, but this is a business opportunity. It's better to try it sooner than later. However, we'll only offer the oil massage part for now and won't do deep-tissue massages. Xiao Jing, do you have confidence?" I replied, "Isn't it just oil massage?

It's not difficult. But is it appropriate to offer it in the bathhouse? Wouldn't it damage your cultured image?" Mr. Gao smiled and said, "It's not difficult for those who can, and those who find it challenging can't. Xiao Jing, you have quite a bit of talent." I said, "Mr. Gao, will you really sink to that level? Oil massage is a step away from erotic massage. Aren't you afraid?" Mr. Gao laughed, "I know the limits. Men and women won't do anything explicit; it's not illegal or criminal to have professional surface contact." Can regulations and rules control such things? People always want more; once we offer oil massage, who knows what might happen. You should know that not all men are gentlemen, and not all women are ladies.

Mr. Gao is a businessman; he knows that in the massage industry, money is easy to make for both men and women. People's living conditions have improved, and they don't mind spending money on beauty and health. He knows that it might be challenging to adopt the practices from Bali in China fully. Besides, it might be hard for the public to accept it openly. If it draws attention from the media and causes a big stir, the bathhouse could be shut down. Mr. Gao printed some exquisite promotional materials and asked us to distribute them to customers first to see their feedback. He also wanted me to train a few staff members who could recommend the essential oil massage to customers on a small scale. While many beauty salons and hair-washing places have secretly offered similar massages, their businesses often need more hygiene and security, and the staff's quality could be better, which makes customers curious but hesitant to try. Since the bathhouse introduced this service, customers were ecstatic.

Experience is accumulated through continuous learning. In my work, I have gained many new insights. Regarding massages, I only knew the surface information. Still, the masseur Ayin has studied authentic

Chinese medicine massage and can recite hundreds of acupuncture points on the human body by heart. She can pinpoint them with her eyes closed. Ayin brought a human body chart and explained in detail the knowledge related to acupuncture points, enlightening me and allowing me to grasp the essentials of Chinese medicine massage. While Ayin is knowledgeable about theory and skilled in massage, she needs more communication with clients. The atmosphere during her massages can feel slightly stifled, making customers less satisfied. On the other hand, I can massage and chat simultaneously, creating a relaxed atmosphere where customers enjoy the friendly exchange. As a result, I have earned a good reputation among customers and gained a prominent position within the staff.

Xiaoshu had taken over my rental room, and I was furious. However, I didn't want to become enemies or openly confront her. Although she came to East Bathhouse before me, she had a lower status. I had the authority to manage her but didn't seek personal revenge, so I didn't make things difficult for her. She was not my friend nor my enemy, and I didn't want to have too much involvement with her. We each minded our business, and nothing was worth further interaction. Even if we crossed paths, I just smiled and passed by. I decided to let her stay in the rented place in Meihua New Village; after all, she would have to pay the rent herself. As for me and Wu Fang, we moved to a residential area, which was more convenient and safe. The community had security guards and electronic doors on the stairs, and our room had a theft-proof door, making it difficult for thieves to break in.

In the spring of 2005, one day in mid-April, we were busy as usual when suddenly, a few police officers walked in. We were somewhat panicked, thinking they were there for a surprise inspection, but they directly took Xiaoshu away while she was massaging a client. The sisters were all puzzled, and I suspected she had been caught engaging in prostitution. It was not until the end of the shift, when Mr. Gao arrived at the bathhouse that we went to ask what had happened. Mr. Gao said, "She committed a crime, a serious one. I'm not clear on the specifics." Later that night, while watching the news, I learned the whole story of Xiaoshu's arrest from a program called "Social Realities."

As it turned out, the night before, Xiaoshu approached a Taiwanese businessman and, after accompanying him back to his hotel room, she tricked him into drinking a beverage laced with sleeping pills. When the Taiwanese man fell into an exhausted state, Xiaoshu and a few of her accomplices looted everything he had, including a laptop, passport, thousands of dollars in cash, several bank passbooks containing a considerable amount of money, and some important documents. During their theft, the Taiwanese man might not have drunk much of the drugged beverage, so he didn't fall into a deep sleep. When they were rummaging through his belongings, he woke up. The Taiwanese man wanted to ask questions, but one of Xiaoshu's accomplices knocked him unconscious with a blow, causing a head injury that bled profusely. After the robbery, Xiaoshu returned to her residence as if nothing had happened. Meanwhile, her three accomplices took part in the stolen items and hailed a taxi to escape towards Shanghai.

The hotel's security noticed suspicious individuals entering and leaving the Taiwanese man's room on the surveillance footage. They immediately checked the room and found the Taiwanese man lying on the floor, the space in disarray. Realizing that he had fallen victim to an anesthesia robbery, they quickly called the police. The 110 police acted promptly; luckily, not much time had passed since the incident. The armed police were stationed at the Jinjihu toll station on Suhu Airport

Road. Nighttime taxis leaving the city must register, so when the taxi carrying the suspects approached, the police routinely stopped the vehicle for inspection. They found three individuals inside looking anxious and suspicious, so several officers quickly surrounded the taxi. Seeing the situation deteriorating, two suspects opened the car doors and tried to escape. The police chased them and got into a scuffle with the criminals.

A heart-stopping scene unfolded: Another suspect in the taxi saw his accomplice being caught and, fearing capture, jumped out of the car and pointed a gun at one of the police officers. The situation was critical, but a nearby armed police officer rushed towards the suspect with the raised gun, trying to wrestle it away from him. A gunshot rang out, and the bullet narrowly missed the officer's armpit. Fearless, the armed police officer continued fighting with the suspect, pressing the gun toward the ground to prevent him from harming innocent people. Several other police officers came to reinforce them, and they successfully arrested all three suspects, handcuffing them and loading them into police cars.

Due to this incident, a "Social Realities" reporter followed the police car and recorded the scene when the arrest happened. The thrilling footage ignited the public's hatred towards the criminals and filled them with deep respect for the police officers' selfless bravery. When I saw this report, I remembered finding tranquilizer pills and foreign currency in Xiaoshu's bag. It turned out that she had been involved in these heinous activities for a while. No wonder they looked sneaky every time they returned to the rented place, staying in the room for extended periods. I initially thought they were engaging in intimate activities, but they were planning these anesthesia robberies. They deserved their fate! It was even more surprising that they had guns; I had unknowingly lived with such criminals under the same roof for several months. Looking back, I felt a bit scared!

Chapter 37

The Desire of Boss Gao

There might be a misunderstanding about my intention to write this diary. Some may think it's for fame, self-glorification, or shamelessly exposing privacy. In reality, I didn't know that far. My purpose was simple - to share my experiences and make people understand certain truths. I will eventually leave this environment, and I hope other sisters will wake up soon, and those girls who are still observing should stay away from this circle as much as possible. Furthermore, I want to let unaware friends know that massage and massage therapists are not dirty; it's a legitimate and healthy industry. The misconceptions arise because of the industry's mixed good and bad elements, making it difficult for us to defend ourselves.

The temptation of materialism is something everyone has to face. Who wants a challenging job and more income? For this, some people walk down the wrong path, tread sinfully, and hesitate. This includes Sister Wu, Xiao Shu, me, and many other sisters from different places. We need experience, and with wise friends to guide us, it's easy to lose ourselves. How can we uphold morality in an unfamiliar place, without family supervision, and in a situation where we can't survive without money? You may criticize or mock us, but who can truly understand the pain and tears in our hearts?

The new massage project at the bathhouse has gradually gained popularity after a promotion period. Some sisters hadn't encountered oil massage before, and I taught them a bit. Only Wu Fang and I were experienced and busy every day. Although Mr. Gao took a bold step, the explicit special services were outside our business scope. Internal body massage and ovarian care services for women have not been introduced yet. However, Mr. Gao is now recruiting male massage therapists and plans to launch these services soon to make a name in Suzhou. Mr. Gao received a tip that a large group of women from Suzhou went to Bali to experience that kind of romantic massage. He saw a potential business opportunity as many women are wealthy and enjoy the finer things. Attracting them here could be a gold mine.

Wu Fang has been going out less recently, behaving better, but she doesn't seem very happy. One day at home, she secretly told me something was wrong with her lower body. She was feeling dizzy with a loss of appetite. After what happened to Ah Lan, I got scared and immediately asked Wu Fang to go to the hospital for a check-up. I asked, "It's not a sexually transmitted disease, right?" Wu Fang replied nervously, "I don't know. I found a few hard lumps some time ago, but they were left alone. Now, things don't seem right. My hair is falling out a lot. What's happening to me?" I said, "It's likely a sexually transmitted disease. You must be careful and learn to protect yourself when going out with clients."

Wu Fang and I went to the gynecological examination together. The female doctor, around forty, changed her expression upon learning of Wu Fang's condition. She scolded, "You're so young, how could you be so careless? This could ruin your life!" Wu Fang was too scared to speak, fearing it might be an incurable disease. The doctor examined her private parts and asked her to do a blood test, but the results wouldn't be available until the following day. The doctor said in the gynecological department, "We need to confirm the test results tomorrow. For now, I'll give you some medicine - injections and a bottle of antiseptic solution for washing your lower body twice daily. Although syphilis is usually transmitted through sexual contact and blood, if the skin rash on your body becomes inflamed and ruptures and the toilet is not thoroughly disinfected, others may still get infected. You can't be careless, but don't be too nervous either. Take the medicine and injections regularly, and visit the hospital for check-ups. There's hope for recovery." The doctor also asked, "Where do you work?" I said, "At the Oriental Bathhouse." The doctor paused and said, "No wonder!" Wu Fang said, "I'm afraid of injections. Can I skip the injections and take the medicine?" The doctor replied, "Even if you're scared, you still need the injections. If you're afraid of pain, don't do such things!"

I checked the medicine box with the prescribed medication and saw labels like "Curing Bacteria" and "Syphilis Clear." I said, "Fang Fang, you don't have syphilis, do you? It's a serious sexually transmitted disease. I remember watching a documentary about preventing and treating STDs in school, and there were many terrifying scenes, like people losing all their hair, their lower bodies looking like cauliflower, and the whole body covered in rashes. It's said that syphilis can remain in the blood and be transmitted to the fetus during pregnancy..." Wu Fang turned pale in fright, "Ah? Is it that scary? Am I doomed?" I comforted her, "It's treatable now; don't worry. You've had a lesson. Just be careful in the future."

The next day, we collected the test results, which showed "positive." The female doctor took the form and glanced at it, saying, "Yes, it's syphilis! When you return home, thoroughly disinfect anything you've used or worn. It's best to buy two new sets of bedsheets and clothes for washing and use boiling water to clean them. Although syphilis is generally transmitted through sexual contact and blood, if the rashes on your body become inflamed and rupture, and others come into contact with them, they could also get infected. Don't let your guard down, but don't be overly anxious. Take the medicine and injections regularly, and visit the hospital for check-ups. There's hope for a cure." The doctor also asked, "It's rare to see syphilis patients today. How did you get infected?" Wu Fang hesitated before saying, "There was one time a man was scratching there a lot. I suspected he had a disease, but still did it with him. Maybe that's when I got infected, that disgusting man!" When women get examined at the gynecologist's, they speak straightforwardly and confidently, and the doctors are used to it. The female doctor said, "So young, why do such things? How unnecessary!"

Listening to the doctor's advice, Wu Fang diligently cleaned herself in the morning and evening. She endured the pain and got the injections. She still went to work but kept the medication with her, taking it after meals. Her sisters joked, "Fang Fang, what's wrong with you? You're not taking contraceptives, are you?" Wu Fang replied, "Of course not. I've been feeling unwell recently, so you should keep your distance in case you get infected." Some sharp-eyed sisters noticed Wu Fang's thinning hair and eyebrows and asked what happened. Wu Fang explained, "I plucked my eyebrows, but without a mirror, I accidentally plucked too many hairs. As for my hair, what's the big deal? Some actresses even shave their heads. I deliberately cut my hair short to make it easier to comb!"

In order to allow Wu Fang to recover peacefully, I requested sick leave from Mr. Gao on her behalf, stating that she wasn't feeling well, and the doctor advised rest. I didn't tell anyone about Wu Fang's STD. Once the other sisters at the bathhouse found out, it could lead to panic. Many people are still unaware of sexually transmitted diseases, and some think you can get infected by just talking face to face. Also, if Wu Fang's condition was known, she might be ridiculed, and that's not good when being sick is one thing, but losing face and confidence in life is another. I brought her to Suzhou and acted as her elder sister since her sister wasn't there. But I didn't take good care of her, and I feel a bit guilty. If she can't be cured of her illness, how can I explain it to her family? They might blame me for leading her astray.

Wu Fang's condition was under control, and her symptoms gradually disappeared. The doctor said, "Syphilis has a relatively long incubation period, similar to the hepatitis B virus. It may seem cured on the surface, but the bacteria remain in the body, and the blood test will still show positive. It usually doesn't have much impact on daily life, but it could relapse when your body is weakened." Worriedly, Wu Fang asked, "Can it be cured completely? Are there any aftereffects?" The doctor replied, "If there's no relapse within two years, it's almost cured. People with syphilis will develop antibodies, and some with less severe or early-stage symptoms can gradually improve without treatment. However, suppose you plan to have children after marriage. In that case, you must undergo strict medical examinations because the virus lurking in your body may be passed on to the fetus, leading to deformities or congenital syphilis carriers. So, you must keep yourselves clean and avoid causing a lifetime of regret for a moment of pleasure!" The doctor's earnest words made Wu Fang feel ashamed and greatly enlightened her.

Wu Fang's painful experience with syphilis taught me to be more cautious in my relationships with men. I am now only with Mr. Fang and have no interactions with other men. I will be fine if Mr. Fang is safe and healthy. Whenever we meet every week, I insist on taking protective measures. I still don't understand why men and women need to be together or what I want from Mr. Fang. His care for me goes beyond his family, and it's something hidden from the world. He won't divorce, and I don't plan to marry him. We are destined to be in a secret relationship. I can't even clearly explain what I like about him. There seems to be no reason; we are just together.

The business at the bathhouse is thriving, and I have gained more appreciation. My steps are lighter, and my smile is more charming. With skillful massages and enthusiastic service, I motivated the sisters to improve the quality of their massages and work ethic. Of course, the happiest person is Mr. Gao. Wu Fang was on leave, so I went home alone after work. Sometimes, Mr. Gao would drive me home, claiming it was on his way, but I knew his home was in the opposite direction. But since he was willing to do so, I gladly accepted. I'm helping him make money and am his capable assistant, so I feel safe sitting in his car. Does Mr. Gao know about me and Mr. Fang? He has never mentioned it, and I only occasionally see them chatting over tea.

That night, Mr. Gao claimed to be on his way again and offered to drive me home after work. In the car, he smiled and said, "Xiao Jing, if all the bathhouse attendants were as competent as you, I'd be set!" I chuckled, "You're still not making enough money? Aren't you content yet?" Mr. Gao replied, "Men are never content. Contentment is a luxury only suitable for you girls. Once you marry a good husband, you'll feel happy. Men are different; we need our careers to succeed to feel accomplished." I joked, "What's the point of success? You'll still eat, drink, sleep, and go to the restroom. Otherwise, you'll come for a massage." Mr. Gao laughed and said, "As you mentioned, I remember now. You are my employee, and you've massaged countless clients. I am your boss, so when will you massage me too?" I chuckled, "Of course, whether you're the boss or a client, I treat everyone equally!"

Chapter 38

Misunderstanding Ends Future

I skillfully applied my massage techniques, sometimes gently like a dragonfly skimming the water, sometimes firmly like rowing a boat against the waves, and occasionally with a soothing touch and a combination of different movements. Under my careful massage, Mr. Gao's originally fair skin took on a rosy glow. After finishing his back, he turned around, and his gaze showed admiration and affection. Mr. Gao, who was more than ten years older than me, exuded a mature charm evident to all. Although he was my boss, he also sometimes felt like an older brother. Right now, he is my client. Each man had his unique charm, and Mr. Gao had a composed maturity, while Mr. Fang possessed a refined elegance. The short-lived pleasure I had with Mr. Fang was full of anticipation and passion, but it was pure and clean with Mr. Gao. I enjoyed his gentle smile and friendly presence; he was a respectable and likable boss.

Lying on the massage bed, Mr. Gao only had a towel covering his abdomen, exposing almost everything. The massage room had central air conditioning running throughout the year, maintaining a comfortable constant temperature. I was dressed in the uniform designed by Mr. Gao, a short skirt and a bellyband that highlighted my graceful figure. I teased, "Mr. Gao, would you like a massage too?" He chuckled, "Why not? I want to see if your skills live up to the legend." I laughed, "It's just a rumor. I'm not a professional massage student. I don't have any real skills." Mr. Gao smiled and said, "Your skills are not to be underestimated. The massage you just gave me on my back had a strength and technique that surpasses that of ordinary masseuses. Your reputation is well-deserved!"

The reason why clients were usually satisfied with my massages was not because I was highly proficient in massage techniques. In reality, it was all about my intuition, honed through experience. By observing a client's body shape, touching their skin, and feeling their muscles and bones, I knew how to provide the best massage. Massages should also be tailored to each individual; some prefer a gentle touch, while others enjoy a more vigorous approach. It all depends on the experience accumulated over time. Whatever the task, attention to detail matters. If my mind was preoccupied or restless during a massage, my movements would be distracted, and the massage effect would suffer, affecting the client's mood as well.

Interestingly, those who sell meat don't usually like to eat meat, and those who raise fish don't particularly enjoy eating it. Although Mr. Gao owns this bathhouse, he doesn't get massages here. Even when socializing with friends, taking baths, or getting massages together, he prefers to visit other bathhouses. This might be to maintain a certain distance or aura of mystery between him and the staff. If he were to accept massages from his employees, his authority might diminish, and the team might lose some respect for him.

Some service attendants might fear the boss, but I don't. What's there to worry about? Will he bully me? Will he eat me? I've massaged many wealthy people, including officials, Taiwanese businessmen, and private business owners. Some have assets worth tens of millions, yet they were all satisfied with my massages. This was a VIP room with complete facilities, suitable for work or rest, and Mr. Gao seemed relaxed. I massaged him from head to toe to warm his skin and mind. I lifted the towel covering him, fully exposing him to my view. Masseurs are similar to obstetricians and gynecologists; their sensitivity decreases as they have frequent contact with the human body. Moreover, our profession doesn't allow us to have fluctuating emotions; otherwise, how could we provide attentive massages? If I were to be anxious before the client, I might make a fool of myself before they even made a move.

In Suzhou, there are alternative names for oil massage. If it's done with hands, it's called "hand service." If it's done with the mouth, it's called "oral service." If it's done skillfully in one go, it's called "excellent service," if massage and special services are combined, it's called "full service." Under my hands, Mr. Gao had a reaction, and it couldn't withstand my rubbing and gradually grew warmer. I was more than just massaging that area but also paying attention to the surrounding sensitive areas. A man's private part is as powerful, sensitive, and fragile as his soul. Under my siege, Mr. Gao eventually surrendered after about fifteen minutes of pursuit and blockage. He grasped my hand and didn't let go for a long time.

Mr. Gao said, "When you massaged me, I felt like I was in a garden full of exotic flowers and plants, with fragrant melons and fruits and a stream flowing. I could smell the flowers, and I even saw the kind of waterwheel I used to play with in that hazy atmosphere as a child. The imagination you brought me is simply beautiful!" Mr. Gao's praise made me feel a little embarrassed. I said, "That's your rich imagination, not the result of my massage. I am just a masseuse; how could I possess such magic to make you see a garden?" After dressing, Mr. Gao's face had a rosy tint, like a young girl's. I chuckled, discovering that even a boss could be shy.

Since then, he started giving me more generous red envelopes, and sometimes I would do a little extra for him, working overtime to give him a massage. It was a win-win situation for both of us. This was our private matter, and although other sisters saw me massaging the boss, they knew that Mr. Gao highly valued me, and their jealousy was useless. I must clarify that until now, I have remained pure with Mr. Gao. He hasn't taken advantage of me, and I haven't thrown myself at him. He has a wife, a teacher from a high school, who has visited the bathhouse a few times. I've seen her, and she is an elegant woman. I also have a man in my life, although Mr. Fang is my comfort, not my destiny. But I am content with that.

One day, tidying up the massage bed, I found a shiny ring. I picked it up and realized it was a beautiful platinum ring with a dazzling diamond. I tried it on my middle finger, and it fit perfectly! I knew diamond rings were precious, even more so than gold rings. TV commercials said, "Diamonds are forever a symbol of eternal love!" I couldn't help but like it, and a thought crossed my mind—to keep it for myself. After all, which girl wouldn't like a diamond ring? Besides, it was such a small thing; I could pretend I hadn't seen it even if someone asked about it. If I took it out of the bathhouse, no one would notice. But then I thought, this diamond ring might be someone's cherished possession. Keeping it would be stealing their love. How could I bear to do that?

Carefully holding the ring, I entered Mr. Gao's office. Before I could explain my purpose, he received a phone call and hurriedly left. I followed him outside. The receptionist reported to Mr. Gao, "This gentleman just had a massage here and said he lost a three-carat diamond ring. Did any of the staff find it? Should we call everyone and ask?" I saw a young man, not yet thirty, tall and anxious. He was the Taiwanese guest I had served just minutes ago. He introduced himself as Mr. Wang, a section chief at a Taiwanese company, earning a monthly salary of 200,000 yuan. I jokingly said, "Mr. Wang, your one-month salary is equivalent to ten years of mine!"

Mr. Wang said, "Could you please help me find it? I wore the ring when I arrived, but it was missing when I returned to the company. I thoroughly searched my car, but couldn't find it. It's possible I lost it while bathing and getting a massage. Please try your best to find it. It's my engagement ring, and inside the ring are three letters representing the first letter of my name. It's worth over a hundred thousand yuan and holds my fiancee's deep affection for me!" I was taken aback that such a small ring could be worth over a hundred thousand yuan, more expensive than the watch that caused me to leave Nanxun! Modern young men could indeed have such deep affection for their wives! Mr. Gao said, "Please don't worry; we will help you find it. Rest assured that if it's lost here, I guarantee we will find it." As Mr. Gao was about to call the staff, I stepped forward and said, "Mr. Gao, Mr. Wang, there's no need to search. I found the ring." Mr. Gao looked at me in astonishment, and Mr. Wang was overjoyed, "Really? Where is it?" I opened my hand, and the ring lay in my palm, sparkling brightly.

Mr. Wang took the ring and said excitedly, "Thank you! Thank you so much!" When he saw it was me, he was pleasantly surprised, "It's you! Your massage earlier impressed me, and I never expected your character to be more noble than this diamond!" Mr. Wang thanked me and even praised Mr. Gao, "Mr. Gao, your staff has such excellent character; it's truly admirable! Thank you so much!" Mr. Wang took out a stack of money from his pants pocket and said, "This is a token of my appreciation. Please accept it, Miss Number 2!" My service number was 2, and occasional customers like Mr. Wang were unfamiliar with my name but remembered my service number. I quickly declined, saying, "There's no need; it's my duty. This ring belongs to you, and returning it is only natural!"

I noticed that the money Mr. Wang offered was in U.S. dollars, with ten bills of 100 each. I had received tips from customers in U.S. dollars before and recognized them. However, I didn't accept his money, even though that 1000 would be equivalent to three months of my salary. Reputation is essential; it is an intangible and precious asset that accompanies us throughout our lives, more important than money. I have forgiven Ge Weiming's mother. Her rejection of me was likely to protect her family's reputation. Although she hurt me at the time, I understand that if I were in her position, I might also prevent my son from marrying a female massage therapist due to societal pressure, something one person can't change.

Mr. Wang would visit for massages every weekend and bring his friends along. Even when I wasn't serving him, he would politely greet me and recommend me to his friends, praising my massage skills and character, which made me feel a bit embarrassed. As Taiwanese, Mr. Wang and his group may have been familiar with the massage industry from an early age, and they showed great respect for us massage therapists. I have read in newspapers that Taiwan has "betel nut beauties," similar to some roadside solicitors in China. However, besides oil massages and some minor connections to sensuality in our bathhouse, there were no blatant indecent services. Most of our customers had specific standards and didn't make vulgar demands. We were content with our job; the overall treatment was good, and we had adapted to it.

Mr. Gao highly appreciated me and encouraged all employees to learn from me. He even considered contacting the media to report the incident and have them interview me, promoting my honesty. However, I didn't like being in the spotlight; it made me uncomfortable as if standing in a hurricane. I told him, "Mr. Gao, please don't praise me too much. The more you praise, the harder I'll fall. I don't want to end up unable to get back on my feet someday. I want to live a simple life, so let's keep it simple, and I'll be grateful to you." Mr. Gao looked at me and said, "Xiaojing, I've come to realize that having you work here isn't just beneficial for you; it's beneficial for me too. You are a great help, and you've elevated my business. I really should thank you!" I smiled and said, "What's there to thank me for? I work for you, and you pay me a salary. Isn't that enough?"

Mr. Gao smiled and said, "Xiaojing, your birthday is coming up soon, right? I want to give you a birthday gift." I happily asked, "Really? What do you want to give me?" He said, "A quick massage training class starts at Yangzhou Vocational School. You'll receive a graduation and qualification certificate if you pass the exam. It will help you learn massage systematically. I've enrolled you, and classes begin on June 1st. How do you feel about this gift?" This was an unexpected gift. Could I not be excited? Although I was enjoying a comfortable life, I had always worried that my massage skills were not up to par and did not qualify me as an actual masseuse. Now that Recharging had become famous, I was considering where to study, and Mr. Gao had thought of a place and helped me realize my plan.

If he weren't my boss but an ordinary man, I would have embraced him and given him a passionate kiss at this moment! Joy is meant to be shared with someone. I smiled and said, "Mr. Gao, why are you so good to me? I can't afford it!" Mr. Gao laughed and said, "It's also an investment. If you return with more knowledge, won't you earn more for me? Although you'll be away for three months, my bathhouse can't do without you, but while you're still young, it's better to learn more; it will benefit you." I sincerely said, "Thank you! I'm not ungrateful; I'll repay you for your kindness!" My repayment meant working harder for him, not anything else.

However, just as I was full of confidence, an unforeseen event, like an invisible net, quietly closed in on me. Wu Fang's illness mainly had improved, and she was still resting at home, following her medication and treatment regimen. I told her about my plan to study, and she was happy for me, asking me to learn well and teach her so she could earn more money. One day in late May, I was packed and ready to go to Yangzhou Vocational School. I stood in the lobby, waiting, as Mr. Gao had promised to take me there, but he suddenly received a phone call and hurriedly left. My colleagues knew I was pursuing further studies and looked at me with envy. I felt like a child about to study abroad, full of beautiful expectations.

At almost ten o'clock, Mr. Gao returned. I happily greeted him, but to my surprise, his wife, Sunjie, stood beside him, her face dark, staring at me. I whispered, "Hello, Aunt Sun!" Seeing the rare sight of the boss's wife, the staff greeted her individually. Sunjie glared at me coldly and said, "So it's you that he keeps talking about. It turns out you look quite good! Gao Xiaohu, you talk to her!" Mr. Gao looked at me guiltily and turned to his wife, saying, "Sunjie, don't make a scene. Her attending the training is beneficial for me too. Why are you stopping her?" Sunjie snorted and said, "Yes, beneficial for you. You stand by her side all the time. Have you stopped caring about me? Do you think I can't see you being extra nice to her? Do you know how many men there might be behind her? How can you be so unthinkingly devoted to her? Do you think she'll come back to work here after graduating from the training? Your heart is too kind!" Mr. Gao said, "Sunjie, can you hold your tongue for a moment? All the employees are watching. It would be best if you didn't say such things in public. Come on, let's go; I still have something to do." Sunjie turned to me and said, "We have discussed this. I won't allow anyone to threaten our family. Now, I declare that, Xiaojing, you are disqualified from participating in the training! And from now on, you are expelled from Eastern Bathhouse! The bathhouse will pay you an additional three months' salary per the rules. Now, Xiaojing, settle your accounts and leave!"

Chapter 39

The Conspiracy of Lover

Fate is not something we can control; external factors can influence it anytime. I was joyful, looking forward to attending a formal massage training class to obtain a qualification certificate that would lay the foundation for my future. However, Sunjie's appearance poured cold water on my dreams and threw them into the cold palace! I never expected Sunjie, a cultured woman, still hold strong biases against massage therapists. It was easy to imagine how society viewed us! People generally see us as outcasts, but this perception is biased! We earn our living with our skills, and while a few may engage in illicit activities, we cannot be judged based on a few bad examples. Even those so-called virtuous wives and mothers might have extramarital affairs, so why do they receive forgiveness while we can't defend ourselves?

I've never been married; men are the heads of the household, and women are supportive wives. But now, I felt that Mr. Gao despite being the boss at the bathhouse, might still be under his wife's control at home.

I could understand if Sunjie didn't want me to attend the training, but to fire me on the spot was too much. Am I that easy to bully? To be called upon at will and discarded just as easily? Do they treat me like a call girl? Despite being a teacher, Sunjie was so rude. I have always respected teachers, but if she fabricated lies and slandered me, I wouldn't be afraid of her! My anger surged, and I didn't care about her status as the boss's wife; if she provoked me, I would have it out with her.

As I was about to argue, Mr. Gao called out, "Xiaosun, what are you doing? Please stop causing a scene. I'm in charge of everything here. You should go back to teaching at school!" Sunjie's face turned red with anger, and said, "Fine! Do you still defend her? If you have nothing to do with her, why keep her here? Let her go; are you afraid you won't survive without her?" Fuming, I said, "Sunjie, how can you speak like this? Anyone can live without anyone else! I'm here to work, not to listen to your complaints!" Sunjie, not backing down, said, "You came to work? Then why do you have your luggage with you? Isn't that a sign that you want to leave? I don't think I know anything. Do you think the bathhouse can't survive without you? We can run it even better without you!"

Why was she attributing the newly launched massage project at the bathhouse to me? Mr. Gao said, "Xiaosun, you misunderstood. I'm the one who thought of promoting the new project. Xiaojing is just helping me with work. Please go back to your classes. Do you want your colleagues to laugh at you for causing a scene here?" Sunjie persisted, "Listen to how affectionate you are when you call her Xiaojing! I want you to decide now. Do you want to fire her or not?" Mr. Gao replied, "She's such a talented person and has attracted many customers to the bathhouse. Why would I want to fire her? You're better at teaching, but you're not familiar with the business. Don't meddle in the affairs here!"

Sunjie said, "Fine, I won't meddle, but only if you don't let her come between us!" Mr. Gao said, "Why can't you be more open-minded? Everything is just your suspicious mind, and there's no real issue!" Sunjie retorted, "Are you feeling guilty? If there's nothing between you, why can't people discuss it? If there's nothing between you, why insist on keeping her? I can tell you have something to hide!"

Listening to their heated argument, I found it all very dull. Sunjie came at me with the suspicion that I had something going on with Mr. Gao, assuming that ulterior motives drove my presence at his side. In reality, she was overthinking things. I am not interested in every man, and Mr. Gao's kindness to me was only something I felt grateful for. There was no romantic involvement; we were just closer than a usual boss-employee relationship, which I had no guilt about. My heart remained calm even when I did the oil massage for him. I never expected that our innocence would be misunderstood! Must all relationships between men and women be romantic or ambiguous? In the local Suzhou dialect, Mr. Gao and I were just "green onions mixed with tofu, clear and straightforward"!

I thought about leaving in anger, but I would be misunderstood even more if I did. Mr. Gao said, "Xiaosun, can you calm down? Don't cause trouble for no reason!" Sunjie said, "Women are all selfish. I don't want anyone else to interfere with our marriage! I didn't come here to quarrel with you; I want to hear your decision!" Mr. Gao asked, "What decision?" Angered, Sunjie said, "At this time, you're acting like you can't hear me. You're capable of doing that! Do you cherish this little lover of yours? Do you want to run away with her? Let me tell you, she's already fired, and I want her to leave immediately!" Mr. Gao said, "Xiaosun, why don't you understand? She's popular at the bathhouse. If we fire her, it will affect our business!" Sunjie said, "Gao Xiaohu, do you care for her? Or do you care for me? Today, you have to make it clear!"

As they argued relentlessly, I became an unwitting "participant." It wasn't appropriate for me to intervene, and the staff stood still, unsure of what to do. It was not yet noon, and there weren't many customers. Seeing the boss and his wife quarreling, some of them shook their heads with a smile and left. This was a private matter that could have been discussed calmly. I didn't understand why Sunjie had to make it public. What good would it do for her? Did she want to gain public sympathy while making everyone condemn me? It wasn't cute, and I couldn't help but feel sorry for her and all women! Why can't women live without men? They become terrified once they realize that the man they depend on is unreliable.

I should make a concession for Sunjie's unfortunate family or her love and marriage! Even if I leave Dongfang Bathhouse, I can find another job. Even with Mr. Gao, my income will be well-spent. I don't want Sunjie to think I'm Mr. Gao's lover. Even if I have a man in Suzhou, he is not Sunjie's husband! If I stay or if Mr. Gao insists on sending me to Yangzhou for training, it will only exacerbate their marital problems. What was once a minor issue would become a major one, and I didn't want to become an inexplicable scapegoat. I tried to break free from this trouble.

I said, "Stop arguing! If Sunjie wants me to leave, fine, I'll go! But I want to clarify that I'm leaving voluntarily, not because you're firing me! As you imagine, there is no inappropriate relationship between Mr. Gao and me. Okay, I won't waste any more words. Mr. Gao, Xiaojing is resigning!" I turned around and left. It wasn't about acting cool; I genuinely didn't want to stay and listen to their arguments. Suzhou people have pleasant speaking methods, but it's not pretty when they quarrel. I heard Mr. Gao say, "Xiaojing, don't go!" Sunjie said, "She's leaving. Gao Xiaohu, go after her!" Ah, why do women have big breasts but small minds? I heard Mr. Gao angrily say, "Xiaosun, don't stir up trouble!"

Sure enough, Mr. Gao caught up with me, grabbed my luggage, and said, "Xiaojing, don't leave yet. Don't listen to her; I'll take you to Yangzhou now!" Ah, Mr. Gao needed clarification. If he did that now, wouldn't it be pouring oil on the fire? If he sent me to Yangzhou today, it would only worsen their marital problems. What was once a non-issue would be seen as valid by Sunjie. I struggled free from his grip and said, "Mr. Gao, it's unnecessary. Even if I don't go for training, I won't starve. You should return to avoid Sunjie accusing me of stealing her husband!" Mr. Gao, in frustration, said with a smile, "Xiaojing, what are you joking about? If you give up the training, you must still stay and work!" I saw Sunjie coming after us with an unpleasant expression. I said, "Sunjie, don't worry, I won't have feelings for your husband. I'm leaving now, wishing you prosperity in your business and happiness in your family. Goodbye!" I hailed a taxi and left. I left; I couldn't be bothered by them.

Having been in Suzhou for over half a year, I had a good job, but because of Sunjie's jealousy, I had to leave Dongfang Bathhouse and join the ranks of the unemployed again. Mr. Gao tried to reach out to me a few times afterward, but I declined to meet him. I didn't want to get entangled in this unclear situation. If there were something between Mr. Gao and me, I would accept it, but there was nothing. Going back now would only fuel the rumors; even a fool would think we had something going on. I didn't care about Dongfang Bathhouse; its current business had nothing to do with me!

I didn't want to find a job immediately; after being busy for half a year, I wanted to take a break. However, I was annoyed outside and also annoyed at home. The neighbors upstairs were renovating, and the drilling noises made staying home during the day impossible. Wu Fang's condition had improved, and she still wore the wig she bought after losing hair. Her golden hair made her look sexier; from behind, some men might even think she was a foreign girl. I jokingly said, "Good thing it's not AIDS; otherwise, you would have lost your life. Are you scared now? Think you won't act recklessly anymore?" Wu Fang grinned and said, "I'm not afraid of death; everyone dies eventually. Life becomes exciting only when you live it to the fullest! I haven't had meat for a few months and can't stand it anymore!" This girl isn't afraid of dying! She was barely alive when she was infected with syphilis, and now she's getting restless.

I laughed and said, "Fangfang, tell me the truth. Can't you live without men? Or can't you live without money?" Wu Fang tilted her head and thought momentarily, "Hmm, I definitely can't do without money. I can't live on air or beg for food! Without men? In the short term, it's possible, but over time, it's not feasible!" I asked, "Why?" Wu Fang chuckled, "Why are you asking me? You're well-fed and don't know what it's like to be hungry! Don't you and that guy with the surname Fang have a close relationship?" I said, "Once you're completely recovered, we'll look for jobs together." Wu Fang said, "Okay, my money is almost gone, and I'll need your help. I'm not as skilled as you in finding jobs." I smiled, "We're sisters who ventured out into the world together. Do I even need to say that?"

Without a job, I became lazy, but my desires became more active. When I was working, I only ate a small bowl of food. Now that I wasn't working, I ate much more, like a lazy pig. When I was complete, I'd sleep, and I didn't want to sleep alone; I wanted a man to accompany me. At first, being with Mr. Fang had a certain charm; we chatted, went shopping, and it had a bit of romance. However, something changed recently; my desire surged, and I became greedy. I wanted to cling to him, spend more time with him, be tireless, and never get bored. Perhaps it was because I had nothing to do, feeling empty and bored, so I needed some excitement.

Something I overlooked led to Mr. Fang's conspiracy succeeding and made me see his ugly face clearly. It made me decisively break ties with him! When we were together, we always took preventive measures. Although he jokingly mentioned wanting a daughter, I didn't take it seriously. Now that I was seeing him more often, out of trust, I didn't check, and I never expected him to plant his seeds inside me intentionally! He even deluded himself into thinking that everything would take root and grow. He wanted to make rice and cook mature rice! I was completely unaware of his scheming actions until I found out I was pregnant...

Chapter 40

Rashly Pregnancy

Lately, I've been feeling bored and a bit crazy. As the temperature rises, my intimacy with Mr. Fang has increased daily. I almost treated him as my exclusive partner, clinging to him every time, not letting him leave. Fortunately, Mr. Fang's situation is different from Mr. Gao's. Mr. Gao is a traditional man who goes home to sleep every day. In contrast, Mr. Fang enjoys more freedom. His wife doesn't seem to care about his whereabouts. Later, I realized that every woman manages her husband differently. Some are keen on "keeping them in check," closely monitoring their movements, and not allowing them to wander outside. Others prefer "letting them roam" as long as they don't get divorced, letting them do as they please. Men are like children; they need to be managed, but there's a bAh Lance, tight enough and loose. Behind a good man, there's always an outstanding woman, his mother or wife.

I didn't visit Mr. Gao's bathhouse after I left, and during phone conversations with Aying, I learned that the business was doing fine. My departure attracted little attention since they had a foundation and a stable customer base. Some customers inquired about my situation, and the staff told them I had personal matters. Aying laughed and said, "Lately, the boss's wife comes to inspect frequently; she's keeping a close eye on Mr. Gao. Poor Mr. Gao, a bathhouse manager, but always looking distressed!" Perhaps jealousy is a common trait among women; even someone like Sunjie, a role model to others, shows an incredibly stingy side regarding family issues. This shows that rich people have various troubles, just like us.

Wu Fang and I went through thick and thin together. After I resigned from Dongfang Bathhouse, she didn't go either. Mr. Gao is good; he transferred 10,000 yuan to my account and 5,000 yuan to Wu Fang's account as compensation after our resignation. The intermediary fee between Mr. Gao and Sunjie was also settled. Now, Wu Fang and I were free agents again. Sunjie contacted me, saying she could help us find new jobs, but I declined. Approaching employers directly would be more convenient; having an intermediate step would mean less income and less freedom. The situation now was different from when I first arrived in Suzhou. Back then, I urgently needed a job, but now, we didn't lack money, so there was no need to rush.

I stopped sending money home now. It's not that I didn't want to, but my family refused to accept it. Ever since they found out I was working as a masseuse, my parents told me not to send money home. My family was not financially well-off, but they had great pride and considered my earnings tainted money. My dad said he would return it or burn it like waste paper even if I sent it. My mom cried, saying that she wouldn't recognize me as her daughter if I didn't return home immediately! I knew it was just her anger speaking; she was upset that I wasn't living up to expectations and brought shame to the family. Others might think my money was unclean, but it was hard-earned! After coming to Suzhou, I didn't make any extra money on the side; my relationship with Mr. Fang was mostly unpaid, just accepting some gifts from him. Since my family didn't want it, I saved it for now. There were 30,000 yuan in my bank account, which would come in handy if I married someone or started a business.

Xiao Hong called and said Sister Wu had returned to Nanxun, and she had broken up with that man. She said it was all their sisterly impulse; the eagle was pecked unthinkingly by the chicken, losing the woman and soldiers in one go! Xiao Hong asked what I was doing now. I said I was having fun, not working. Xiao Hong said, "Then come back; the Haitian Paradise where you used to work has several people coming here asking about you. They miss you." When I arrived in Suzhou, I changed my phone number, and my old friends couldn't contact me. I said, "I'm fine here, better than when I was in Nanxun. Xiao Hong, you, and Sister Wu could also come to Suzhou. Whether doing massages or working in nightclubs, there are many opportunities here. Sister Wu and Wu Fang should have reconciled by now, right? There's no need to let a worthless man ruin your sisterly bond." Xiao Hong said, "Being a hostess is easier than doing massages. I've done massages before, and it's tough work. As a hostess, I can earn 50 yuan for each 100-yuan session, and sometimes I can serve multiple clients in one shift. If there's a business trip, the income will be even higher. Sister Wu knows she's made a mistake and often regrets it. If we have time, we'll come to Suzhou to see you guys."

It's often said that actors and prostitutes have no feelings, but that's probably not entirely true. We are not actors or prostitutes, but our social status as masseuses is similar to theirs. In reality, we have strong emotions and loyalty among us sisters. If one of us has a headache or fever or gets robbed, we would be there to care for and help her through the difficulties. While we engage in erotic activities during work hours, we are no different from other girls once off the clock. Why do people always look at us through tinted glasses? To be blunt, your lover, girlfriend, or partner might have been a masseuse before. Or maybe she's secretly seeing someone else behind your back? You don't know. We are open about our jobs; they are discreet. That's the only difference.

Work feels tiring, but I also think weary after resting too long. Having nothing to do every day is like being a walking corpse. Seeing Wu Fang's health has improved, I told her, "Idleness for three years at sea will rust one's skills. Should we consider going back to work?" Wu Fang replied, "Sure, going back to work is fine. Even when staying home without illness, one can still become unwell. Being sick is painful, but it also made me gain weight. Look at my measurements; they are much larger than before, right?" I laughed and said, "Bigger is good. Don't all men like women to be curvy?" Wu Fang jokingly replied, "No, there's one type of man who doesn't like women to be big; they prefer them to be petite!" I chuckled, "Enough. You must be careful in the future. We're here to do massages, not to entertain men." Wu Fang protested, "If you want me to be a nun, that won't work!" I said, "You should moderate yourself; don't pick up bad habits. When Sister Wu comes to see us, she might blame me." Wu Fang said, "Is she coming? I don't want to see her yet!" I said, "Let it go; it's all in the past. Your sister regrets it too. Why hold grudges over someone who wasn't worth it? Sisterly love is what matters most!"

After massaging for a long time, just like any other job, we also develop occupational hazards, especially psychologically. Like people who spend a lot of time online and constantly think about the internet, we always think about massages. It's been a while since my fingers were busy, and I feel a bit itchy in my heart. I want to experience the pleasure of giving a massage again. We have grown accustomed to massage techniques and the satisfaction they bring to our clients. However, we are not used to the prolonged inactivity of our limbs. I once heard a client say that he became addicted to massages after coming for three months. If he doesn't get a massage for three days, he feels uncomfortable all over, especially with his skin; he feels inexplicably uncomfortable and finds the day uninteresting. At that time, I found it funny, but now I understand. It's not just the clients who get addicted; we, the massage providers, also get addicted.

Working as a masseuse is not something anyone can do like not everyone can do embroidery. As a masseuse, the first thing you need to overcome is psychological barriers. After practice and exploration, you'll naturally find your way into massaging. The skill level depends on one's insight and hands-on experience. I've only heard about traditional Chinese health massage; I have not received formal training. The few moves Aying taught me were bare, and I could only grasp the essence of massage with proper training. Frequent massages are like flowing water; they bring vitality to people's lives. Although Wu Fang's skill may be better than mine, it's still decent. Regarding income, traditional Chinese health massage practitioners may not earn more than us. Our erotic massages may be on the edge of breaking the rules, but they're not illegal. Nowadays, society is more open, and the market is relatively tolerant. More and more massage parlors are bringing us closer to the public.

I heard that there is a new Hai Tang Chun foot spa on Bei Huan Road. The grade of foot spa is slightly lower than that of bathhouses, but they may also offer various massage services. Wu Fang and I are planning to apply for jobs there. The advantage of a newly opened establishment is that all the employees start from the same starting line. It will take a little while for the skill level to show, and with our experience, we have a good chance of getting the attention of customers and the boss. If we were to join an established place, we might face exclusion since there are already experienced staff. Nowadays, every field is highly competitive, and there are plenty of ordinary masseuses. Still, the chances of standing out are much higher for experienced massage therapists like Wu Fang and me.

On that afternoon, the office of Hai Tang Chun foot spa was crowded with people coming for job interviews. The applicants were from all over the country. Some looked like sixteen or seventeen-year-olds, probably just fresh out of school, and some were very beautiful, with excellent figures and looks comparable to models on TV. The foot spa was hiring only fifteen female attendants for the first time, but over forty people came to apply, including Wu Fang and me, standing in line at the back. Those with a poor appearance were immediately eliminated on the spot. Fortunately, they prioritized applicants with work experience in massage. Those with no massage experience but good appearance and physique would receive simple training before officially starting their job.

I felt confident and even smiled at Wu Fang, but suddenly I felt nauseous and had a strong urge to vomit! I held it in, thinking I could get through the interview first. When the person ahead of me finished the interview, the manager of the foot spa left with her resume, and the girl went happily. I sat down to fill out the form, and Wu Fang followed closely behind. Just as I finished filling out the record, I couldn't bear it anymore. I felt a surge of acid rising from my stomach to my throat. I couldn't hold it back and "vomited" on the railing by the corridor! My stomach was churning, but what came out was just a puddle of yellowish liquid with a few grains of rice, mostly making me feel uncomfortable.

Wu Fang probably finished filling out the form, but she rushed out and supported me before her interview, saying, "Jing Jie, what's wrong? Why do you look a bit pale?" I said, "It's okay, help me to the restroom; I'll rinse my mouth." In the restroom in the corridor, I rinsed my mouth with tap water a few times, and although I still felt a bit unwell, I felt much better. Wu Fang said, "Could it be food poisoning? We only had egg-fried rice for lunch and ate nothing else." I said, "I don't know what happened. Food poisoning usually accompanies diarrhea, but I only feel discomfort and want to vomit." Wu Fang suggested, "How about skipping the interview today? Let me accompany you to the hospital." I said, "The recruitment ends tomorrow. The opportunity is rare; you should go inside, and I'll stay in the corridor to get some fresh air." Wu Fang said, "Jing Jie, let's go to the hospital for a check-up first. I'm afraid of getting sick; don't wait until it happens to you."

I followed Wu Fang's advice, and she didn't go in for the interview. We went downstairs and took a taxi to the nearby hospital. Wu Fang helped me register, and I went into the internal medicine outpatient department with her. The young female doctor, who was only a few years older than me, probably just graduated from medical school, asked me some questions and took my blood pressure and heart rate. She gave me two lab test forms and asked me to do a blood and urine test. I had accompanied Ah Lan to the hospital before, so I knew how cumbersome it could be to see a doctor. Nowadays, doctors rely on medical equipment for everything, even for a common cold, patients need to do various tests. Technology brings convenience, but it also makes doctors dependent. In the past, doctors could diagnose a patient's condition with just "look, smell, ask, and touch," but do doctors still do that now?

Since a small amount of blood was required, I got the lab test results in a few minutes. There was also a urine test form, but I couldn't understand the printed data. I handed the two papers to the female doctor, and after looking at them, she glanced at me and asked, "Are you married?" I said, "I don't have a boyfriend yet." She smiled and said, "I don't know if I should congratulate or remind you. You are pregnant!" What? Am I pregnant? I thought I heard it wrong. The female doctor said, "Yes, you're pregnant. You need to have an ultrasound to know more about the baby's condition. Would you like to do it now or later?" My mind was a bit chaotic, and the word "pregnant" confused me all at once! How could I be pregnant? Didn't we use protection every time? Aren't condoms safe? This is strange!

With the ultrasound form, I realized I had been pregnant for over two months. In other words, it happened shortly after I quit the Eastern Bathhouse and had intimate moments with Mr. Fang. Did he do it intentionally or unintentionally? I'm pregnant, and that's a fact I must face now! The child cannot be born. It's not that I lack humanity and want to terminate a budding life; it's just that this fetus is coming at the wrong time. Can I raise a child in my current situation? I haven't mentally prepared for this. I still feel like I haven't grown up and am an irresponsible girl. Can I be a mother now? And in what capacity would I raise the child? As someone's mistress? Or lover? This Mr. Fang, I trusted him so much and never asked anything from him, yet he took such liberty with me without even considering my situation. He's genuinely despicable!

Wu Fang said indignantly, "Jing Jie, do you understand now? No man is a good person! If you don't play them, they will play you! He got you pregnant without any intention of informing you about it, which shows he had bad intentions from the start! If it were me, I would trouble him until he can't live a peaceful life! Let's see how he handles it?" I said, "I will find out the truth. If it was unintentional, an accident, then I'll let it go. But I won't let him off easily if he did it on purpose!" Wu Fang said, "Exactly, that's how you deal with men. They are heartless, so don't blame us for being ruthless! Doesn't he have a wife? Go to his place and make trouble; make his life miserable! Doesn't he have money? Make him pay for it; don't spare him!"

When I was feeling agitated, my phone rang. It showed an unfamiliar number, so I pressed the answer button and said unkindly, "Who's this? Speak up if you have something to say; otherwise, don't waste my time!" There was a moment of silence, then a polite male voice said, "I'm sorry for disturbing you. May I ask if you are Xiao Jing?"

Chapter 41

A Date with a Bad Guy

Unexpected pregnancy caught me off guard. I decided to confront Mr. Fang. I'm only 21 and haven't officially found a partner yet. He secretly allowed me to get pregnant, and it's just too selfish and despicable! I prefer sincere and straightforward men, not those with petty and dishonest behaviors. He didn't seek my opinion, didn't get my consent, and dared to play the trick of using me as a "surrogate," treating my body as his "private territory." Hmph! I won't let you succeed. Let's see how this ends!

The call came from Haibian Spa. When the manager, Mr. Wang, confirmed I was the "Xiao Jing" from Dongfang Bath, he excitedly said, "Is it you? That's great! If you can come to Haibian Spa, it's exactly what we were hoping for! If it's convenient, could you come over for a face-to-face discussion about work and compensation?" They may have seen the application form I filled out and my name and resume, so they contacted me. I didn't expect that a small massage therapist like me would have some reputation in the eyes of these big bosses. My hard work was worthwhile, and my sweat was well-spent.

I decided to delay dealing with the pregnancy matter for a while. After leaving the hospital with Wu Fang, we went to Haibian Spa. As we entered the manager's office, I saw three men inside: one was tall and thin, one was the guy responsible for the recruitment, and there was another very fat man, all in their thirties. When the chubby man saw us, he came up to shake hands, smiling, and said, "Miss, it's a pleasure to meet you! My surname is Wang, and I'm truly sorry for not recognizing you during the interview, but as soon as we saw your information, we guessed it was you, so we immediately got in touch. We sincerely invite you to join Haibian Spa!" I smiled and said, "Don't be so polite. I'm just an outsider, and I'm grateful that you big brothers take notice of me. I'm here looking for a job, as long as I can have a bowl of rice to eat, I'm more than happy!" I've learned some social niceties after two years of experience in this line.

Mr. Wang pointed at the skinny guy and introduced him warmly, "This is our Haibian Spa's owner, Mr. Chen. Miss, please meet him!" I smiled briefly at the thin Mr. Chen and said, "Mr. Chen, please take care of me." I've encountered hundreds of bosses before, and they usually puff their chests and act important, but seeing Mr. Chen, who was as skinny as a bamboo pole, was quite rare. He seemed astute and capable. Mr. Chen said, "Miss, welcome to work at Haibian Spa! Listening to Mr. Xu, you left after filling out the application form. Did something happen? Do you need help?" It was our first meeting, and he was already expressing concern. It showed that he had a humane side. I replied, "It's nothing, just a private matter. This is my good friend Wu Fang, also a skilled masseuse. She wants to join Haibian Spa with me." Mr. Chen said, "That's great! We welcome Wu Miss as well." Wu Fang added, "Thank you, Mr. Chen! I'm coming with Xiao Jing, wherever she goes, I go too!" Mr. Wang laughed, "Alright, that's settled. You can officially start working tomorrow. Now, let's have dinner together!"

The fact that the owner invited us to dinner was a first, indicating that they value me and Wu Fang. I had good relations with previous bosses, like Sun from Nanxun and Mr. Tian and Mr. Gao in Suzhou, but there was always a hierarchy. At Dongfang Bath, I was closer to Mr. Gao, often visiting his office. Still, it was unusual for regular employees to interact with the boss, let alone have dinner together. Yet, before even starting work at Haibian Spa, I was already receiving much attention, which was somewhat surprising. Wu Fang and I also had some drinks, and everyone was laughing and having a good time.

Manager Xu explained, "Although we're called a foot bath place, we have multiple business segments—sauna, foot bath, massage—and we plan to offer accommodations on the fourth floor. Initially, gaining recognition and customers is quite crucial. We have to accumulate continuously and provide high-quality service to retain customers. Since we're newly opening, we can set the prices lower. The staff's image and qualities are also critical, and we've already selected the first batch of service staff, including you, Xiao Jing, and Wu Miss. There will be twenty of you in total. You can start training tomorrow, and we'll have a soft opening. One week from now, on August 18th, Haibian Spa will officially open." Mr. Chen added, "Good plan. Let's go with that. Also, Xiao Jing, if you could guide our newly recruited staff, it would be great. We want them to get into their roles as soon as possible." I said, "No problem. Since I'm joining Haibian Spa, it's like joining a family. All of us sisters are one family!" Mr. Chen said, "Xiao Jing, I appreciate your dedication and teamwork spirit! It's truly commendable for someone as young as you!" I replied, "I don't know about dedication and spirit; you should work hard. It's good for everyone."

Mr. Wang said, "We've prepared two salary structures: one is a monthly salary, and the other is an hourly wage. Those with work experience will be on a monthly salary, and we'll agree on the monthly amount. We'll use an hourly wage for newbies, with a 10 yuan bonus per hour. About tips, we'll split them fifty-fifty as usual. Xiao Jing, do you have any requests or suggestions?" I said, "No objections, it sounds good." Mr. Wang asked, "Do you mind sharing your previous salary? We promise not to offer anything lower." I smiled and said, "I was making 4,000 yuan, and Fang Fang was making 3,000 yuan. While more money is always good, we're not just here for the money. We must also consider the work environment, intensity, and days off." Mr. Chen said, "Although this is our first meeting, I believe in your abilities. We'll offer you 4,500 yuan per month and 3,500 yuan to Wu Miss. You'll have Sundays off, and we'll pay extra for overtime. How does that sound? If you have any requirements, please feel free to share; we'll seriously consider them." Wu Fang and I exchanged a knowing smile and said, "That's great. We're delighted."

The next day, we started work. Five 18 other service staff had previous massage experience, while the remaining thirteen were new. Haibian Spa hired a specialized teacher for basic knowledge training, and I provided some guidance during their practical training. Even though the official opening hadn't happened yet, most attendees were friends of the three bosses. I also made a bit of a splash—there's a saying, "An expert will know in an instant." I only did a simple back massage, and the new service staff were watching. Mr. Wang and Manager Xu were there as well, observing. I seized the opportunity to show off a bit. Wu Fang also did well and earned everyone's applause.

Don't be fooled by our casual demeanor. When massaging clients, one moment, it flows like a stream. The next moment it's as focused as a monk's strike of the gong. We might seem confident, but massages also require physical effort. After massaging seven or eight clients, I felt sweat on my body. I also provided a few foot massages that day, using techniques like kneading, pushing, pulling, tapping, rubbing, and scraping. Everyone who experienced my massage praised it, saying it was comfortable. Massage requires skillful hands. Watching from the side isn't enough; you must practice hands-on. The new service staff were practicing clumsily at first. They were curious about the massage work but also a bit apprehensive. I was once in their shoes, feeling the same. Over two years, I had transitioned from a newbie to an experienced therapist and from innocence to maturity.

If you're taking someone's money, you have to work for them. My salary was the highest at Haibian Spa, and naturally, my labor wasn't easy. This Haibian Spa foot bath was a partnership among the three bosses. They collectively invested over three million yuan, with Mr. Chen contributing the most at 70%, Mr. Wang at 20%, and Mr. Xu, the manager, at 10%. Businesspeople invest in making money and implementing bold strategies to recoup their investment quickly. It was deceptive while they were officially a foot bath place; apart from the sauna, foot bath, and massage, they planned to offer hotel services. According to Manager Xu, for approval convenience, the fourth floor was presented as a relaxation area associated with the foot bath, but it was actually operated as an accommodation service. This aimed to achieve a one-stop entertainment strategy at "Haibian Spa." Businesspeople are often like this; as long as they can make more money, sometimes they might deviate from ethical practices.

After the official opening of Haibian Spa, business was good. In summer, enjoying a sauna might seem out of season, but the allure of a "battle" was what they were going for. I was almost three months pregnant, experiencing some morning sickness. Sometimes, I suddenly felt nauseous and vomited. If the work were busy, I would feel lower back pain and couldn't take it. Mr. Xu was responsible for this area, and he was considerate. He asked Wu Fang and a few other staff members to cover for me. There weren't many skilled masseuses; the newcomers could only manage an essential foot massage. Our experienced therapists were relatively busy. Due to this, I hadn't had the time to confront Mr. Fang lately. I felt that as the carrier of the fetus, I held the power. If I disagreed, this child wouldn't be born. I was determined to demand an explanation from Mr. Fang.

I was a core massage therapist at Haibian Spa and a practical assistant to Manager Xu. He valued my experience and insights, and his trust in me was evident. He confided that Haibian Spa would learn from competitors and introduce some massage services with erotic undertones to enhance attraction and profits. He asked, "What other types of massage are you familiar with?" I said, "I know a few, but not many." Manager Xu continued, "Things like 'oil massage,' 'breast massage,' 'ice and fire,' 'savage dragon,' do you know them? If you're familiar, we could make you the head masseuse in charge of related training." I honestly replied, "I've done oil massages and breast massages. As for 'ice and fire' and 'savage dragon,' I can't accept them. I've never tried them." "Ice and fire," also known as "Ice and Fire like Heavens," involves alternating hot and cold water on the client's body, aiming to thrill by alternating sensations. "Savage dragon" refers to using the tongue to stimulate a client anally. Though it's another sensitive area, it felt too dirty. Even though I was a masseuse, in my eyes, "ice and fire" seemed like torture, and "savage dragon" was bordering on perverse. I wouldn't accept such practices.

On this Sunday, Wu Fang and I had a day off. Wu Fang said, "Go find him! Confront him and see how he explains himself." I said, "What if he denies everything and claims he didn't know?" Wu Fang said, "If he says that, then terminate the pregnancy and demand financial compensation. After all, he's the one who got you into this mess!" I had a plan in mind. Wu Fang and I went to a restaurant, and then I called Mr. Fang to set up a dinner meeting. I said, "I've found a new job. We haven't seen each other in a while, and I've missed you. Please come over!" Mr. Fang, in a smug tone, said, "Really? Missed me, huh? Want me to perform well?" I playfully responded, "Yes, with the new job keeping me so busy, you haven't come to comfort me. I've been having sleepless nights, you know?" Mr. Fang agreed to come right away. Wu Fang chuckled, "Jing, maybe you should quit your job and become an actress. Your acting skills are quite impressive!" I laughed, "Don't flatter me. When he arrives, you better cheer me on!"

About fifteen minutes later, Mr. Fang hurriedly entered the restaurant. In his thirties, his face was flushed and exuded a mature charm, much more attractive than those young boys. He walked up to me, affectionately patted my head, and said, "Xiao Jing, what made you think of treating today? Have you struck it rich?" I calmly replied, "Oh, where? We women work hard all year round, and our daily income doesn't compare to yours!" After he sat opposite me, he smiled and said, "Why do I feel like you and your friend are giving me some predatory looks? Is this an ambush?" Wu Fang chimed in, "Do you have money with you today? Whether it's an ambush or not, in any case, we're treating you, and you're footing the bill!" Mr. Fang chuckled, "Alright, I see. So, you want to blackmail me, huh?" Wu Fang said, "Mr. Fang, please don't make it sound so harsh. We've never extorted anything from you. You shouldn't be stingy as a man and a big boss!" Mr. Fang probably sensed a bit of an aggressive tone from Wu Fang's words, but he continued to smile, "You're not hungry, but I am. Let's order!"

Deal with essential matters after we've eaten. To avoid an unpleasant meal, neither Wu Fang nor I confronted Mr. Fang directly. Mr. Fang kept serving me food, seemingly oblivious to Wu Fang. Once we were finished with the meal, Wu Fang said, "Mr. Fang, is it only Jing who matters to you? Are there no other women in your eyes? You're treating me like a third wheel, or is your nearsightedness that severe?" Mr. Fang apologized, "Oh, I'm sorry. I'm used to having meals with just Xiao Jing. You're sitting there, and I overlooked it. My apologies!" I said, "Mr. Fang, are you truly good to me? Or is it all pretense? Or perhaps you have ulterior motives? I'd like to hear your honest opinion." Mr. Fang seemed a bit startled. He said, "Xiao Jing, what's wrong with you? Why are you suspicious? There's only you in my heart; I've never been with any other woman." Wu Fang smirked and said, "Mr. Fang, before you tell a lie, maybe you should draft it first. You have a wife and child. To claim that there's only Jing in your heart, isn't that blatant lying? If you truly care about Jing, you should have divorced and married your wife properly. What's this situation now? Sneaking around—what if Jing gets pregnant? What are you going to do?"

When Wu Fang mentioned the word "pregnant," a glint of delight appeared on Mr. Fang's face. He turned to me and said, "Xiao Jing, you won't tell me you're pregnant, right?" I neither confirmed nor denied it, saying, "If I were pregnant, would you be happy or troubled?" He probably fantasized about me having his child; he blurted out, "Of course, happy!" As soon as he said it, he realized something wasn't right and corrected himself, "But I'd worry about you, Xiao Jing. You feel the same, right?" I replied, "How would I know what you're thinking? Let me ask again: If I were pregnant, would you prefer I get an abortion, or would you want me to have the baby?"

Chapter 42

Fatal Love Turns Heartless

They say women are cunning at heart, but in front of men, women are all fools. Otherwise, how could the saying "Women in love are fools" exist? Although Mr. Fang and I were not in love, we still had some mutual affection. Initially, I willingly stayed with him without expecting anything in return. However, I never saw his true feelings. He deliberately got me pregnant and even wanted me to keep the child! He was using me with a calculated plan! When I realized this, I found his smiling face hypocritical and despicable! He had deep schemes, disregarding whether he hurt me with his actions.

Mr. Fang didn't directly answer; instead, he asked me, "Xiao Jing, tell me, are you pregnant?" I replied calmly, "Please pay attention to the order. You answer my question first, and then I'll tell you." Mr. Fang pondered for a while and said, "From a legal and moral perspective, if you are pregnant, you can only have an abortion and end the innocent life in the womb. But from an emotional and humane perspective, I hope you can keep the child. He is a new life. You and I will be his parents. As for how to raise him, you don't need to worry about that." I said, "So, let the child be a bastard, and I'll be the bastard's mother? Dear Mr. Fang, I'm not even married yet. Do you think what you said makes sense?"

Mr. Fang said, "Xiao Jing, you didn't explicitly say it. I was just assuming. So, tell me, are you pregnant?" I replied, "If I am pregnant, can you give me a clear answer?" Mr. Fang guessed that I was indeed pregnant, and he excitedly stood up, grabbing my arm, "You went for a check-up, didn't you? You are carrying my child, aren't you?" Wu Fang coldly said, "Mr. Fang, please show some respect. This is a restaurant, a public place, not your company!" Mr. Fang realized he had lost his composure and sat back in his seat, "I understand. It's true. So, let's discuss it." Wu Fang smiled, "What do you want to discuss? Do you want Jing to continue being your mistress and raise the child to adulthood?"

I placed the medical record on the table and said, "Take a look for yourself!" He picked it up and looked at it joyfully, "It's true! Xiao Jing, this is your record from a month ago. So, you already knew. Why didn't you tell me earlier?" I said, "I was just about to ask you, how could I be pregnant?" Our table was situated near the window, and there were no people at the nearby tables; otherwise, if they heard our conversation, they would have already stared at us. People are used to seeing couples, but illegitimate children still arouse various opinions.

Mr. Fang scratched his head and said, "I don't know either. Nowadays, there are many defective products, and maybe it's a false positive?" Wu Fang stared at Mr. Fang, smiling slyly, "I'm afraid someone intentionally made it show as a false positive, right?" Mr. Fang looked at Wu Fang strangely and said, "Fang Fang, this is a matter between Xiao Jing and me. Do you have to meddle in it?" Wu Fang chuckled, "You don't need to get so worked up. I want to meddle. What can you do about it?" Wu Fang had a more assertive personality than me; she dared to say and do whatever she pleased, regardless of what others said. Since I moved to Jiangnan and worked as a masseuse for two years, I've become less temperamental. I don't know how to get angry anymore, and my job doesn't allow me to get angry at customers; offending them is something we service staff avoid. Over time, my personality has become more gentle.

Mr. Fang asked the waiter for the bill, then said, "It's not convenient to discuss this here, right? Xiao Jing, let's find a place to talk, okay?" I was about to agree, thinking that arguing on the spot would be laughable. Wu Fang said, "Why not? What's the difference? Don't daydream. Jing won't be fooled by you again!" Mr. Fang gave her a sideways glance and said, "What do you mean? This is between the two of us. Is there any need for you to butt in?" Wu Fang smiled, "Look, Jing, his true colors are showing. Mr. Fang, a man should show some grace!" Mr. Fang got a little upset; he didn't want to argue with Wu Fang, knowing that she and I were close friends, and he couldn't do anything about her. Afterward, he stood up and said, "Xiao Jing, let's go outside to talk!" We came to hold him accountable, so we couldn't let him leave just like that. Wu Fang and I exchanged glances and followed him outside.

Mr. Fang parked the car at the restaurant entrance and waved to me, "Get in the car!" I complied and got into the car, and without hesitation, Wu Fang opened the car door and got in too. Mr. Fang knew that Wu Fang and I were inseparable, so he couldn't pick a fight with her and could only tolerate her. The car drove to Jinjihu by the garden area, and Mr. Fang parked the car by the roadside. We got out of the vehicle. The lakeside avenue here is beautiful, with lush flowers and plants, and right next to it is the rippling Jinjihu. The water area of Jinjihu is even more significant than West Lake in Hangzhou. Initially located in Suzhou's suburbs, it has become a part of the city due to urban expansion. Citizens love Jinjihu for its serene environment and fresh air. Some couples also come here to talk about love, and young mothers bring their children to bask in the sun. This place is closer to nature than Suzhou's gardens and is well-liked by people.

We sat on the lawn. Mr. Fang said, "Xiao Jing, since you're pregnant, let's keep the child, and I'll cover all the expenses!" Wu Fang said, "Keep the child? You say it so casually! How old is Jing? Do you want her to be an unwed mother? How do you expect her to live? You are so selfish!" I said, "I don't want to have the child. I can't even care for myself. How can I take care of a child?" Mr. Fang eagerly said, "Why not? Whether it's a boy or a girl, as long as you give birth, I'll give you a large sum!" I looked at him strangely, "Do you think money can buy everything and solve all problems? Do you think I'm after your money?" Mr. Fang hurriedly explained, "No, that's not what I meant. I meant that if you have a child, there will be a lot of expenses." I deliberately gave him a hard time, "If you want me to have the child, then divorce your wife and marry me immediately. Only then can I have the child legitimately? Following you without a clear status is not possible!" Mr. Fang looked troubled, "Xiao Jing, this issue... Didn't we agree in advance that you wouldn't affect my family? She has done nothing wrong, and I have no reason to divorce." I said coldly, "Is there still a need for a reason to divorce now? It seems in your mind your wife is still more important than me! Saying that you love me the most, it turns out it was all a lie!" He became anxious and pleaded, "Xiao Jing, I didn't lie to you. I truly love you; my feelings for you are genuine! Please keep the child, and I will compensate you!"

Wu Fang sneered, "What kind of compensation? Is it emotional or financial?" Mr. Fang said, "Xiao Jing, don't worry. As long as you agree to give birth to the child safely, I promise to give you much compensation. At the very least, you won't have to work anymore." Wu Fang said, "Don't you have a wife? If you want a child, have it with her. Why involve Jing?" Mr. Fang replied, "She is too old and unsuitable for having children anymore. Besides, she already had one child and can't have another. Xiao Jing, you are young and beautiful, and I want to have a child with you. Please agree, I'm begging you." I moved to the bushes on the side and squatted down, vomiting. I had eaten hot and sour fish and boiled chicken for lunch, and it all came out. After taking a deep breath a few times, Wu Fang handed me a water bottle. I rinsed my mouth, and accidentally some water splashed on Mr. Fang's clothes and face, making him frown.

Mr. Fang said, "Xiao Jing, look at yourself. You're feeling so uncomfortable. Why do you still want to work? Quit your job and rest at home!" Wu Fang retorted, "Quit her job? Who will support us then? You? Can you support us for a lifetime? We won't feel secure relying on your money!" Mr. Fang shook his head and said, "What do you mean 'us'? I'm talking about Xiao Jing, not you. It's none of your business here, doesn't overstep." Wu Fang angrily replied, "Who do you think you are? Liu Dehua or Kim Jong-wu? You're just a stinking rich man who thinks he's something special—accusing me of overstepping? Ha! What a joke! Take a look at yourself in the mirror first. What kind of person are you? Jing trusted you too much and fell for your lies! Now she's pregnant with your child. How are you going to deal with it? Whether she gives birth or not, you can't escape responsibility!"

Wu Fang's words were resolute, leaving Mr. Fang stunned and

speechless. I said, "Mr. Fang, how about considering my situation? Can I give birth now? Aren't you the one causing harm to me? If you were a real man, you'd devise a reasonable solution instead of daydreaming!" Mr. Fang said anxiously, "I've thought about it. As long as you have the child, I will care for you for the rest of your life. The child belongs to both of us! It's because I like you that I want a child with you. Do you understand? I'll leave all my wealth to you and our child in the future." Wu Fang laughed, "Mr. Fang, aren't you thinking too far ahead? The present issue hasn't been resolved, and you're already thinking about inheritance?" I said coldly, "The fetus is in my womb, and I have the final say. No matter how much money you offer, I won't give birth to the child!" Mr. Fang disappointedly said, "Why? Xiao Jing, you're heartless!" He, who had done something wrong, dared to accuse me of lacking compassion? Wasn't he trying to shift the blame? I retorted indignantly, "Who are you talking about? Who lacks compassion? You do! I'm just a young girl, and you want me to have a child for you. Have you ever considered my feelings? I still have to live my life and get married. I won't sneak around with you for the rest of my life! I see through your true colors now! You've disappointed me!"

He still tried to justify himself, "I haven't done anything wrong. I love children, and there's nothing wrong with wanting one. Xiao Jing, don't forget, this child carries my blood even though it's in your belly!" Wu Fang shouted, "You have no shame! How can you say such things? You're just toying with Jing, deceiving her from the beginning! You've been scheming all along, never considering others! Regardless of whether Jing decides to give birth, do you know how much damage you've caused her?" Mr. Fang still refused to admit his mistake, "I have money, and I will compensate Xiao Jing. She works hard, and I want to support her so she doesn't have to work for those men. Is that wrong?" I wanted to slap him, but I restrained myself. Wu Fang was right; he was inherently selfish, appearing gentlemanly on the surface but misleading me.

Wu Fang said, "Enough with the nonsense, Mr. Fang. First, bring 200,000 yuan and let Jing go for the surgery!" Mr. Fang was surprised, "Why surgery? It wouldn't cost that much; a few thousand yuan would be enough if she's going for an abortion. Why should I give her money?" Wu Fang scolded, "Are you even a man? If it weren't for your actions, would Jing be pregnant? Do you think terminating the pregnancy is all it takes? What about her nutrition expenses, compensation for mental distress? Aren't you responsible for that? Moreover, we've been informed by the doctor that the surgery requires anesthesia, which carries risks to her life. Can you handle that?" We asked for money to gauge his attitude. As for the amount, I don't care. Asking for 200,000 yuan was Wu Fang's idea; we didn't discuss it beforehand. But Mr. Fang's disappointing behavior made me feel sad and heartbroken. Among the men I've encountered besides Mr. Zhang, Mr. Fang left a good impression, followed by Mr. Gao and Mr. Ge. But he betrayed my trust; he never truly liked me.

I calmly said, "The 200,000 yuan Wu Fang mentioned is the minimum. Mr. Fang, if you divorce your wife within a month and marry me, I won't ask for a cent. I will give birth to the child. Otherwise, there's nothing to discuss!" Mr. Fang hesitated, "How can I just get a divorce? If I do, I'll have to give her half of my property, and my company won't survive!" Wu Fang said, "That's why you'd better be sensible and transfer the 200,000 yuan to Jing's account as soon as possible. Otherwise, I'm afraid your family won't have peace if we come to your place." Mr. Fang glared at Wu Fang and asked, "Are you trying to blackmail or threaten me?" Wu Fang looked up to the sky, not bothering to look at him, and said, "Why would I threaten you? You deal with it yourself! Don't even think about any tricks with me as your advisor!" I said, "Mr. Fang, you might be a good businessman, but you're not a good man! Can't you bear 200,000 yuan? I didn't even ask you for more. Besides, I felt deceived, causing my body and mind to suffer. Even if you were just a customer, I've accompanied you for so long. Isn't this amount insignificant?"

This negotiation ended in our complete victory. Mr. Fang was afraid that I'd cause a scene at his house and saw that I insisted on not giving birth to the child, so he had no choice but to compromise and agree to my demands. The next day, he transferred 200,000 yuan to my account. Despite receiving so much money, I didn't feel joyful. I learned my lesson this time. As the saying goes: "You can't trip over the same stone twice." He had helped us rent the house in the garden area, but now that we had cut ties with him, he secretly negotiated with the landlord to terminate the lease. Fortunately, the landlord was understanding, and after learning the situation, he didn't kick us out but continued the lease with us, with the rent paid by ourselves.

I wanted to abort the child in my belly as it was my burden. I knew the child was innocent, and the responsibility lay with the adults, but he came at the wrong time, and I couldn't let him enter this world. Ending it would put an end to everything. To be honest, if I were a bit older and had a stable job, I might consider giving birth, but now I couldn't bear the reality of being an "unwed mother."

Chapter 43

Boundless Love

In the era we live in, temptations are everywhere. Men pursue desires, and women chase after wealth. How many can remain untainted? As long as women are willing to loosen their morals and men are eager to open their wallets, any transaction can be made. Sometimes, "love" is merely a deceptive mask, a mere pretense. In reality, it's all just a play, a mutual exploitation. Once the value of exploitation is lost, or when the novelty wears off, one might be easily cast aside, and some may choose to play the game of disappearing.

The night in Su Zhou is adorned with flowing lights, and the bright street lamps have transformed this thousand-year-old city into a place that never sleeps. In some dimly lit areas, you'll find women heavily made-up, secretly casting flirtatious glances at passersby. This scene exists in every city at night. They are not massage therapists; they merely use "massage" as an excuse for illicit activities. Some come to work unthinkingly, with a college degree or experience, finding it easier to secure a job. So, they find temporary shelter in some hair salons, earning a living. A few girls also prefer an easy life and voluntarily gamble their youth for a better tomorrow. Among the single migrant workers, they also need to fulfill their physiological needs, and those sordid places offer them convenience. Sauna cities, hair salons, beauty salons, everywhere you go, there are no shortages of female service personnel, and business is always bustling.

I once read a poem by Gu Cheng: "The night has given me dark eyes, but I use them to seek the light." Standing by the window, gazing at the vast night and the flickering neon lights, where can I find my share of brightness? My current profession is more respectable. When will this path reach its end? Tomorrow, I will go to the hospital for surgery to remove the little life inside me and send it to heaven. I asked for a week's leave, saying I'm visiting a friend in Zhejiang. Manager Xu didn't inquire further and agreed. The foot bath center needs me, but he knows he can't offend me, as I am a prominent figure for Haitangchun. Wu Fang wanted to take leave to accompany me, but Manager Xu disagreed. He said, "I hope you both understand my difficulties. If both of you take leave, our business will suffer."

I tidied up my emotions at dawn and arrived at the hospital alone. I felt calm, nervous, and lonely. I saw other girls who came for obstetrics and gynecology check-ups with their boyfriends while I was alone. I had previously made an appointment with the doctor, and all kinds of examinations were done. Today, I only needed to undergo the procedure. The doctor told me, "If you do a painless abortion, it's best around two months of pregnancy. It's very convenient, and if your physical condition is good, you can go home after the procedure. You've already exceeded three months, so we can only perform an induced labor." The doctor handed me some papers to sign, and I didn't read them carefully.

Still, I vaguely remember they were about the risks associated with the surgery, and the patient must bear the possible adverse consequences. The doctor also asked my family members to sign with me, but I smiled and said, "My family is in Chongqing, and they can't come here to sign. You can rest assured I'm willing to take full responsibility for the surgical risks myself so you won't be bothered." The doctor asked me to write "I am willing to take full responsibility for the surgical risks" underneath my original signature. I complied. However, I wondered: How can the hospital transfer the surgical risks to the patient?

I was pushed into the operating room, and after general anesthesia, I lost consciousness. I didn't know how long it had passed when I finally woke up. After waking up, I didn't feel any pain, maybe because the anesthesia hadn't worn off completely. But I felt weak all over, and my limbs couldn't exert any strength. I was pushed into the ward, lying on the bed, looking at the IV drip, drop by drop, flowing into me. My hands felt icy, and I felt a bit lost. After a while, I felt a stinging pain in my lower abdomen. An unborn life was abandoned like this. I felt sorry! I felt a bit guilty, hoping the soul in heaven could forgive my heartlessness. Reality can be cruel sometimes, and I had no choice but to make this decision for survival.

At other bedsides, there were people to accompany the patients, but mine was empty. I thought of the scene when Ah Lana was hospitalized, with our sisters talking and laughing together. Having relatives and friends accompanying you might alleviate some pain. Besides being seen by an intimate man, a woman's body is often exposed to doctors. Men are keenly interested in my body, but the doctors performing the surgery remain indifferent. I heard some hospitals have male doctors in the obstetrics and gynecology department. That would be interesting. If it were me, I would let a male doctor examine me. There may be a sense of mystery, and that's how a sense of professional sacredness can be maintained. If they become indifferent, they might lose their passion for work.

After work, Wu Fang came to accompany me, and there was also a colleague, Xiao Zhu, who got along well with us. I didn't have to worry about her spreading anything outside. With them keeping me company, I felt much better. The doctor said I could be discharged after resting for four or five days, but I would need more rest once I returned. I couldn't engage in heavy physical work temporarily. Wu Fang asked, "Can you work after being discharged? We can't take leave." The doctor said, "It depends on what kind of work she does. If it's office work, of course, it's no problem. But if it involves physical labor, it's better to resume work after a full recovery to avoid leaving any after-effects." Without thinking, Wu Fang said, "What if it's massage? Is it okay?" The doctor looked at us with doubt and said, "Massage? Are you both massage girls?" Wu Fang replied, "Yes, what's wrong with being massage girls? We're self-reliant too." The doctor nodded and said, "Take care of yourselves, rest well, and eat nutritiously. Don't overwork yourselves."

Being sick has its benefits; it forces you to rest and put everything aside for your health. Only when you are ill, do you realize the fragility of life and the uncertainty of the world. The hospital is filled with many patients, and every day there are some who pass away, some due to overwork, falling ill, and becoming bedridden. After being discharged, I should focus on making money and pay attention to my health. I once read a metaphor in a magazine saying that one's health is like a "1," and all other things like wealth, status, and family are the "0"s behind the "1." When the "1" stands, the "0"s have meaning. However, if the "1" falls, meaning when one's health is compromised, the "0"s are just "0"s, losing their significance.

On the third day of my hospitalization, Wu Fang and I were having lunch at noon. Wu Fang was on the night shift and knew I must feel lonely at the hospital, so she came to keep me company and talk during the day. Suddenly, we heard loud wailing from outside, and Wu Fang, curious, ran out of the ward to take a look. After a while, she came back. I asked, "What's happening outside? Did someone else die?" It's common to see patients passing away, but for the families of the deceased, it's a devastating blow. When I was with Ah Lana, I witnessed the heart-wrenching grief of cancer patients' families, and Ah Lana's departure also left us sisters heartbroken. Life is precious but also unpredictable.

Wu Fang sighed, "It's so pitiful! A six-year-old boy has leukemia, and his whole family is crying downstairs. The boy's mother is only in her thirties and fainted from crying!" Hearing this news made me feel sad. My years as a massage therapist haven't hardened my heart. I said, "Leukemia? Isn't that life-threatening? Why do so many people get this unlucky disease?" Wu Fang replied, "Who knows? When someone's unlucky, even drinking cold water feels sour to them! When a child falls ill, the whole family suffers!" There's a TV drama called "Blood Suspicion," and its protagonist has leukemia. This disease costs a lot of money and is tough to cure. If an ordinary family has someone with this disease, their happiness will be almost destroyed. Where do so many demons of illness come from in this world?

Five days later, I was discharged but didn't immediately return to work. Instead, I asked Wu Fang to help me take another week off. Manager Xu didn't know about my hospitalization, and he wondered Wu Fang, "She's not back yet? I already gave her face by letting her take two weeks off. If it were someone else, I would have asked them to leave!" Wu Fang replied, "It's easy to find many people, but it's hard to find someone like

Sister Jing, a good massage therapist. You can't find her just anywhere." When Wu Fang told me about this, I laughed and asked, "What did Manager Xu say?" Wu Fang smiled and said, "What else could he say? If he acts tough, I'll take half a month off too. Let's see how he explains it to Mr. Chen, then?" Mr. Chen seldom appears, and he always looks cold. He doesn't talk much with the employees. When he comes, he makes a quick round like he's doing a secret inspection. If he finds any service staff without their name tags or if there's any litter lying around, he instructs Manager Xu to deduct money according to the rules. He doesn't show leniency, and some service staff fear him. However, I agree with his statement: "If someone can't even handle small matters well, how can they do big things?"

While resting at home, Wu Fang and I would walk by the Golden Chicken Lake after she finished her shift. When I was working, the days felt long, but during my rest, several days passed in a flash. When I returned to work, Mr. Wang held a meeting for us and said that the city was cleaning up and regulating entertainment venues, including foot massage centers. However, the situation was better for us than for dance halls, bars, and KTVs. They only required us to obtain a health certificate and a temporary residence permit for service staff. Manager Xu took us for a medical examination in the afternoon, but it was just a formality. We got a few stamps on the medical examination form and paid some money, but they didn't do an ultrasound or blood test. We would receive the essential health certificates for work in a few days. We also handed in our photos; the foot massage center would help us get the temporary residence permits.

During these days, I thought about a child with leukemia. Although I didn't know him or his family, I knew they were probably helpless. How much money does it take to treat this disease? I thought I had money in my account, right? Mr. Fang gave me 200,000 yuan, and I haven't touched a penny. One morning, I told Wu Fang, "Let's go to the hospital and see that child with leukemia." Wu Fang looked at me as if she didn't recognize me and said, "Sister Jing, what's gotten into you? What are you going to see? Why bother yourself with someone else's illness? Don't you know that doing good deeds nowadays might not bring good karma?" I said, "Don't say that. Didn't Wei Wei sing 'The Dedication of Love'? It's normal to offer some love as long as it's within your ability! Didn't we donate money when there was a major earthquake in India? This is something close to us. If I didn't see it, it would be fine, but now that I know, I can't help but keep it in my heart." Wu Fang sighed, "Sister Jing, you are destined not to have money. As soon as you have it, you start thinking of being like Lei Feng daily. Are you full and bored? Why act so foolishly? I really can't understand you!"

Wu Fang couldn't argue, so she accompanied me to the hospital. We asked several doctors in the outpatient department, and they all said that they hadn't seen the child recently, but they provided some information about him. I learned that the sick child's surname is Lu, and they are from Xuzhou, Jiangsu. His family had been in Suzhou for a few years. The child's parents work on a construction site, and the child was diagnosed with leukemia at the beginning of the year. They have been accompanying the child for chemotherapy, but it's possible that they ran out of money recently, which is why they haven't come. Another doctor said that to save the child, he heard that the child's mother plans to get pregnant again and give birth. They want to use the newborn's umbilical cord blood to save the unfortunate son. The doctor said that using the umbilical cord blood from a sibling can potentially treat leukemia, but he didn't know where that family lives.

Wu Fang said when we left the hospital, "They probably found a way to save the child, so you don't need to worry anymore. Besides, we don't even know where they live. Will you stay at the hospital, waiting for them to show up?" I said, "I will find a way to locate them. Pregnancy takes ten months, but that child's life is in danger at any moment. They might not be able to wait for ten months. Since Mr. Fang gave the money to me, and it's not mine, I plan to give it to them for the treatment!" Wu Fang almost jumped and said, "Sister Jing, have you gone mad? The money is in your account, so it's yours! If you have too much money, why not give some to me? It will save me from working so hard! Why give it to a stranger? Isn't that foolish?" I smiled and said, "Good steel should be used on the blade. The money is of little use to me, and if it can save lives, wouldn't it be more meaningful?" Suddenly, I remembered that the TV station had a social documentary program when Ah Lana passed away. They might still recognize me. Why don't I find them and ask for their help in locating the child with the surname Lu?

I waved my hand at Wu Fang and said, "Let's go. We're going to the TV station!" Wu Fang was taken aback and asked, "Why? Are you going to broadcast a missing person announcement? Do you have so much money that it's driving you crazy? Do you have to spend it all to feel at ease?" I laughed, saying, "I need money, but I have to earn it myself. As for what others give me, I will also give to others!" Wu Fang smiled and said, "I understand now; you're borrowing flowers to offer Buddha, right?" I said, "Come with me; we'll ask the TV station for help finding that child." Wu Fang understood and couldn't help but tease me, "Sister Jing, are you addicted to being on TV again? It looks like you're going to become famous again!"

Chapter 44

Doing Good is Hard

In the city, there are many beautiful women, but most of the ones we see on the streets are not locals but migrants. These migrant women know how to dress up, and they dare to wear revealing clothes. Suzhou girls usually wear light makeup, and only married women would put on makeup to hide their age. My confidence comes from within, as well as my work experience. I treat others with courtesy. Even though I don't have a college degree, I have the skill of massage to support myself. I am no longer afraid of not finding a job.

I didn't think about donating money to become famous; it was genuinely out of concern for that child's misfortune. Why shouldn't I extend a helping hand to his family when he is so young and has leukemia? Society is like a big family; helping each other is a virtue. It's an honor for me to be able to help others! There's another reason I want to donate to help leukemia patients. When I arrived in Suzhou, the TV station reported a story about a girl named Chen Xia. She was in her twenties and very beautiful but unfortunately got leukemia. After media coverage, the public spontaneously donated over 300,000 yuan to her. A hospital in Taiwan also found a bone marrow match for Chen Xia, ultimately saving her life. Due to everyone's enthusiastic help, a leukemia patient on the verge of death was given a chance to live a healthy and happy life among us. What a wonderful thing it is! Why can't massage therapists do noble things? No matter what kind of operation the boy with the surname Lu needs in the future, whether it's a bone marrow transplant or umbilical cord blood therapy, it will undoubtedly require many medical expenses. Will my 200,000 yuan be enough for them? If it can ease their urgent situation, that would be great!

We arrived at the TV station and found the team responsible for the social news program. Many people were busy, so Wu Fang and I stood at the door without disturbing them. After a time, Wu Fang pulled me and said, "Let's go. Can't you see they're busy? We shouldn't just stand here like wooden statues." I said, "Since we're already here, and the matter isn't settled yet, how can we just leave like this?" As we were talking, a male colleague approached us. He saw us peering inside the door and asked, "Whom are you looking for? Is there something you need?" I glanced at him, feeling familiar, and he seemed to recognize me too. Slowly, he asked, "Who are you?" I smiled and said, "I'm Lai Xiao Jing. Your team reported on me before." He slapped his forehead and exclaimed, "Right, you're that massage therapist! Our program was a great success, and we even won an award!" Wu Fang and I laughed, and Wu Fang asked, "Did you get a bonus?" He chuckled, "Money is a small thing; encouragement matters! Oh, do you have something to tell us today? Please come inside. Just now, I thought you two were new interns!"

We entered the room, and several people inside saw us. A woman in her thirties approached and said, "You must be Lai Xiao Jing, right? I'm Su Min. We met last year, and I remember you very well!" I smiled and said, "Su Jie, I remember you too. You were the one holding the microphone interviewing me." Su Jie said, "Let me introduce them. This is Ding Hui, this is Yang Yang, and this is Tian Jing. The four of us interviewed you last year. Do you remember?" How could I forget? My good sister Ah Lana received immense love from the people of Suzhou when she tragically passed away, and these respected TV journalists all donated money to Ah Lana's parents. Thanks to their reporting, we received widespread understanding from society when we returned to work. It's an honor, a sign of respect, and a reward that material things cannot replace. I am full of gratitude and admiration for these journalists with loving hearts!

I said, "I often think of you all too. I came to Suzhou last year, and now I work and live here." Tian Jie smiled and said, "Really? Why don't you come and hang out with us? We'll treat you to a meal." I chuckled, "I should be the one treating you all. You helped Ah Lana and us so much, and we haven't thanked you enough!" Yang Ge said, "I just saw someone at the door, but I didn't expect it to be you. We were caught up with some work, and I didn't say hello. I apologize!" I smiled and said, "I saw you were all busy, so we didn't come in." Yang Ge asked, "Is there something you need? Just tell us; don't treat us as outsiders." Wu Fang said, "Jing Jie is trying to retake the limelight; she wants you to help her find someone!" Ding Ge became interested and asked, "Oh, who do you want to find? It's not a lost brother. In that case, you don't need to search; I'm your brother! Haha!" I didn't expect the journalist to joke like that, and I laughed, saying, "No, I'm not looking for a brother; I want to find a young boy surnamed Lu." Su Jie said, "You're looking for someone? Don't rush; come, drink water, and tell us slowly."

Wu Fang picked up from where I left off, saying, "She's not looking for her biological brother; she wants to find a little boy surnamed Lu!" Ding Ge asked, "Why do you want to find a little boy? Who entrusted you with this task?" I said, "No one entrusted me; I don't know the boy personally. But I learned he has leukemia, and his family has exhausted their money for his treatment. Now, I don't know where they live. I have money and want to donate it to help with his treatment. So, I want to ask for your help in finding this young boy." Upon hearing my words, they all looked stunned. Tian Jie said, "Leukemia may not be easily cured, and the treatment costs are very high. You work hard now, and earning money isn't easy. Even if you donate all your salary, it may not save them from their urgent situation. However, we can create a unique missing person announcement and mobilize the public to find this sick child. Kind-hearted citizens who see the program will extend their helping hand and donate to them. This is a tradition among the people of Suzhou; similar programs have been aired before with a positive social impact." Ding Ge said, "Xiao Jing, you're impressive! You're a source of pride for the new people of Suzhou!"

I said, "I have 200,000 yuan. I don't know if it will be of any help to them. Time is of the essence for this disease. I hope we can find the boy soon to ensure he receives proper treatment." Su Jie surprisedly said, "Where did you get so much money? It's not stolen, is it?" I said, "Definitely not stolen, nor found. Please rest assured! I have my salary, which is enough for myself. I want to donate this money to those who need it more." Yang Ge said, "It's rare to see such a kind heart in you! Then get ready, and we'll film you to help find that child." I shook my head and said, "Don't film me; I don't want to be on TV again. I'm not doing this to seek attention." Ding Ge said, "If you don't say anything, just broadcasting a missing person notice won't have a significant effect. It will be more effective when you speak from your heart in the program and say what you think. The boy's family will see the program and come forward to accept your donation." Wu Fang said, "We don't want to show our faces. We still have to work. Jing Jie wants to be a good person, which is right, but we should also pay attention to the method, right?" Tian Jie said, "That's right. Let Xiao Lai appear in the program and discuss her wish to find the little boy. We can use her back or side profile to avoid showing her face directly. This way, we can achieve the goal of publicity and finding the child without causing any negative impact." Yang Ge said, "The eyes of the public are sharp; we will find that unfortunate child!"

I said, "When you broadcast the missing person notice, it's best not to disclose my profession, okay? I don't want others to misunderstand." Due to some people's prejudices, if the public knows that I'm a massage therapist, they might look down on my actions. If the boy's family knows my identity, they may not accept my donation. They might think my money is not clean, from an unknown source, or even suspect it's "kept woman money" from some boss. Would the Lu family be willing to accept my money then? Su Jie smiled and said, "You're very thoughtful. Okay, we won't disclose your true identity. Hopefully, we can find that little boy as you wish."

The following evening, "Social Fax" aired the "missing person announcement." The program's team made appropriate technical adjustments to prevent the audience from recognizing me and disturbing my life. Most of my appearances were shown in profile; occasionally, a mosaic obscures my front image. It was Monday, and Wu Fang and I were working the early shift. We watched the program at home that night. Wu Fang chuckled, "Jing Jie, it seems you're becoming famous again." I shook my head, saying, "I don't want to be a celebrity. Look at those stars. Once they gain a little fame, they become incredibly arrogant. Even trivial matters are turned into news. It's ridiculous. On the surface, they may seem glamorous, but they lose their freedom. People follow them everywhere, and even their love lives become the subject of gossip. I don't like that kind of life; I'd rather be an ordinary person, unburdened."

Wu Fang said, "Then what's your intention in donating so much money? I thought you wanted to become famous and marry a wealthy person!" I laughed, "I didn't have any intentions. I just felt sorry for that little boy; he's so unfortunate. His family is now living in poverty because of his illness. That 200,000 yuan I had, I never really considered it as my own. I feel relieved now that I've used it to help someone in need." Wu Fang said with a smile, "That's just like you. But in any case, I couldn't do it. If I had money, why not use it for myself? Giving it away for nothing, isn't that foolish? If you want to be like Lei Feng, he's already dead!" I laughed and said, "I'm not emulating anyone; it's just something I want to do. Our salary is pretty good now, and I've saved some money. I won't be so silly as to go hungry while helping others. I didn't earn this money, so I don't mind donating it."

On Tuesday afternoon at 2 o'clock, I received a call from Su Jie saying they had found the little boy. His family was at the television station and wanted to meet me immediately. I had to start work at 4:30, and two hours remained. Would I be late if I returned to work afterward? But they were waiting for me at the television station, indicating that they had high expectations. Wasn't it me who wanted to find them? Now that they were found, why wouldn't I go to meet them? I also wondered if the little boy's condition had improved. I told Su Jie, "Alright, I'll come over immediately. Should I bring my bank card?" Su Jie replied, "Let's first sign a donation agreement, and the money can be given to them on another day. But you can give it to them now if you want."

Wu Fang accompanied me to the television station. In the reception room of "Social Fax," I saw a family of three. The little boy had a pale complexion and a bald head, likely due to leukemia and chemotherapy.

His parents were in their early thirties and dressed. His father's face was dark, and his mother's eyes showed confusion. However, I noticed her slightly bulging belly, perhaps indicating that she was already pregnant and wanted to use the newborn's umbilical cord blood to save her son. Last time, I heard from the doctor that they worked at a construction site, likely much harder than our massage job, and they earned less money. Their child had this illness; how could they not be anxious? When they saw Wu Fang and me walking into the room, their eyes seemed to glimpse hope, and they showed joy and gratitude.

Su Jie introduced us, and the little boy's father tightly held my hand, tears welling up in his eyes, and said, "Thank you! Thank you so much! I never expected there would be such a kind-hearted person in this world!" I smiled and said, "It's nothing. I hope the child's illness gets better!" He touched his son's bald head and said, "Go on, call her auntie!" I quickly replied, "Lu Jiawei, you don't have to call me auntie. Call me sister." The little boy was very obedient. Despite suffering from such a severe illness, his little eyes shone brightly and clearly. He walked up to me and softly said, "Sister! Sister, you're a good person!" I hugged his head and pulled him close; tears almost fell. He was only six years old; why did the disease ruthlessly torment such an innocent and adorable child? Six years old, he should be in kindergarten, but instead, he left school, parted with his playmates, and fought tenaciously against the disease. It's genuinely heartwarming and heart-wrenching.

I saw Yang Ge and the others pointing the camera at us, and I said, "Isn't there no need to film? I'll give them the money." Yang Ge said, "We must film it. Not only that, but we also need to film it well! Nowadays, there are too many heartless wealthy people in society. People like you are just too rare! We want to awaken people's compassion and make Suzhou's spiritual and cultural construction vibrant and dynamic!" Ding

Ge said, "You all come over here. There's an agreement on this table. One party is willing to donate, and the other is the recipient. Both parties need to sign to confirm. We have also invited a notary to issue a notarized certificate for you." I laughed, "Do we need notarization?" Yang Ge chuckled and said, "With the agreement and notarization, it has a legal effect, and you can't easily go back on your word!"

As Lu Jiawei's father and I approached the table, Wu Fang's phone rang. She walked outside to answer it and returned to me, saying, "Jing Jie, Manager Xu said that you must go to work immediately. The massage room has hired a few new service staff, and they want you to train them." Lu Jiawei's father looked puzzled as he stared at me and said, "Miss, you work at a massage parlor?" I knew it wouldn't end well, and for a moment, I didn't know how to respond. Wu Fang, however, said, "Yes! So what? Jing Jie is kind-hearted and insists on donating to your family. I admire her! If it were me, I wouldn't do it. We work hard to give massages and can barely make enough money." I angrily shouted, "Wu Fang, can't you keep your mouth shut?!" But it was too late; Lu Jiawei's father seemed to feel deceived, looked at both Wu Fang and me angrily, turned around, took his son and wife, and shouted, "We don't want this money! No matter how poor we are, we can't accept this money! Jiawei, let's go!" Yang Ge, Su Jie, and everyone else in the room watched in astonishment, but no one tried to stop them.

I glared at Wu Fang, somewhat angry, and said, "Wu Fang, couldn't you keep quiet for once? Now look, they've left! It's a case of being good for nothing and making a mess of things!" Wu Fang apologized with a guilty look, "Jing Jie, I'm sorry! I didn't mean to!" I said, "You just had to say a few words and scare them away! Did you see that child? He might be in danger if we don't help him quickly!" Wu Fang muttered, "There are so many sick people in the world; you can't save them all.

They left; so what? Aren't you worried that the money won't be used well?" I sighed, frustrated, and said, "Wu Fang, can't you just shut up? Can't you pretend to be mute for a while?"

Su Jie said, "It's okay, Xiao Jing. You two can go back first. We'll explain to them and contact you again when there's news, alright?" Ding Ge said, "In my opinion, just let them know your true identity. What's the big deal about being a massage worker? Don't think negatively. A massage worker with such a kind heart is more valuable and worthy of society's praise and reflection!" Tian Jie said, "Xiao Ding, don't cause trouble. We should respect the wishes of those involved. If the Lu family doesn't want to accept the donation, we'll suggest another way to persuade them. Saving the child is the most important thing!"

Wu Fang and I left the television station, called a taxi, and headed to the Haitangchun Foot Bath Parlor. I was feeling a bit down, silent in the car. Wu Fang repeatedly apologized, "Jing Jie, I'm sorry! I never thought things would turn out like this! If I didn't go with you, maybe this wouldn't have happened!" I looked out the window; the scorching sunlight was dazzling, people and cars bustling around, and everyone seemed busy. I sighed silently: Why is it so difficult to do a good deed?

Chapter 45

Seeking Pleasure Alone

When we arrived at the entrance of Haitangchun, Wu Fang and I hurriedly got off the taxi and rushed into the hall. This Wang brother knew how to show off, as at the hall's entrance, he had placed a vast Suzhou embroidery screen featuring "Red Carps Playing in Water." Just as I turned around the screen, I suddenly felt empty-handed and shouted, "Oh no, my bag!" I had left my small bag in the taxi, containing my bank card with over two hundred thousand yuan! While in the cab, I absentmindedly left the bag beside me due to my troubled emotions. I regret my actions and think about the Lu Jiawei's family. What if they didn't accept my money? My mind was a bit chaotic, and I just remembered that I needed to take the bag with me in the confusion!

I became anxious and started to sweat. It was a considerable sum, and I intended to use it to help Lu Jiawei with his treatment. Now, heaven seemed to be against me as I had lost it! The frustrating part was that I never asked the driver for a receipt, as what's the use of it? You can't claim expenses with it! But now, I needed to find out which taxi I left the bag in because I needed to see the license plate number. Wu Fang showed no urgency and gloated, saying, "It's better this way! Now, you can't go on giving others money all day. Let's see what you'll use to give now?" I scolded, "Wu Fang, how can you be so heartless? Quickly help me think, recall, what was the taxi's number?" Wu Fang said, "What's the use of being anxious? You should report it to the police quickly!"

I dialed 110 and reported the situation, saying that five minutes ago, I lost my bag containing a bank card in a blue Santana sedan taxi driven by a man in his forties. Still, I need help remembering the license plate number. The operator asked me where I got off and where the taxi was heading. After answering, the 110 operators said, "Please don't worry. Taxis have positioning and calling systems. If the belongings are still in the taxi, we will remind the driver to pay attention. Once there's any news, we will contact you immediately!" My heart gradually calmed, and I was no longer in such a hurry. Although the bank card was in the bag, it had a password, so they couldn't withdraw money even if someone found it. If I couldn't retrieve the card, it would be troublesome, and I would have to go to the bank to report it lost. I had seen police reminders advising people not to put bank and ID cards together to avoid theft. I followed that advice, and now it proved helpful; otherwise, if someone found the card and withdrew the money, that would be a disaster!

Wu Fang and I stood by the roadside, waiting for that taxi to appear. However, cars came and went, passing by without any sign of stopping. I felt discouraged and said, "Maybe we shouldn't wait any longer. I'll go handle the loss procedures tomorrow." Wu Fang shouted, "You should've said so earlier! If I knew your card couldn't be lost, I wouldn't have bothered to stand here with you in the dust!" I was about to turn around when my phone rang. It was from 110. "Did you find my bag?" I asked. The police on the other end said, "Yes, the driver has handed over your bag to the city's Public Security Bureau. You need to bring your ID to claim it." Wu Fang smiled and said, "It's really found? It seems like there are still many good people around!" I laughed and said, "Yes, Suzhou is paradise on Earth; of course, there are many good people!" I asked Wu Fang to cover for me for a while. I took a taxi to the Public Security Bureau to retrieve my bag. I had lost it and then found it again, and nothing inside was missing!

Some time ago, while resting at home and feeling bored, I went online to the nearby internet cafe. Playing computer games and giving massages were similar; both involved using hands. The air in internet cafes could have been better; men were playing games, and women were video chatting. That was the case most of the time, with a few browsing web pages. Nowadays, going online is mainly entertainment; few are there for studying. While chatting in the chatroom, I met a few like-minded people and added them for private chats on QQ. When I turned on video chat, some internet friends would exclaim, "The internet is a dinosaur world; I never expected to find beauty here!" I didn't think I was charming, but looking around the internet cafe, finding someone better looking than me was hard. After chatting a few times, some people would suggest meeting in person, but I always used "remembrance is better than meeting" as an excuse. I wasn't afraid of "seeing the light" and revealing my identity, but I felt that online friends were just that - online friends. As long as we enjoyed our conversations, why did we have to meet in real life? Meeting in person might ruin the sense of openness we had. Distance adds beauty and the so-called online love is just romantic illusions. I wouldn't say I liked daydreaming.

Lately, due to worrying about Lu Jiawei, I didn't go online. On the other hand, Wu Fang wasn't afraid of fatigue and stayed up all night after work. She secretly told me that she wanted to "fish" online. I knew her intentions; she tried to find lustful men online and use their lust to toy with them. I repeatedly advised her to be cautious and not go too far. It was okay to earn some money, but she must never break up someone's family. Also, she should be mindful of her safety; she shouldn't get pregnant or contract a disease, and she definitely shouldn't get caught by the police or be deceived by men! Wu Fang didn't care and said, "I've long developed a keen eye; a man who can deceive me hasn't been born yet!" Horses stumble, and people slip. I was apprehensive that while Wu Fang was fishing, she might get caught instead. The internet is full of scammers, deceivers who are after money or pleasure; they can be anyone. I didn't want to take that risk; anyone who wanted to meet me in person, I ignored them all. The internet is a virtual world, and those who blabber online might be kind-hearted in reality, just as I might be an ordinary masseuse in real life.

After returning home late at night, I couldn't sleep and was bored, so I lazily started watching a TV drama. The one currently airing was a Korean drama called "Dae Jang Geum." Korean dramas and Taiwanese dramas are similar, slow-paced with family-oriented plots, something I used to dislike. However, I unexpectedly got hooked this time, binge-watching four episodes every night from 1 a.m. to 4 a.m. I became fascinated by the beauty, intelligence, strength, kindness, and tolerance of the main character, Dae Jang Geum. She had many admirable qualities, and I truly admired her! Talking with my colleagues at work, I found out they were also watching it and thought it was the most captivating Korean drama. In China, we have numerous historical dramas, and just for the Qing Dynasty alone, there are countless TV dramas. But once watched, they are easily forgotten. None were as good and touching as "Dae Jang Geum."

When Wu Fang returned in the morning, she excitedly described her gains from last night. I was half-asleep and too lazy to pay attention to her chattering. I'm generally not talkative, only opening up more with close friends. On the other hand, Wu Fang is different; she's warm and friendly toward people. A stranger could become her old friend within half an hour if she's in a good mood. We are close in age; she's one year younger than me, but we have many differences, not just in character but also in physiological needs. Her desires are much stronger than mine. I have had experiences with men but am not obsessed with them. They are neither essential nor indispensable to me, and the idea of being unable to sleep due to thinking about men is almost impossible. Wu Fang, however, is different. Her appetite is much bigger, and she occasionally desires to explore new experiences.

I see through the true faces of men. Unmarried people are too immature and lack financial stability, so I don't like them. As for those who are married, they are someone else's husband. Besides, they are often just looking for a short-term fling; all they need is carnal desire and a confidante to add excitement to their lives. While snatching someone else's husband is not impossible, such a man needs to be exceptional. Wouldn't I become a second abandoned wife if he's just inconsistent? However, I believe that a man is waiting for me somewhere in this world. It's just a matter of whether we'll meet.

Su Jie from the TV station called me and told me that they visited Lu Jiawei's family and are currently working on persuading them. Lu Jiawei's parents are considering accepting the donation due to their child's urgent medical needs. Once they agreed, Su Jie said she would inform me immediately. Although I have never given up on the idea of helping them, there was also a part of me that considered backing down. I found it amusing and even self-defeating. People in need are looking down on those who want to help them. It's truly ironic, and I couldn't help but feel slightly disappointed. Fortunately, "Dae Jang Geum" gave me a lot of inspiration. It made me understand the importance of persistence; otherwise, I would only achieve something.

After half a month, the TV station finally called to inform me that Lu Jiawei's father would accept my donation. I told the reporters I wanted low-key coverage; I didn't want to become a public figure. This time, I went alone and returned to the reception room. Lu Jiawei's father apologized and said, "After listening to what the journalists said, I realized that you are a good person. Your job is hard, and earning money is not easy, yet you selflessly offered to help my family. I don't know how to thank you. I offended you last time, and please forgive me!" I only hoped for mutual understanding and respect; I wouldn't hold any grudges against him. We, who work in massage, are no different from those working on construction sites. We are all laborers striving for a better life. We took a photo together, and I told Lu Jiawei, "Focus on getting well. Sister will come to see you often." The TV station respected my request and didn't exaggerate the donation to the news sensation. They only made a simple report, stating: Lu Jiawei's family, who is, unfortunately, suffering from leukemia, received a generous donation of 200,000 yuan from a kind-hearted person. He is currently receiving treatment in the hospital, and they are actively searching for a matching bone marrow donor. They hope to cure the young boy's illness and have him return to school soon, healthy and happy!

Since donating the money, I felt very pleased. Only Wu Fang, Lu's family, and a few reporters knew about this, and they didn't publicize it, so my life remained unaffected, unlike the attention I received after appearing on TV for the first time. I felt that life was good now. Going to work, coming back home, and sometimes riding my bike around, I enjoyed this peaceful life. With a steady income, happiness was closer to us. When I worked, I interacted with clients, providing enthusiastic service and a smiling face. In return, the clients also became polite with me. Some clients require more exciting services, and I recommend oil massage or other massages which other massage therapists would perform. Wu Fang voluntarily transferred to the second massage department because the service there was more open, and she could receive more tips and interact with more passionate clients.

I can't explain why, but I don't like being a supervisor or managing people. I prefer treating my colleagues as equals and doing my job well. In this aspect, I can't compare myself to Dae Jang Geum; she had noble ideals and, after many hardships, ultimately achieved her dreams. My life might be simpler, but I find it fulfilling. My reputation at Hai Tang Chun gradually rose, and clients needed to make reservations to see me. Massage has become my profession for survival, and clients found relaxation in massage, making it a win-win situation.

Sometimes, our actions can subtly influence people around us, like giving up our seats or acting bravely in the face of danger, setting an example for others. However, some actions can only be responsible for oneself and cannot control others, like my roommate Wu Fang. She likes to do as she pleases, enjoys seeking pleasure alone, and ignores my advice. Character shapes destiny, and the environment can change nature. I would like to know if I will change tomorrow. I hope we achieve our dreams and life becomes colorful and beautiful.

Chapter 46

Sisters' Reunion of Love

Life is like a big tree, plucking a leaf randomly reveals a colorful poem; life is like a river, every wave carries a unique hue. We can blend into the current of reality, low-key and unnoticed, but we must not remain indifferent or underestimate ourselves. The paths we have traveled or are currently on, regardless of roughness or smoothness, success or failure, gain or loss, will always accumulate some experiences and lessons. We will find a few sparkling pearls in the hourglass-like flow of time. I write about my experiences, and though it records fragments of life, I hope that the places I have been leave behind markers, enabling those beside and behind me to see the direction to move forward.

During the 2006 Spring Festival, we celebrated with great joy and excitement. Several sisters from Nanxun came to Suzhou, including Sister Wu, Xiao Hong, A Ju, Ah Chun, Ah Fang, and Sister Xu, who used to tutor me in massage. They accepted my invitation to come and play. Hai Tang Chun had an eight-day break, and we could spend time together. We bought many quilts and slept on the floor in the rented room to chat freely.

Sister Xu mentioned that she was still running a training class, and business was doing well. Many girls from Jiangsu and Zhejiang areas couldn't find suitable jobs for a while, but there was a high demand for massage therapists, and after simple training, they could find employment. I understood their situation, as I was once in the same predicament when I first entered the massage field. There's no denying that it's a quick way to make money, and many girls in the entertainment industry find it challenging to stay in control. Those so-called "massage parlors," essentially venues for cash and sex exchanges, make it easy to get into this situation. "Getting on board is easy, but getting off is hard." Once aboard this treacherous ship, it's challenging to get away from it. Besides facing societal rejection, their minds will also be corroded. Only a lucky few will encounter a good man and be able to break free from the shadows, living a sunny life. Most of my sisters are merely muddling through.

Sister Wu and Wu Fang have made amends; the two sisters embraced each other, crying and laughing like children. Blood is thicker than water, and family bonds can resolve any hatred. It was just a moment of confusion, and now they understand it was not worth it for an unworthy man. Sister Wu and Xiao Hong are still in nightclubs; they've been in the industry for a few years and are getting too deep into it. I advised them to develop in Suzhou, but they were reluctant. Xiao Hong said that Nanxun is getting stricter, with some entertainment venues closing down, but they are managing okay. They've gotten used to living there and consider it their second home. Once they've saved enough money, they will return and marry. If no man is willing to marry them, they'll live as single women. I said, "When will you earn enough money? Living like that, it's easy to age. When women get old, there will be no one interested in them. It's better to settle down sooner." Xiao Hong laughed, saying, "I'm already old now, but I'm still attractive to men. It's not that I'm old; my heart is just tired. I don't care anymore. When I make a million, if I can't get married, I'll keep a toy boy to serve me!" Although Xiao Hong laughed, I could sense her helplessness.

Sister Wu was my guide in my massage career. She helped and might have hurt me, but I don't hold any grudges against her. A person's destiny is predetermined and self-selected, and I can't blame others; everything results from my choices. If I were willing to endure hardship, I might not have become a massage girl, and I could have worked as a laborer on a construction site. If I could remain steadfast, no matter how much money a man offers, he wouldn't be able to touch my heart. However, can I indeed be so noble? Vanity is a common problem for girls, and I also yearn for an easier job, a higher salary, and dressing up beautifully every day. However, those dreams can't come true. I can only strive as much as possible in my current life circle, digging for gold or, if not, brass. However, where will we find rewards if we don't give first? We may not have talents, but our capital is our youth. I hope to return to the right path and do what I believe is right in the messy massage industry.

We chatted incessantly and played cards together, and Sister Wu, Sister Xu, Xiao Hong, and Wu Fang were playing Mahjong. There were wins and losses, but it was all for fun, just a tiny matter to enjoy ourselves. I planned with Ah Chun, Ah Fang, and A Ju to visit Ah Lan's parents in Yancheng during the Qingming Festival to pay respects and clean her tomb. Ah Lan's fate was unfortunate, leaving us at such a young age. It was such a pity. Whenever I mentioned her, I couldn't help but feel sad and sigh. People's destinies are fragile; one day, they are here, and the next, they may be gone. Yesterday, they were carefree children; today, they've already experienced life's vicissitudes.

The wages in Nanxun are lower than in Suzhou. I advised them to come here and live together. Ah Fang said, "I've worked at Hai Tang Chun for three years; I have some attachment and many familiar customers. I also rely on it, and I'm too lazy to leave. If they close down, we'll come to seek refuge with you." I smiled, "Seek refuge with me? I'm not some big boss! I can only help you find a job." A Ju chuckled, "When we have enough money, we'll open a massage center together, be our bosses, and earn money for ourselves. We won't be oppressed or exploited by others anymore!" Ah Fang laughed, "You're daydreaming! Do you think it's easy to open a massage center? If you don't have connections, it won't last three days before someone kicks your business over! If you don't have the right connections, you won't be able to get the required licenses. What's the point of trying?"

Wu Fang couldn't keep the secret and revealed the story about me having a man in Suzhou, getting 200,000 yuan from him, and then donating the money to others. Everyone except Sister Xu, was extremely shocked. Sister Wu said, "Xiao Jing, have you gone mad? That money was compensation you deserved. How could you give it away like that?" Xiao Hong said, "That's right. Earning money isn't easy. You were hurt, and getting 200,000 yuan is some consolation. How could you so willingly give away the hard-earned money? Are you confused?" Wu Fang said, "I've advised her many times. I told her she was an idiot! Who still acts like Lei Feng these days? What does it have to do with her that someone else got leukemia? There are so many sick people in the world, and that's what the civil affairs department and the Red Cross should care about. What's the connection with us massage girls? She must be bored with nothing else to do!" Ah Fang and Ah Chun also said, "Ah Jing, what you did was wrong. Good people shouldn't be like this, right? We massage therapists don't need fame; we need practical benefits!" I could only smile without defending myself.

Sister Xu said, "I think Xiao Jing did a good thing. She thought of saving a life and could give away 200,000 yuan without hesitation. Her kindness is remarkable!" I felt embarrassed and said, "Sister Xu, you're praising me too much; I can't handle it." Sister Xu continued, "Xiao Jing is just a person like us. She works hard all day and only earns a hundred yuan, barely enough. But her kindness is something we should learn! Do you all remember? No matter where Xiao Jing works, she wins everyone's love. This isn't accidental; it shows she's doing things right and well, gaining everyone's respect! We work for money, but we can't just work for money; we need to change people's views by changing ourselves. I admire Xiao Jing's efforts. They're for herself and all massage therapists, creating a positive image for us all!" Sister Xu, in her thirties, is the oldest among us, and many are still her students. Everyone was receptive to what she said. Sister Wu and the sisters said, "Sister Xu is right, Xiao Jing is a great role model, and she's our favorite good sister!"

Sister Xu asked, "I wonder how the little boy is doing now? Has he recovered from his illness?" Wu Fang said, "Not long ago, the television station aired a special program about the little boy, Lu Jia Wei. The China Bone Marrow Bank found and successfully operated a matching donor for him. He's currently undergoing recovery treatment. The TV station mentioned Xiao Jing's donation again, saying that it was because of the 200,000 yuan that Lu's family could afford the expensive surgery, saving their son's life!" Sister Xu said, "Xiao Jing has transformed from an ordinary massage therapist into an angel-like young lady. She's truly remarkable, even better than I imagined!" I sincerely said, "Sister Xu, everything I've done is because of your influence. The words you said to me and the guidance you provided have taught me many life lessons. I should thank you!"

During these days, we tasted various local snacks, such as Lu Yang's wontons, Lu Changxing's noodles, Huang Tianyuan's pastries, Cai Zhi Zhai's preserved fruits, Ye Shouhe's candies, Lu Gaojian's cooked meat, and braised dried tofu, among others. I bought each of them half a pound of high-quality Bi Luo Chun tea and jokingly said, "Drinking tea is better than drinking alcohol; it helps with weight loss and beauty." Wu Fang chuckled, "Drinking tea is not good at all. I drank her tea once and couldn't sleep at night. I wanted to find a man, but she didn't let me. She made me suffer." I laughed, "Who asked you to snore while sleeping? I want you to fall asleep a bit later, so I can quietly watch TV." Sister Xu said, "Xiao Jing, you watch TV even though you finish work late?" I replied, "It's rare for me to watch TV. The drama 'Dae Jang Geum' was good, so I watched it daily." Sister Xu said, "That Korean drama was pretty good; I watched it too." Ah Chun chuckled, "We watch it when we go home too. During that time, we were exhausted, couldn't sleep during the day, and had to work at night. But when we got home, we couldn't resist watching it." Sister Wu said, "I never watch TV. What's the fun in that? I prefer spending time with men, drinking, dancing, and making money." Sister Xu laughed, "You've fallen into the money trap!"

For dinner, we ate at home. Sister Xu was excellent at cooking and prepared a table full of delicious dishes. The eight of us ignored our ladylike manners and devoured the food with gusto. Sister Wu said, "Anyone who can marry Sister Xu would be truly blessed. You'd have a good appetite every day!" Sister Xu smiled and said, "I prefer living alone. When I'm full, my whole family is full. As for men, I only use them when I need to. Otherwise, I can't be bothered with them!" Wu Fang laughed and said, "Men are my money pockets. If I don't have money to spend, I beckon, and they line up to give me money!" I playfully scolded, "Shameless! Do they give you money if you don't get along with them?" Sister Xu smiled and said, "Like sister, like sister. I see you two sisters. You'll never lack men or money in your lives!"

When the three women get together, and all eight of us are in one place, we become lively, laughing and chatting like a flock of sparrows holding a meeting. Even the neighbors upstairs and downstairs would knock on our door, asking us to keep it down as they couldn't rest. Wu Fang glared and said, "It was even noisier than this during your renovation. Did we complain? We rarely get together as sisters, so we want to have some fun. Please don't bother us! If you find it noisy, go on a trip!" The family was angry and couldn't say anything. I quickly said, "It's only a few days during the Spring Festival. Friends came to visit; please be understanding! Don't worry; we'll be careful!" I was afraid they would call security to handle it. If they made the sisters move out, it would ruin our mood. It's better to have peaceful coexistence among neighbors.

Despite our playful antics when together, everyone felt a bit sad when the time to part came. Wu Fang enjoys liveliness and prefers a festive atmosphere every day. As she hugged Sister Wu, she even shed a few teardrops. I hugged Sister Xu, Ah Fang, Ah Chun, and A Ju individually. There might be a farewell kiss for men and women, but among us women, we can only hug each other to express our affectionate goodbyes. I said, "Don't be sad. It would help if you had come here happily and left with joy. Whenever you have time, feel free to come and visit! Suzhou has many great places you haven't seen yet!" Sister Xu said, "Xiao Jing, Wu Fang, now only two of you are left here. Take good care of yourselves!"

Chapter 47

Rekindled Love

The fortune teller had mentioned that I had a "peach blossom" fate, which meant that before 30, my relationships with men would be somewhat chaotic, but after 30, I would become more steadfast and pure. For men, having a peach blossom fate was considered fortunate, indicating good luck in love. However, it was considered a calamity for women, which meant their love lives would be troubled. I had to wait until I turned 30 to distance myself from men, but that seemed distant since I was only 22 now, with a whole eight years ahead of me. The thought of this fortune-telling added uncertainty and anxiety to my heart.

That day was entertaining. Wu Fang and I visited the Xuanmiao Temple and saw a fortune teller setting up a small booth, attracting customers. We stopped to watch Despite knowing he was making things up. Someone had just paid him fifty yuan, claiming his predictions were highly accurate. I thought the fortune teller possessed some mystical power, but it turned out he had accomplices. He charged only two yuan for each reading but would ask for additional fees if he predicted any critical junctures in someone's life. These vital junctures were moments when a person might encounter disasters, and if they wanted to turn bad luck into good, they had to buy the fortune teller's help to avoid the calamity. Although his words were extravagant, I was skeptical. Wu Fang said, "Well, it's just two yuan. Let's have him read our fortunes."

The fortune teller was quite skillful. When he read Wu Fang's fortune, she only gave him her birthdate and time of birth, but he surprisingly told her she had a sister, leaving me amazed. He also said that Wu Fang could earn money but spent it as quickly as water flowing. He told her life was ordinary, and while she wouldn't face hardships, she didn't have strong support. Wu Fang asked, "Can you tell me if I'll meet my Prince Charming?" The fortune teller calculated and replied, "You won't meet a Prince Charming, but you'll encounter many men." I couldn't help but chuckle, and Wu Fang glared at the fortune teller, visibly annoyed. In the end, since Wu Fang's life was generally smooth and didn't require critical measures, she paid only two yuan. She was somewhat displeased and said, "If you had told me something more positive, I would have paid you two hundred yuan! Two yuan for my fortune is too ordinary!"

My experiences were similar to Wu Fang's, so I decided not to get my fortune read. After all, fortune-telling was superstitious, and a few words couldn't determine one's destiny. As I turned to leave, Wu Fang held me back and said, "No, you have to get your fortune read too. It's just two yuan. Let's see what he says." The fortune teller carefully observed my birthdate and said, "Miss, you have a peach blossom fate, but beware of love misfortunes. This year, you'll face more misfortune than good luck!" I retorted, "I'm working well. Where would I find any misfortune?" The fortune teller continued, "I won't hide it from you. In your lifetime, you'll be deceived by men three times, impacting your future. You've already experienced two, and there's one more crucial event. If you become careless, it could lead to a disaster!" Deceived by men? Twice? I racked my brain, thinking: Mr. Fang deceived me in Suzhou, which counts as one time. But what about the other time? Mr. Gao? Mr. Sun? Mr. Zhang? It didn't seem like them! Suddenly, I remembered being inexplicably cheated by someone wearing a watch at Sea Paradise, costing me over ten thousand yuan! That's right; it must be that time! But the fortune teller also said there would be one more severe case. When will that happen? I felt uneasy and anxious.

Wu Fang urged, "Tell her quickly! What's this one more case? You've said it; now, are you afraid we won't pay?" The fortune teller raised a finger, and Wu Fang said, "10 yuan?" The fortune teller shook his head, and Wu Fang said, "100 yuan? Are you too greedy? We agreed on two yuan; how did it jump to 100 yuan?" The fortune teller said, "The price depends on different destinies. Ordinary people pay two yuan, but I don't charge any money to those with terrible fortunes. However, the price differs for those with danger or great wealth in their destinies!" I MIGHT AS WELL HEAR HIM OUT since I had asked him to read my fortune. "Fine, tell me. What will happen to me?" I asked. The fortune teller said, "Based on your birthdate and the five elements of your fate, your life is good, and men find you attractive. You'll live a comfortable life, but at 25, you'll encounter a man with a rival fate. If you're not careful, it's possible to suffer physical harm. If you're cautious that year, don't trust others unthinkingly, and avoid disputes with men, you'll remain safe!" He continued, "Although you'll face accidents, you'll also encounter noble people who will help you avoid calamity. So, don't worry!" He said I'd encounter a rival fate at 25, and there were still three years ahead. Who knew if what he said was true or false? He also mentioned engaging noble people in the future; who could say if that would be true? People's destinies are unpredictable. "Good fortune may turn into misfortune, and misfortune may turn into good fortune." No one can predict it for sure.

Time passed quickly, and in the blink of an eye, it was already March of the following year. I had been in Suzhou for nearly two years. March in Yangzhou was known for its beautiful scenery, but I couldn't visit. During the Qingming Festival in early April, I had already planned with Sister Xu and others to go to Yancheng to pay respects at Ah Lan's tomb. I recalled reading Zhu Ziqing's prose "Hastiness," and he described it so well: "Time passes during washing hands, eating, and moments of silence..." Yes, like a river flowing eastward, the days were slipping away, and there was no way to retain them. I wanted to know how long I would continue working as a masseuse and if I would remain in Suzhou. There's a saying, "The more one thinks, the more troubles they have," and perhaps it was true. I did and thought a lot, but my life wasn't as joyous as Wu Fang's. She moved freely among the men, and I rarely saw her looking unhappy. She hummed the song "Traveling with Ease" all day, confidently tucking customers' tips into her bra and flirtatiously batting her eyes at them. Though we were as close as sisters and did the same work, we had different paths.

The second massage department was continuously hiring, not for regular employees but for part-time help on weekends. The newcomers were relatively young, around twenty years old, and had decent temperaments; some were very beautiful. Manager Xu didn't arrange any training; they went directly to serve customers. Wu Fang was in the second massage department, and I asked her about the new hires. She said, "Don't you know? They are university students working part-time during holidays and weekends!" I was puzzled and said, "This is considered part-time work for university students? Isn't it inappropriate?" Wu Fang replied, "University students are very open-minded now. They are stealing our business. You and I may become unemployed in the future. Nowadays, men prefer cultured women. When they hear 'female university student,' they get excited as if a cat saw a mouse. Without loyal customers, I would have struggled to make ends meet!" I was surprised. How could university students take on such a job? It seemed very unworthy!

Wu Fang said, "Nowadays, girls don't care what they do. They pursue fashion, wear stylish clothes, and use brand-name cosmetics. With just their pocket money, can they afford that? When I chat with them, I hear that wealthy men already support many beautiful girls. Every day after school, there's a car waiting to pick them up. Those with average looks who have yet to find a rich patron come to do part-time work. They call it 'social practice' at university. Some well-behaved girls work at KFC or McDonald's as temporary employees. The less attractive ones focus on their studies." I exclaimed, "How could this be? Even if they don't have pocket money, they shouldn't degrade themselves like this! I can't understand!" Wu Fang said, "Don't worry about them. They don't care! They say being a lover is wholesale, and being a mistress is retail. Since girls in society can do this, why can't they?" I was speechless. These university students must be the minority.

With university students doing part-time massages, it became a challenge for us. I wasn't worried about them taking my job. Instead, they added competition for regular masseuses, but it wasn't enough to affect my livelihood. They had the advantage of education; some could speak English fluently, which allowed them to entertain foreign clients. With good manners and a certain cultivation level, they could attract customers even if their massage skills needed to be improved. The second massage department at Hai Tang Chun was explicitly for men with a passionate mindset. The staff didn't need outstanding skills; they just had to be bold and able to let go of their pride, as it guaranteed them generous tips. I felt sorry for them; I didn't know where things went wrong for them to abandon their dignity so casually. They didn't understand that it was easy to tarnish themselves but difficult to cleanse themselves.

One day after work, I saw Wu Fang stepping out of the foot bath house, and a black car was waiting by the roadside for her. She smiled at me and got into the car before driving away. It was true that "women become bad for money." Now there were more passionate men than summer mosquitoes, and it was easy to make money from men. I had also encountered many men trying to be close to me, and they hoped I would leave the foot bath house and become their exclusive lover, promising me generous rewards. I declined their advances. I no longer needed to work part-time; I could save two to three thousand yuan each month. To others, it might not be much, but I was content. I couldn't control Wu Fang, but I could control myself.

I felt a bit bored at home in the evening, so I went to the nearby Auchan supermarket to buy some underwear and shower gel. I had dinner outside since Wu Fang wasn't home, and cooking alone felt like it could be more appealing. I didn't eat at KFC; it was too expensive, and the money I spent on four chicken legs there could buy a whole chicken at the market. Besides, it wasn't nutritious. I heard that regularly consuming grilled chicken legs could lead to weight gain and other health issues. I preferred eating Lanzhou noodles and "Da Niang" dumplings. They were cheap and delicious, filling my stomach well.

Leaving the supermarket with a shopping bag, I headed towards my rented place, which was not far away. It would only take ten minutes to walk, so I didn't take a taxi. As I reached an intersection, the traffic light turned red, and I stood on the roadside, waiting to cross. Just as the green light appeared, and I was about to walk across the road, I suddenly heard someone calling my name, "Xiao Jing! Xiao Jing, is that you?" Confused, I turned around, and a Honda car stopped beside me. When I looked at the driver, I was stunned! It was none other than Mr. Zhang! He smiled at me so familiarly and warmly!

He opened the car door and smiled, "Xiao Jing, I didn't expect to run into you here. Where are you going? Get in!" I got into the car, feeling somewhat excited, "Mr. Zhang, why is it you? This is such a surprise!" He chuckled, "Yes, time flies. It's been two years. How have you been, Xiao Jing?" I nodded, "Mr. Zhang, why are you in Suzhou? I thought you were in Huzhou?" I used to address him as "您" to show respect, but now, I directly call him "你," which feels more intimate. Mr. Zhang replied, "I just returned from Changshu and had business discussions with a few wholesalers there. I didn't expect to see you at this intersection. Xiao Jing, you're still so young and beautiful!" I smiled, "I was young to begin with. It's only been two years, so there hasn't been much change." Mr. Zhang said, "Where are you heading? I'll take you." I said, "I'm going home. Are you heading back to Huzhou?" Mr. Zhang replied, "It's okay. I'm alone now, and it doesn't matter if I go back a bit later. Let me take you home first."

My rented place was in the nearby community, and we arrived in a few minutes. Mr. Zhang parked the car, and we got out together. I said, "Mr. Zhang, you mentioned you're alone now. What happened?" Mr. Zhang lightly smiled, "The child has grown up and settled down. My wife got divorced, so I'm the only one left now." I couldn't believe it. Mr. Zhang was in his fifties; how could he get divorced from his wife? Their family had been together for over twenty years. How could it fall apart so easily? It was unbelievable! Mr. Zhang chuckled, "She didn't want to live with me anymore, so we had to divorce. Now, I feel that being alone has its benefits. I can go wherever I want without anyone nagging or monitoring me. Just like you, so free, isn't it?" I never got married, but I believed people need to keep growing—dating, marriage, and having children are essential parts of life. Mr. Zhang said, "Which floor do you live on? Let me take you up." I nodded, and we walked into the building together.

He was my first man; he used the money to buy my virginity. However, I willingly agreed to it so I couldn't blame him. His generosity gave me a sense of warmth and safety, changing my perspective on men and making me realize that there are good people among them, and not all are heartless. After learning about Ah Lan's situation, he readily gave me 100,000 yuan, which was not a small sum. He could have had his first time with dozens of girls with that money. Of course, Mr. Zhang would never do such a thing. I trusted him. That 100,000 yuan of lifesaving money was far more precious than the 200,000 yuan compensation I received from Mr. Fang later. We only met twice, and the second time, I even made an excuse to get away, but he didn't get angry. He was amiable, and I never had any repulsion towards him. I had always been grateful to him. It had been almost two years since we parted, and this accidental reunion brought me joy, and I wanted to chat with him properly. If it weren't for the feeling that he was unattainable to me, I would have wished to be his goddaughter and receive his fatherly love. Now I brought him home, and I didn't feel anything inappropriate.

I made a cup of tea inside the room and casually asked, "Mr. Zhang, have you eaten?" Mr. Zhang shook his head with a smile, "I haven't eaten yet. I had some drinks over there at noon. Since I needed to drive back, I didn't dare to drink again in the evening. Xiao Jing, have you eaten? How about we go out and eat something together?" I smiled, "I've already eaten. You can wait a while, and I'll cook for you." Mr. Zhang stood up and said, "No need, it's too much trouble for you to cook just for me." I smiled and said, "You can't go hungry either. You're a guest now, so you have to listen to me. I don't have many ingredients at home, so make fried rice with eggs for you." I turned around and went to the kitchen, asking Mr. Zhang to wait in the living room. Making fried rice with eggs was something I often did. It was relatively simple and saved the effort of buying and cooking vegetables. The taste was decent, and Wu Fang liked it.

A little over ten minutes later, I placed a steaming plate of fried rice with eggs on the coffee table in front of Mr. Zhang. I smiled and said, "There's nothing fancy, please bear with it." Mr. Zhang replied, "I didn't eat anything for lunch. I only had drinks and some dishes. Now, smelling your food, I'm starving." He lowered his head and quickly devoured the plate of fried rice, not leaving a single grain. I chuckled, "Even the big boss gets hungry sometimes. Just having fried rice might seem a bit humble." Mr. Zhang wiped his mouth with a tissue and smiled, "It's delicious! Tender and smooth, not inferior to the Yangzhou fried rice I've had. Xiao Jing, you should know that businessmen may enjoy delicacies, Maotai, and Fen liquor, but a simple homemade meal is more practical. Those fancy banquets are just for socializing in the business world. Even though we know it's wasteful, we have to attend them. Many people have stomach ulcers because they drink without eating." It was like two worlds apart. I was just a masseuse; how could I understand their life filled with many frustrations?

Being with Mr. Zhang, we had endless things to talk about. It felt like we were family or old friends, sharing our experiences over the past two years. I hid nothing and told him about leaving Haitian Paradise, working at Dongfang Bathhouse in Suzhou, my misunderstandings, and the deception I experienced from Mr. Fang. My desire to vent found complete relief, and speaking out made me feel lighter, mainly because he was sincerely listening. Living with Wu Fang, we rarely talked about our inner thoughts; we mostly just joked around. Mr. Zhang gave me the feeling he could understand my words and empathize with my emotions. Even if he quietly listened without advice, I felt comfortable and reassured.

He also shared some of his situations, such as the reason for his divorce, his concern for my friend Ah Lan, and his thoughts about me. He said he had no regrets; his child had become independent, and he would retire in a few years. But he didn't want to accept aging and was considering starting his own company and exploring investment opportunities. I joked, "Those in positions of power nowadays tend to embezzle a lot of money. Are you like that too?" Mr. Zhang laughed, "That thought does exist, especially at this stage. When you're about to retire, sometimes you might consider taking advantage of the remaining power, but I don't want to end my life on a bad note. So, I can confidently say that I haven't embezzled; I am clean." I laughed, "It's good that you haven't embezzled. If you commit a crime and end up in jail, I won't be able to see you again!" Mr. Zhang said, "With my current salary and bonuses, I earn two hundred thousand yuan a year, which is enough for me. Xiao Jing, if you ever feel that your current job isn't good enough, while I still have some power, I can help and transfer you to my department." I shook my head with a smile, "I like it here. The job is fine for now. Let's see about the future."

We had a great time chatting, and I made Mr. Zhang burst into laughter several times. The conversation brought us closer; it was already past nine in the evening. We were still interested in talking, and my mood was a mix of excitement and joy, with no sign of sleepiness. Mr. Zhang didn't mention leaving either, and I could sense that he was also in a good mood. Two years worth of experiences couldn't be discussed in just one evening. Should we sit down and chat all night? Should I ask Mr. Zhang to leave or invite him to stay?

Chapter 48

Intoxicated Night of Passion

On this quiet and late night, being alone together in one room with mutual affection, how could there not be any issues? In the eyes of a young girl, a man's age is not necessarily a problem. Men with power and influence, like Director Zhang, would likely captivate not just me but many other girls as well. He was wealthy, caring, and subconsciously, I had already regarded him as a benefactor. My feelings for Director Zhang were not love; they were more about gratitude. Nevertheless, I was willing to do anything for him.

As if we had an unspoken understanding and expectations, I led him into the room, and we embraced each other. My heart surged with passion and tenderness as I leaned against his shoulder, feeling a fleeting sense of being at home. It had been several months since I last had intimate encounters with a man, and sometimes, the spring desire would emerge. However, I didn't want to go down that path again. The past was like a dream. I had been intimate with many men during my time at Heaven Sauna, primarily due to my ignorance, confusion, and vanity. I was initially a traditional girl, and I admitted that I had been indulgent in the past. However, I didn't want to let myself continue down that path of evil.

I caught a faint smell of sweat from Director Zhang; it was a masculine scent, but I preferred something more refreshing. I led him into the bathroom and turned on the hot water. We stood together under the showerhead, and I washed him while he applied shower gel to me. Despite his age, he seemed like an obedient child. He said he had never taken a shower with his wife during their more than twenty years of marriage. Naturally, his wife had never given him a back rub either. Today was the first time he enjoyed such treatment, and felt immensely gratified. Exchanging details like this between men and women could add much fun to life.

After drying ourselves, he hugged me, and we were like lovers in the throes of passion as he laid me on the bed. He gently kissed my lips, and the rough stubble on his face made me a little uncomfortable, but I didn't shy away. The slight pain and itchiness made me infatuated. He caressed my skin, lightly laughing, "You used to massage me. Today, let me give you a massage." Though he lacked the skill of a professional masseuse, the sensation of his hands gliding over my body still stirred my heartstrings. He skillfully teased me, making me unable to help but let out a faint moan. Finally, we merged, experiencing the joy of reunion after a long separation...

With Wu Fang not at home, it was just the two of us, and we thoroughly enjoyed ourselves. His middle-aged body was still full of unending passion. I treated him as a man of passion, not just a wealthy boss. He laughed, "You've reignited my vitality." I asked with a smile, "What will you do when you miss being with a woman after your divorce?" He replied with a smile, "I'll endure it. I can't explain why I'm meeting you today, but the flames in my heart were ignited." I chuckled by his side, "I'm pleased to have met you." Perhaps, deep inside, girls never forget their first intimate encounter with a man.

His skin was smooth without any wrinkles, and his face had a healthy flush. Warmth and kindness radiated from his eyes, making me feel comfortable around him. I slept beside him, feeling as content as a hungry baby being fed, and I smiled sweetly, feeling a sense of relief and tranquility. I knew that I wouldn't be with Director Zhang for long. This time, I consider it as my repayment to him. I wouldn't place my love and hopes on him; it wasn't because I found him old but because I understood that we only had a destined connection, and he wasn't my final destination. He couldn't lead me to the shore of happiness.

In the past, there was a classic legend: by the roadside, there was a human skeleton exposed to the elements, ignored by everyone. One day, a scholar traveling to the capital to take the imperial exam passed by and saw the skeleton. Feeling compassionate, he covered it with a mat made of grass. Later, a merchant discovered the skeleton under the mat and was moved by pity, so he buried it properly. In the cycle of reincarnation, the skeleton transformed into a beautiful woman in the next life. She fell in love with the scholar and ended up marrying the merchant, and the two of them grew old together. If I compare myself to that woman, Director Zhang would be the scholar. His kind-hearted help made me genuinely grateful, but our story would end here; it wouldn't continue indefinitely.

At daybreak, I got up because I had to go to work at 7:30. Director Zhang was still sleeping, and I didn't wake him. Seeing him sleeping so peacefully, I inexplicably felt pity for him. He was in his fifties, divorced, and his children were not by his side. He was lonely, and no matter how much money and power he had, what was the point? He could find a moment of comfort with me, allowing him to temporarily set aside the worries that had consumed him for half a lifetime, and that made me happy. Perhaps our encounter was destined, and we couldn't explain the nature of our relationship. Sometimes I treated him as a father, sometimes as an elder brother, and sometimes, I felt he was like a child. I felt gratitude, repayment, and tenderness towards him—all willingly given. This was a complex yet simple emotion, and I couldn't fully explain it. Maybe it was karma from a past life that I needed to repay in this lifetime.

As I was about to leave, Wu Fang returned home. Her eyes were filled with redness, and dark circles surrounded them, indicating her tiredness. I quickly asked, "Wu Fang, what happened? Are you sick?" Wu Fang tearfully replied, "I was exhausted last night, and they only brought me back in the morning!" Shocked, I opened my mouth and angrily said, "They used you all night? That's too much!" Wu Fang waved her hand and said, "Sigh, it's my own doing! They kept me busy all night, and now I'm sore." I scolded, "Are you out of your mind? How much money did they give you to make you act like this?" Wu Fang said in pain, "The three of them gave me 1,500 yuan. I got the short end of the stick!"

Wu Fang's eyes widened as she noticed a pair of men's shoes on the shoe rack by the door. She couldn't help but jump up and exclaim, "Jingjie, you broke the rules! Did you bring a man home overnight?" I whispered, "He's an old friend of mine. He's a good person. I happened to run into him while shopping last night." Wu Fang chuckled, "You had a good time while I was away, didn't you?" I laughed, "No, we didn't do anything that bad." Wu Fang playfully tapped my forehead and said,

"Don't lie. Who's this man that has captivated your heart?" I held her back and said, "Stop being silly. He's sleeping right now. Don't wake him up. Wu Fang, I have to go to work. What about you?" Wu Fang leaned back on the sofa and said, "I'm too tired. Can you help me ask for a day off?" I said, "Fine, but if you act like this again next time, I won't care even if you die!" Wu Fang exclaimed, "You're so heartless. We're like sisters in the same trench!"

Wu Fang stayed at home, and I was a little worried. Director Zhang was sleeping in my room, and Wu Fang was resting at home. I genuinely worried that something might happen between them. Although I wasn't Director Zhang's lover, when he was here with me, he belonged to me. If someone had ideas about him, it would be an infringement on my "rights." I knew Wu Fang's character well. If she learned that Director Zhang had power, money, and good looks, she wouldn't hesitate to pursue him, even though he was my guest. Wu Fang had quarreled with her sister over a man before, so what would stop her from doing the same with me? I didn't know if Director Zhang could resist her temptation rationally. Of course, my worries might be unnecessary, as some things are destined to happen, and no one can avoid them.

I went to Manager Xu to ask for a day off for Wu Fang, and he agreed without asking too many questions. It didn't matter if the Massage Department was short-staffed for a few days, and besides, Wu Fang had voluntarily changed from a fixed salary to a commission-based salary. She earned a percentage of each business transaction, so the harder she worked, the more she made. I still enjoyed a fixed monthly salary, but as a massage therapist in the Massage Department, my treatment was much better than that of the averaLady Gessage girl. No matter what profession you pursue, you could find a foothold in today's society if you master specific skills. You could see that even ragpickers and beggars sometimes struck it rich.

One thing caused quite a stir among us. The building opposite Hai Tang Chun, where a building materials shop used to be, was undergoing grand renovations. It was rumored that several businessmen from Zhejiang had bought the building to open a "Floral ALady Gessage Parlor." This was an intense competition, clearly aiming to steal our business. Zhejiang businessmen always had vision and ambition. Sichuan people were known for working as migrant workers, while Zhejiang people were known for their business acumen. The three bosses of Hai Tang Chun were getting nervous, and they spent the past few days behind closed doors discussing countermeasures. Manager Xu sent some staff to gather information to find out what services they planned to offer in their massage parlor. It was said that they intended to provide similar benefits to those in Bali, offering massages for both men and women. They recruited minority girls from Yunnan and other places as female attendants, while the male massage therapists were recent graduates from formal massage training schools. I thought about how Old Gao from Oriental Bathhouse had plans to do something similar but failed to achieve it, and now these Zhejiang businessmen might beat him to it.

During work, I was constantly thinking about home. Did Director Zhang leave? Did Wu Fang strike up a conversation with him? What was happening between them? As soon as I finished work, I hurriedly rushed back home. When I passed by an alleyway, I saw several men standing there. I rode my bicycle and rang the bell, trying to avoid them carefully, but they wouldn't let me pass. My bike's front accidentally bumped into a man's waist, and I quickly apologized, "I'm sorry, I'm sorry!" Unexpectedly, they all stood there like mute statues. No one said a word, and then they suddenly crowded around me, trapping me in the middle!

Someone held my arm, someone grabbed my waist, and someone had my legs, dragging me off my bicycle! Panicked, I shouted, "Let me go! What do you want?" They quickly moved and pushed me into a nearby van, my mind was in a daze, and I couldn't understand what was happening. They slammed the car door shut with a loud bang, and with me inside, the van sped away toward the outskirts...

Chapter 49

Youthful Stirrings

This was my first time encountering such an unexpected situation, and I felt extremely nervous! I had seen scenes like this on television before. Could they be kidnapping me? I yelled in the car, "Stop the car! I want to get out!" However, I was sandwiched between two men and couldn't move! I thought, "This is bad. Where are they taking me? What are they going to do to me? Assault and murder? Or do they want to extort money from me?" But I was just a masseuse, where would I have any money? I felt terrified, and even though I tried to remain calm, my body couldn't help but tremble.

After driving for about ten minutes, we arrived at an industrial area and stopped in front of a semi-new building. This was the first time I had been to this place, but based on their route, it should be in the northeastern corner of the industrial park. This area used to be a village, but now it belongs to the industrial park. It was remote, and I had never been here before. The three men and the driver surrounded me and took me to a second-floor office. Inside, I saw two young men sitting there. One was short and fat, while the other was tall and handsome with a slender figure. When they saw me coming in, they scolded the men who brought me in, "What's going on? We asked you to bring a lady here, not kidnap her! How will you handle more important matters if you can't even handle such a simple task? Apologize to the lady!" Those men approached me and bowed, saying, "Miss, we're sorry for what happened earlier. Please forgive us!" I thought to myself, "Are they mute? Why didn't they speak earlier? Why did they bring me here without any explanation?"

I used to be nervous when facing unexpected situations, but once I calmed down, I wouldn't be so afraid anymore. What's the use of being scared? I needed to figure out their intentions and find a way to leave immediately. I asked, "I don't know you, and you brought me here. What is the meaning of this?" The short and fat man smiled and said, "Miss, it was a misunderstanding! We brought you here to discuss something with you." He seemed genuine, but I didn't know their identities. If they were thugs or gangsters, it would be troublesome. Some of my friends had encountered such situations, being extorted for protection money. I said, "We don't know each other, and there's nothing to discuss." Then, the handsome man named Wu Jianhao said, "Miss, please don't be nervous. We don't have any ill intentions! We brought you here because we wanted to ask for your help. Please, sit down, and we can talk."

He told the other men at the door, "You can leave now. This is none of your business." Then he introduced himself, "Let me introduce ourselves. I'm Wu Jianhao, and he's Tian Dajun. We are good friends. You are Lai Xiao Jing from Haitangchun, right?" I almost laughed. Was he called Wu Jianhao? Wasn't that a celebrity from F4? But the star Wu

Jianhao wasn't as handsome as the man before me. I nodded and said, "You know me, but I don't know you. Why did you bring me here halfway? My bicycle is still on the roadside!" Tian Dajun chuckled, "Miss, as long as you agree to cooperate with us, we can give you more than just a bicycle. Even if you want a Xiali car, it's just a matter of a word!" I looked at him in surprise, "What do you mean? I don't understand."

In the office, it was just the three of us. Tian Dajun politely said, "Don't be so nervous. Inviting you here was inappropriate, but our sincerity is genuine. We've been running a mold factory in Suzhou for a few years and often enjoy our leisure time. Recently, we want to start a new project. You must have seen it—across the street from Haitangchun, we bought a building almost ready for renovation. Our business project is somewhat similar to yours but more creative. We are planning to open a "Splendid Youth" massage parlor. We invested several million yuan and will adopt the business model of Bali, aiming to expand the massage industry in this excellent Feng Shui spot in Suzhou!" They were wealthy, around thirty years old, and making significant moves. They were not simple characters! I said, "Oh, so that's your place. Opening a business across from us isn't very nice, right?"

Wu Jianhao said, "From a traditional perspective, it might seem like we are taking away Haitangchun's business, and I'm sure your boss thinks that too. But in reality, more shops lead to a bustling market. If our two businesses open together, we can attract more customers. Competition leads to development, you know? Do you know about Pepsi and Coca-Cola? They both sell similar drinks and face fierce competition, but aren't they both world-renowned multinational companies now? So, we shouldn't fear competition; we should turn it into motivation..." He treated me like an employee, conducting a meeting with me. I interrupted him and said, "I don't understand these high-sounding principles. I want to know why you brought me here. I have guests at home, and I need to return soon!"

Wu Jianhao said, "Since Miss Lai is straightforward, let's cut to the chase. We invited you here today because we want you to join our Splendid Youth. Not only you but also your colleagues. Of course, you can rest assured about the rewards. We will offer you a salary several times higher than what you are getting now! Miss Lai, how does that sound?" I was dumbfounded! Were they asking me to poach employees from Haitangchun? How could I do such a thing? I replied, "Didn't you already hire good service staff?" Tian Dajun said, "We have hired some, and the school is currently training them. But they are all newcomers. Although they are from ethnic minorities and have some appeal and novelty to the guests, they lack influence. We are inviting you not necessarily to serve the guests directly but as the image spokesperson for Splendid Youth. We will put up your large portrait outside as an advertisement. Your fame in the massage industry will surely have a great promotional effect. Additionally, we would like you to head to the massage parlor. What do you think?"

Their proposal sounded reasonable and tempting. At least, it offered better conditions than my current job. But could I accept it? I wouldn't say I liked the ungrateful and treacherous type of people. Even if I were to join Splendid Youth and gain fame and more money, would I feel at ease? Cash is always good, but I will only accept things against my principles. Don't think that masseuses only care about money; we also have emotions, kindness, and principles. Some masseuses might deceive men for their feelings and cash or engage in questionable activities, especially those fake masseuses at roadside shops, which damages the overall image of masseuses. However, no matter what, I couldn't hastily accept the offer from Splendid Youth, let alone take colleagues away from Haitangchun.

I firmly said, "This is impossible! I cannot agree to your request!" Tian Dajun asked, "Why? You can quit your current job and work for us; they can't do anything about it. What's wrong with that?" I replied, "I can't do that. My job is going well now. Why should I quit? How would people see me if I just left like that? Won't I become a traitor?" Wu Jianhao said, "Water flows to low ground, and people seek higher ground. This is reasonable. Don't worry about it. As long as you are willing to come, we guarantee to give you a car. You won't have to ride a worn-out bicycle to work anymore. Why not take this opportunity?" I shook my head again and said, "I don't want to leave Haitangchun for now. If I ever consider leaving, I will consider applying to your place. It's already getting dark; please let me go. I have friends waiting for me at home!"

Wu Jianhao said, "Miss, we respect your decision. Take your time to consider; we will always welcome you to join us! We apologize for taking the liberty to invite you today. Also, we hope you won't make our meeting public, okay?" I nodded, "I understand. But my bicycle is gone. How do I get back?" Tian Dajun said, "Come with me, and I'll accompany you to buy a new one!" He drove me to the supermarket, and in no time, he pushed a brand-new Giant bicycle in front of me, smiling, "How about it? You lost an old one, and we gave you a new one. As they say, out with the old, in with the new!" My old bicycle was only worth a few dozen yuan, and this new bicycle was worth several hundred yuan. I didn't lose out; I even made a profit. I said, "You kidnapped me and bought me a bicycle. You got off cheap!" Tian Dajun chuckled, "What's just a bicycle? If you come to Splendid Youth, we'll have much better things to offer you!"

When I returned home, Wu Fang was busy hanging clothes. It was pretty unusual; she usually wouldn't even bother washing her socks, wearing disposable stockings that she would throw away after a day's use. She wouldn't even bother throwing her clothes into the washing machine when they got dirty. I laughed and said, "Did the sun rise from the west today? Why are you suddenly so diligent?" Wu Fang replied, "You get to be an all-around handywoman, and I'm not allowed to become self-sufficient?" I chuckled, "Alright! I won't have to do it alone with you doing laundry and cooking. I have a good helper now." When I approached her, I noticed her left cheek was slightly swollen and asked, "What happened to your face? Do you have mumps?" Wu Fang touched her face and said, "It's nothing. I must have slept on it the wrong way."

I was not concerned about Wu Fang but about Mr. Zhang. When I went to work in the morning, he still slept in my room. Now, why couldn't I find him? I opened my room, but there was no one inside. The bed was neatly made. I asked, "Fang Fang, did he leave?" Fang Fang hummed in response. I continued, "When did Mr. Zhang leave? Did he leave a message for me?" Wu Fang said, "Isn't his car downstairs? He was waiting for you at home, and it bothers me that you didn't return. He might have gone to find you, or he might have left." Wu Fang's ambiguous words confused me. Did he go back or come to find me? Did he not leave any message at all? I asked, "Did he say anything before leaving?" Wu Fang looked at me strangely and asked, "Why would he say anything? In his eyes, there's only you, Xiaojing, where do I fit in? If he had something to say, he would only tell you, not me."

Wu Fang's jealous tone left me puzzled. I knew Mr. Zhang liked me, but he had never said sweet words to me. He was reserved and understood that we didn't have a future together. But why would he leave without saying goodbye? Was Wu Fang content to stay in her lane, or was she trying to tempt Mr. Zhang proactively? I couldn't imagine a man ignoring an opportunity that was right in front of him. Could he resist Wu Fang's youthful charm? Did Mr. Zhang stay at my place all day long? Has he left? I faintly felt that Wu Fang's expression was strange as if she had encountered some setbacks, lost in thought. I worried that she might be seeing Mr. Zhang behind my back. Or perhaps she was jealous of my connection with Mr. Zhang and drove him away?

Initially, Mr. Zhang was unrelated to me, but our encounter changed that. After our first meeting, we could have gone our separate ways, but I went to find him later, and he readily helped me. Last night was our third encounter, and we became intimate again. Ultimately, I respected him and was also captivated by his generous character. Women are selfish creatures, and even though he doesn't belong to me, I didn't want other women to share his affection. I wished he could stay a little longer and we could spend more time together. In the future, I will remember him, and I will love my future husband. He will become a beautiful memory in my heart.

Chapter 50

A Bewildering Enigmatic Fire

There's a saying that if a woman can't even control her body, she won't be able to keep a secret. The truth speaks louder than words, and Wu Fang was such a person. I didn't ask her about Mr. Zhang's departure, but she couldn't hold it two days later and voluntarily confessed. Her words made me have more respect for Mr. Zhang. He was a decent man, although a bit lecherous, he knew when to draw the line. Nowadays, the situation is different from before, being too straightforward won't get you far, and one may even be eliminated. I couldn't deceive myself; he was my benefactor, not my lover. This decision was not based on societal norms; it was my heart's answer.

That morning, she was too tired and fell asleep on the sofa. She didn't even bother to check if a stranger was in the room. When she woke up in the afternoon, she was covered with a blanket, which puzzled her. Upon reviewing the room, she discovered a middle-aged man taking a nap. She then remembered that he was my friend and didn't wake him up. Feeling hungry, she went to the kitchen to find something to eat. There, she saw several dishes on the table, obviously prepared by the man since no one else was home. After enjoying the meal, a thought crossed her mind – this man was good. Why did Sister Jing have such good luck while the men she encountered were all scoundrels?

Wu Fang approached Mr. Zhang, intentionally lying on my bed and trying to seduce him with her words and gestures. Unexpectedly, Mr. Zhang remained like a monk, not only unresponsive to her advances but also advised her to be a sensible and good girl, not to misbehave. Wu Fang disagreed and expressed her willingness to be his mistress, even curling up in his arms and acting spoiled. In response, Mr. Zhang sternly rebuked her and even slapped her! Wu Fang said she was furious and quarried with Mr. Zhang, even scratching his face with her nails. Wu Fang also claimed that Mr. Zhang had initially intended to wait for my return, but her persistence made him leave with a visibly unpleasant expression. I asked, "Did he say nothing when he left?" Wu Fang said, "He did. He said he would come to see you when he has time."

I assume that what Wu Fang said was mostly true, but there might be some omissions regarding her face. How could he slap her if she didn't do anything excessive with Mr. Zhang's status and demeanor? Moreover, it's likely he preached many principles to her. Otherwise, how come I found her behaving better when I returned home? I was curious if there would be another chance to meet him. Even if we meet again, what then? Time will turn everything into the past. Regarding Mr. Zhang, Wu Fang had heard from her sister that he was a sophisticated boss. "Marrying (hitching with) a rich man" is a girl's dream. When Mr. Zhang appeared in front of her, she might unilaterally promote herself, ultimately scaring Mr. Zhang away.

I didn't believe that marrying a rich man would lead to happiness. How deep is the courtyard in the rich man's home? Many women who married into wealthy families ended up being neglected, full of regret. The fickleness of rich men is often unreliable. Businessmen are busy with work and social engagements; they may indulge outside while remaining indifferent to their longing wives. The saying goes, "The home may be flying the red flag, but colorful flags are waving outside." Those who frequent nightclubs and massage parlors are 80% married men, reveling in the night, seldom thinking of giving gifts or warmth to their families. The most admired loving couples are primarily ordinary working-class people who diligently endure hardships together. Marrying a wealthy man may gain wealth, but you could lose the person.

In Suzhou's main streets, there were fully armed police patrols. I saw them carrying submachine guns, exuding an aura of authority as they walked through the streets, giving citizens a sense of security. The public safety here is relatively good, and with these police, they can prevent problems before they occur and swiftly deal with illegal activities. In our Hai Tang Chun, although it is not a major thoroughfare, we often fear the presence of criminals when leaving work late at night. Now it's different, no need to worry anymore. I stopped engaging in transactions involving money and favors, and my heart became more at ease. I no longer needed to avoid the gaze of the police when I saw them. After dating Ge Weiming, I understood that the police are ordinary people too. They don't have any grudges against us; they maintain social stability. If we don't break the law, we can live peacefully and worry-free.

Wu Jianhao and Tian Dajun haven't come to see me these days. They might have given up on the idea of cooperating with me. No matter their conditions, I'm afraid I have to disagree. Yesterday, I saw that "Floral Elegance" has been partially renovated, and workers were installing neon lights. These neon lights emit dazzling brilliance at night. The decoration of Floral Elegance, both inside and out, is much more upscale than our Hai Tang Chun. Local businessmen have conservative thinking; although they develop new marketing strategies, their implementation is slow and indecisive. They need to gain the daringness of businessmen from Zhejiang. For instance, Mr. Gao thought of emulating Bali's massage concept but has yet to act. Now, Floral Elegance has taken the lead. I may need help understanding business, but I comprehend the meaning of seizing opportunities. Opportunities are fleeting, and if seized in time, they will stay put.

Floral Elegance stands out conspicuously in this area. Its pink exterior walls are adorned with numerous roses, making the whole building look like a luxurious palace with a bright and tasteful style. Even before its official opening, it has already caught the attention and interest of passersby. I didn't become their spokesperson; their current outdoor advertisements feature stills from the movie "In the Mood for Love," showing Maggie Cheung and Tony Leung gazing affectionately at each other, creating a compelling appeal. They are scheduled to open on March 18th, and the service staff wearing ethnic minority costumes have already caught people's attention with their beautiful attire. I can faintly see their massage beds from the second floor of Hai Tang Chun. From here, I'll be able to see how their business fares in the future.

March 15th is Consumer Rights Protection Day, and newspapers, television, and shopping malls are all actively engaged in activities. Some complaints that had been unresolved have finally reached a satisfactory conclusion today. Why have these businesses waited until today to address consumers' concerns? Some even invited television stations to report the news, giving the impression that they were putting on a show and not genuinely serving consumers. Sometimes, dealing with these unscrupulous businessmen requires using clever tactics. Wu Fang bought a pair of leather shoes at a shopping mall, and the heels came off the next day. She went to seek an explanation, and although the store agreed to repair them, they refused to exchange or refund the shoes. Wu Fang was furious and decided to stay at the shoe counter, planning to retaliate in kind! Whenever someone came to look at the shoes, she would say that the shoes' quality was subpar and that they were selling counterfeit products. She warned people not to buy them, as the store won't offer refunds. After hearing her words, who would dare to make a purchase? Unable to deal with her, the store was afraid of her negatively impacting their regular business and had to give her a full refund, compensating her with an additional thirty yuan for transportation expenses. Wu Fang said, "This is called 'gracious before force'; they showed no mercy, so they can't blame me for being unyielding!" Those businesses that don't treat consumers seriously need to be shown a little tough love, so they understand that disrespecting consumers will lead to dire consequences!

The new store's opening chose a supposedly auspicious date, like the 8th, 18th, or 28th, for a "prosperous" start. It's the same with weddings; whenever there's a date with an eight, the streets are filled with wedding cars, and everyone rushes to get married on the same day. Do they all plan to have children on the same day too? There's a saying that last year was the "widow year," and next year will be the "bachelor year." So, this year, many people are rushing to register for marriage. It's amusing; today, why are people still so superstitious? As long as two people genuinely love each other, any day is good for getting married. Even the most auspicious date won't bring them happiness if they don't cherish their love.

On March 17th, probably a little after 11 pm, I had just finished giving a massage to a client and was washing my hands by the water basin when suddenly, I heard the piercing sirens of a fire engine coming from the road! We opened the curtains to take a look and were shocked beyond words! What we saw sent shivers down our spines! The Floral Elegance massage parlor diagonally across the street was engulfed in raging flames! Sparks flew from the windows, and black smoke billowed from the rooftop. We could hear occasional crackling sounds, and the choking smoke wafted our way. One fire engine after another sped toward the scene, leaving us in a state of bewilderment!

Didn't they finish renovating and plan to open tomorrow? How could it suddenly catch fire tonight? As massage therapists, we didn't need to take pleasure in others' misfortunes. Even though the owner of Hai Tang Chun is not in the store, if they find out that a massive fire is devouring Floral Elegance, they might be unable to contain their laughter, right? The rival they worried about may have just vanished into thin air! The girls just stared blankly, with no one uttering a word. Who could have done this? Who is behind this dark act, destroying Floral Elegance on the eve of its grand opening? If this were intentional, it would be fierce and heartless! People can do business in their way, each with their unique methods, but to deliver a fatal blow from behind seems quite evil. Is the business world a battlefield where one must fight to the death?

While the fire over there was still not extinguished, I saw a group of people not fighting the fire but instead holding sticks, aggressively charging toward Hai Tang Chun! An ominous premonition flashed through my mind! I called the police on my phone while quickly running to the second-floor entrance and shouted to the startled girls nearby, "Quick, help me close the iron grille door in the corridor!" Some of them also saw the group of people about to storm into Hai Tang Chun and realized the danger. They rushed to help. We had just locked the iron grille when we heard a loud bang from downstairs, followed by smashing things. The people downstairs could not reach the second floor, and we bought some time by locking the door. That loud noise seemed to be the embroidery screen at the entrance being shattered! A cacophony of voices came from below, with several people shouting and screaming. Among the chaos were sounds of things being destroyed and female staff members crying out in fear! The scene downstairs must be in utter disarray. We exchanged anxious glances and waited eagerly for the rescue from the police!

Chapter 51

No Part-Time Jobs for Me

The situation escalated beyond our expectations. Those people came with great force, and at night, with our boss absent, who knew what serious consequences could unfold? We were a bit panicked. I immediately called the police, and they assured me they were already on their way. I also called Manager Xu, who sounded frantic and said, "How could this happen? I'll notify Mr. Chen and Wang, and you report it to the police immediately!" I told him I had already done so, and he replied, "I'll be there soon. Be careful!" A few minutes later, several police cars arrived with sirens blaring. From our window, we saw that group of people, armed with sticks, rushing out of the lobby and dispersing in all directions. The brave police officers chased after them, apprehending a few and loading them into police cars.

My colleagues and I opened the iron grille door in the corridor and rushed down to the first-floor lobby. Everything was in disarray—embroidery screens, service counters, windows, chairs, and stools were all shattered and scattered across the floor. In just a few minutes, the lobby became a sorry sight! We had never experienced such a scene before. The fire at Floral Elegance was already horrifying enough, but we never expected our foot massage parlor to suffer! The police questioned the frightened staff members, who were not physically harmed; those people had only vandalized the place without attacking them. Some staff members told the police that the vandals mentioned coming for revenge, intending to damage and set fire to the site! My heart trembled at the thought that the people upstairs would have nowhere to escape if they had put it on fire! Fortunately, the timely arrival of the police prevented further deterioration.

Upon seeing the lobby in ruins, Manager Xu arrived and asked in bewilderment what had happened. None of us knew, and it was bizarre that those people had charged in and wreaked havoc. Shortly afterward, Big Brother Wang also arrived, and upon witnessing the fire at Floral Elegance across the street and the disorder in his establishment, he began to piece things together. He said to Manager Xu, "It might be a misunderstanding." Big Brother Wang then called the staff members from the second and third floors to clean up and tidy the first floor. After everything was in order, they were allowed to go off-duty. The police took Manager Xu, Big Brother Wang, and several staff members from the first floor to the police station for questioning and to give statements.

The fire at Floral Elegance had stirred quite a sensation, attracting the attention of the media and the public. They advertised in newspapers and on television to gain publicity, announcing the grand opening on March 18. Now, with the fire ruining their plans, it was inevitable that rumors and speculations would arise. Seeing their million-dollar-decorated massage parlor turn into a charred building was truly heart-wrenching! I arrived at Hai Tang Chun early the next day to inquire about the situation. It was said that the boss of Floral Elegance had hired the group of people. Upon learning that Floral Elegance, about to open, caught fire, Wu Jianhao immediately suspected that Hai Tang Chun was behind it. As Floral Elegance's opening would inevitably impact Hai Tang Chun's business, he guessed that Hai Tang Chun had used underhanded tactics. Outraged, he ordered the factory workers to bring weapons and vandalize Hai Tang Chun, seeking revenge! Manager Xu and Big Brother Wang vehemently denied any involvement in the arson. Big Brother Wang claimed that Floral Elegance was merely located next to Hai Tang Chun and that he would never do anything so outrageous. They had wronged us!

The people from Hai Tang Chun returned last night. The vandals who came to smash and destroy our things were all apprehended by the police and detained at the police station, undergoing further investigation. Around noon, Mr. Chen rushed back from Nanjing. He was in Nanjing for business negotiations, planning to open another massage parlor. He hurried back quickly after hearing about the fire at Floral Elegance and the inexplicable attack on Hai Tang Chun. After inspecting the situation, he asked Manager Xu to take photos of the lobby. Then he contacted the decoration company to repair the first-floor decor and restore operations as soon as possible. He also mentioned that if the closure lasted too long, loyal customers might be lost, as they would find other places to go, and it would be hard to attract back. Manager Xu gave the staff members a three-day break, and they would resume regular work after three days.

Two days later, I received news that the police had concluded that the fire at Floral Elegance was not a deliberate act but an accidental fire.

The police had found the ignition point and identified the actual cause of the fire. As it turned out, Floral Elegance was brightly lit the night before the grand opening to celebrate the occasion. The central air conditioning was also running. Due to poor electrical circuit design during the renovation and subpar materials used by the electricians, the wires did not meet the required standards, resulting in overheating and igniting the interior decorations, causing a massive fire! The private rooms of Floral Elegance were all decorated with logs, and when the fire broke out, everything went up in flames, reducing the three-million-worth renovation to ashes! The two bosses acted impulsively, thinking that their competitors were to blame, and their first suspect was Hai Tang Chun. Consequently, they resorted to sending people to vandalize our establishment.

On March 21, Hai Tang Chun reopened its doors after a fresh renovation. The new decor had even more local characteristics. The entrance was adorned with a moon cave gate, and in the middle of the lobby, there was a small pavilion and an artificial mountain, complete with stone benches where customers could sit and rest, feeling like they were in a garden. The corridors of the private rooms on the second and third floors were paved with crushed eggshells, which, when walked on barefoot, had health benefits, making it more relevant to a foot massage parlor. Surprisingly, Chen, the boss, took inspiration from the attack, which was commendable. Manager Xu confided that after mediation by the police, the bosses of Floral Elegance had compensated Hai Tang Chun with a total of three hundred thousand yuan, including the value of damaged items, renovation costs, and the revenue lost during the three-day closure. The vandals received punishment in the form of administrative detention.

Manager Xu also mentioned that Chen and the boss of Floral Elegance were discussing the possibility of purchasing the burned building and opening a branch of Hai Tang Chun opposite the road to expand their business. If the deal were to be struck, the previously recruited staff members could also stay. I chuckled, remarking, "Isn't Chen taking advantage of the situation?" Manager Xu replied, "In Zhejiang, a burned building is considered inauspicious, and people usually sell it off cheaply. But in Suzhou, a lively and prosperous business is encouraging!" Businesspeople's minds can be peculiar. What is good about a building that caught fire? I felt sorry for Wu Jianhao and the others. A natural disaster coupled with artificial trouble—no one could predict it. Their investment of millions went down the drain, and they had to pay an additional three hundred thousand as a painful lesson.

I learned that Chen and Wu Jianhao had yet to agree a few days later. Wu Jianhao wanted to sell but wanted to sell to something other than Chen. Perhaps it was due to the narrow-mindedness of businessmen; they were unwilling to see their competitors succeed. In light of the fire, the public security fire department conducted a comprehensive inspection of all entertainment venues in the city to eliminate potential hazards and prevent accidents.

Although the fire at Floral Elegance had caused some lingering fear, it was over now, and our work and life had returned to normal. I thought I would work for another three years, accumulate some capital, and then open my beauty salon. I'd start with a small one, experiencing the feeling of being a boss. I could follow Sister Xu's example and run a massage training course if I wanted something more accessible. The income should be good too, as people were spending more and more on leisure and entertainment. Nowadays, finding a job requires many certificates, and fake certificates are ubiquitous. There are even phony virginity certificates now. Yet people believe in these lies and deceive themselves and others.

Recently, I met an online friend who was studying in Australia. He said, "In China, prostitution is illegal, but it seems everywhere. It's easy to find one, but in Australia, it's legal, yet not so easy to find." I asked why, and he replied, "The tighter the control, the stronger people's curiosity. When it's more relaxed, people become accustomed to it, and very few are interested in prostitutes." I asked him playfully how much it would cost for such services over there. He said it was 160 Australian dollars, equivalent to 1000 RMB. I laughed and said, "That's not expensive." He said that not everyone in foreign countries is wealthy, and rich-poor disparities exist everywhere. Women engaged in such work in Australia mostly come from impoverished areas, and this is the means they use to survive.

We had an amiable chat. He knew I was a massage therapist and asked if I did part-time work. I honestly replied, "I used to, but not anymore." As we were chatting online, and he was overseas, I wasn't worried about him harassing me. So, I felt at ease talking to him, but we were both polite and knew where to draw the line with our jokes. I heard that nowadays, many people engage in online sexting, which is even more shameless than being a prostitute! Those women are hypocrites, and those so-called gentlemen are self-righteous. We don't care to play such boring games.

He told me that if he were in China, he would come and find me, hoping to be just ordinary friends. He didn't believe that being a masseuse was a stain. After all, no one is perfect; as long as your heart is kind, your virtues can overshadow imperfections. He introduced himself as Mr. Fan, 26 years old, and he would return to China after completing his studies abroad. I joked, "You're not a descendant of the character Fan

Jin from the Chinese classic 'Rulin Waishi,' are you?" He laughed and replied, "So what if I am? Fan Jin's madness was not his fault; he was also a victim. How many others have been misled by the civil service examination system?"

This overseas student, Mr. Fan, claimed to have read many books. He said, "Objectively speaking, there is a certain gap between Chinese literary works and foreign classics. On the one hand, Chinese works are not translated and are hard to find overseas. On the other hand, domestic works often have limitations in their themes, era, and self-expression. They are either superficial or fabricated, lacking the compelling power and vitality to touch people's hearts. Unlike the four classic Chinese novels and a few beautiful folk legends like 'The Butterfly Lovers' and 'Legend of the White Snake,' which have a broader influence, modern novels are barely noticed, lacking lasting appeal. China is a great country with a profound cultural heritage and has produced numerous literary talents. Still, contemporary literature seems to be lost in confusion. Literature should speak to people's souls, but current works are disappointing and hardly worth reading." I said, "Talking about literature with me is like preaching to the choir." He replied, "No, in ancient times, the brothel courtesans were well-versed in various arts, such as music, chess, calligraphy, and painting. Nowadays, most women in that line of work have poor education. Their image would greatly improve if they had a certain cultivation level."

I admitted he had a point and said, "I have an idea; I want to take some time to write a diary, recording my experiences as a masseuse." He enthusiastically said, "Great! I support you! What belongs to the nation belongs to the world, and what's personal is also part of the era! Don't worry about what others say; write truthfully! Remember works like 'The Amber Ball,' 'La Dame aux Camélias,' 'Crescent Moon,' and

'Fusang.' They depict this aspect of life and reflect a certain aspect of society, depicting the bitter lives of the lower-class people. It's meaningful! If you write well, you might even become famous!" I laughed and said, "I'm just writing for fun; I don't care about becoming famous. If nobody criticizes me, I'll be grateful!"

I made an appointment with Mr. Fan to chat once a week. Being friends with educated and cultured people can be inspiring. Recently, I stayed up all night at the internet cafe talking with him. He is my most profound online friend, and I feel like a semi-transparent person in his presence. In late March, I contacted my sisters in Nanxun, and on April 5, I went to Yancheng to visit Alin's parents. Alin was no longer with us, but we were like their daughters.

Chapter 52

Injured Body

Despite being younger than me and joining the massage industry later than I did, Wu Fang had skills in dealing with men that I couldn't match. She always found a way to get close to the customers, and within a few days, she could complete the journey from strangers to bed partners. She said, "Flies don't bite seamless eggs. Don't blame me; blame those men for having twisted minds." I advised her, "Protect yourself and don't go too far. Otherwise, you might get burned." Wu Fang replied, "Jing, don't worry. I'm taking advantage of them; I won't let them be disgraced. How can I survive otherwise? Money comes easily, but my pockets seem to have a hole. I can't save money and know where it all goes."

Wu Fang and I were on different shifts, and our schedules differed. She worked in Massage Department 2 and earned commission-based wages, which gave her more freedom. She often stayed out all night, and sometimes a car would pick her up right after work. So, recently, I have been going to and from work alone. She was an adult, and we weren't related, so I felt uncomfortable saying too much to her. Wu Fang jokingly said, "Jing, how about I set you up with someone? Men will surely line up for you once you're willing to provide services! You're a normal woman. Why act like a nun? You're wasting your potential!" I laughed and replied, "It's not wasting; it's called being prudent! You are excessively extravagant, and it's not good for your health."

In recent years, Suzhou's economy has boomed, becoming as fashionable as a young girl dressing up. The water in the Suzhou River had become much more apparent, and people would fish by the riverside during weekends. I thought they didn't care about catching a few fish; they were feeling in a leisurely state of mind. Suzhou had built several expressways, making transportation more convenient, and there were plans to build a subway. I still rode my bicycle, which was suitable for getting around. There were more and taller buildings in the industrial park, with clusters of villas and mixed-use buildings rising on the east bank of Jinji Lake, providing a breathtaking view of the lake. Nowadays, housing prices are high; buying a house would cost at least 400,000 RMB or more. With my current income, I could save around 30,000 RMB a year, but it would take over ten years to afford a house. It seemed only possible to settle down and make a home in Suzhou if I took a shortcut and married a local man. However, could we meet a man worth marrying in our work?

It took about ten minutes to ride home after work. The Giant bicycle that Tian Da Jun gave me was very light. Even though I didn't lack money for taxis now, I still preferred riding my bike as it helped me maintain my figure. In the middle of the night, the streets were filled with the shadows of trees under the streetlights as cars sped by. Pedestrians were rare. The city had fallen asleep, and I was riding alone at night, heading back to my rented place in the industrial park. After work, Wu Fang would disappear like a fried fish. She hardly stayed at our place, so it was understandable that she complained about paying for the apartment alone. I understood that my life wasn't exciting and sometimes felt lonely. However, I felt at ease, not having to flirt or deceive, and I slept soundly. With no man to embrace, I would hug my pillow as I fell asleep.

Every time I passed that alley entrance, my heart would skip a beat. Not long ago, I was held captive here by the people from Huayang Nianhua. They scared me half to death, and the shadow of that experience lingered with me. When I rode my bike here, I would feel anxious, afraid that someone might jump out and block my way in the darkness. It was true, "Once bitten by a snake, one is afraid of good ropes for ten years." The night was calm, and I felt slightly tense, fearing someone would come out and stop me. I pedaled harder, hoping to speed up and pass-through this dim stretch of the road. As long as I reached the well-lit intersection up ahead, I would feel safe again.

The more I feared something, the more it happened! Because I wanted to rush forward, I was riding fast and vaguely saw something dark and blurry on the road ahead. It might have been an oil stain or a pothole, but I couldn't brake in time. I felt the front wheel sink suddenly as if I were falling off a cliff. My body lost control, and with the inertia, I was thrown forward like a stone flung from a catapult, tumbling over the bike's handlebars with a loud thud, landing on the ground! I was momentarily dazed, my mind buzzing, and I lay motionless on the floor. After a while, I felt a burning pain in my palms, knees, and arms. But the worst was the intense pain in my lower abdomen, wave after wave! When I fell, my lower abdomen hit the bike's handlebars; damn it! What should I do now?

I tried to get up, but every slight movement made my palms and knees ache terribly. I was afraid I had broken bones, which would be unlucky! What was that dark thing that caused me to crash? I propped myself up halfway and carefully examined the ground. It turned out that the dark and blurry thing was a hole about the size of a saucepan lid! The lid had probably been stolen, leaving a gaping mouth that could devour people! Those people were despicable and heartless. They stole the lid and left a dangerous hole that threatened nighttime pedestrians. I had seen on TV that some children fell into similar holes and lost their lives! Fortunately, I was on a bicycle, and the front wheel got stuck at the edge of the hole, preventing me from falling in. I might have fallen into it with my bike if the gap had been bigger. Whether it was cables or sewage underneath, falling into it would be fatal or cause injuries. Wasn't that terrifying?

It was late at night, and no one could help me. The road was lined with green belts about half a person's height. The passing vehicles couldn't see me lying on the ground due to the dark lighting in this area. If I couldn't get up, I might lie there all night without anyone noticing. I didn't call for help; it would be in vain even if I did. Not to mention at this late hour, even during the day, when someone falls, there's no guarantee anyone would be willing to lend a hand. People nowadays seem somewhat numb, following the mentality of "not my business, just ignore it." They don't actively care about others; how can you expect them to help you when you're in trouble? I had no one to rely on; who could help me? At a critical moment, I thought of the police.

My cell phone was in my bag, which I remembered was in the bike's basket. The bicycle's front wheel was still stuck in the hole, with the rear wheel suspended and spinning rapidly. I didn't know if the bag wrapped around the handlebars was still there or if it had fallen onto the road or into the hole. It was just my luck that this intersection was always causing me trouble. I struggled to get up, supporting myself on the ground and then squatting. The pain in my palms and knees, which had been rubbed against the ground, was unbearable, but my face had luckily avoided making contact with the ground; otherwise, it might have been bruised. If that happened, everything would be ruined. Feeling the pain from below each time, I took a small step and gritted my teeth.

To my relief, I saw the bag next to the hole; it almost fell into it. Thankfully, I had wrapped the bag strap around the bike's handlebars, or else it would have been gone. Inside the bag were my cell phone, bank card, and ID. If I lost my ID, that would be a big problem, and I would become undocumented. My bank card and ID were usually left open in the bag, but today, the company needed a copy of my ID to issue the salary card, so I brought them together. Ha, Tang Chun used to pay us in cash, but now they switched to depositing the money into our accounts directly. Other companies had done this long ago, but some private businesses still paid in cash. If I lost my bank card and ID, I would become needy. I needed my ID to apply for a replacement bank card. I picked up the bag, took out my cell phone, and dialed 110. I couldn't go home now; I needed their help.

After about five minutes, a police tricycle arrived and stopped next to me. Two police officers got out, helped me onto the tricycle, and hung my bike at the back. One of the officers asked, "Should we take you home, or do you want to go to the hospital?" I was fine everywhere else, but my lower body hurt so much that I couldn't bear to touch it in front of them. I replied, "Thank you, but my injuries aren't severe. Please take me home." When we reached my rental place, one officer supported me up the stairs, and the other helped push my bike into the garage. From the time I got to know Ge Wei Ming, I began to lose my fear of the police, and the police in Suzhou were polite and good-looking, which made me feel safer.

I went into the bathroom and took off my clothes. A pool of dried blood was at my knees, and my palms were scraped and bruised, showing some bruising. My delicate body had taken such a harsh fall on the concrete ground; it was inevitable that I would get hurt. Not having suffered any fractures was already a stroke of good luck. But what angered me was when I removed my bra, I saw a hard lump about two to three inches below my navel, with a bruise the size of a copper coin. When I touched it, it hurt a lot! I had this hard lump on my body for no reason, and I feared it might affect my future fertility.

Faced with such an accident, I didn't know whether to go after the thief or complain to the management unit responsible for the well cover. Or should I accept my bad luck? As I massaged the painful area, I felt frustrated and restless. I had a few bottles of essential oil that I had stolen from the shop and used occasionally for self-massage. But what use was applying essential oil now? It wouldn't alleviate my pain and disappointment if I covered myself in gold dust. I knew my parents loved me but couldn't truly understand me. Perhaps they were blaming me for bringing shame to the family, and to put their minds at ease, I couldn't share the hardships I faced outside. Living independently was both painful and happy, and I had to bear it alone. If someone were by my side at this moment, even if they didn't take care of me, just offering a comforting word would make me feel warm and empowered.

I had no love, insurance, or housing that belonged to me. I treated this place as my home, but it wasn't mine. Ultimately, I was just a working girl, a massage therapist, and a wandering child in a foreign land. People only saw our professions, only the money we earned, but they couldn't see our exhaustion and sadness, couldn't see our humiliation and helplessness. I had no medical insurance, and every time I caught a cold, I had to pay for the medical expenses out of my pocket. I had no retirement insurance, and I had to rely on my savings from my youth to cover future costs. We could only silently endure the injuries we suffered and couldn't cry in front of others. We could only shed tears in silence. Who could understand that we also have sensitive hearts? Many of our peers still lived under their parents' protection; how could they know the struggles of our wandering lives?

I curled up in bed, unable to fall asleep. I knew I was insignificant. Despite having a small reputation in the massage industry, what did it matter? I was still just a massage therapist, attached to the lights and temptations of the city, serving well-fed and well-clothed clients, trying to earn a meager means of survival. Pain tormented me, and I decided to endure it for now and see a doctor tomorrow.

Chapter 53

Fragrance of the Soul

I am not a lotus flower and don't possess that level of aloofness; I am an ordinary person destined for a fate similar to grass. No matter what we do, we cannot ignore the dignity of our personality. Although a massage therapist's income might be higher than that of an average working girl, our social status is relatively low, and the risk is high. I haven't given up this job because it can support me, and I find it somewhat manageable. Moreover, I am not the inexperienced person I used to be; I now know how to protect and cherish myself rather than focus on self-indulgence.

Lying on the bed, the pain surged like waves. I need to examine my body tonight to check for fractures or muscle injuries. My hand covered the swollen area, feeling like a raised mound. Although I could walk earlier, lying down now made me feel sore whenever I moved. I forced myself up and took a painkiller. I dialed the emergency number 120, and after about fifteen minutes, I was picked up and taken to the hospital.

The doctor on duty in the emergency room was a man. There were female nurses, but they didn't handle medical cases. A male doctor asked, "What's bothering you? Stomach pain?" I shook my head and said, "I want a female doctor. Find me a female doctor!" The male doctor, experienced in various situations, guessed that my condition might involve privacy concerns. Without saying a word, he immediately called a female doctor living nearby. She entered the examination room, looked at my injuries, and gently pressed them, saying, "Were you hit? It's likely muscle damage, and there may be internal bruising. I'll give you some medication and ointment. Rest for the night and see how you feel. We'll take an X-ray tomorrow to see the extent of the injury." She applied disinfectant on the superficial wounds, saying they were not a problem.

The following day, I called Wu Fang and asked her to come to the hospital to keep me company and help me request a leave from work. Manager Xu asked, "Why do you keep asking for leave?" Wu Fang replied indignantly, "Jingjie is feeling unwell, and I'm here to accompany her! Who doesn't feel unwell sometimes? Can you guarantee a lifetime without any health issues?" Manager Xu was speechless. Wu Fang arrived at the hospital, heard what happened, and angrily said, "Find them! They should compensate for your medical expenses! What if it was an older adult who fell? They might have been killed!" I smiled wryly, "Who do we look for? The thief or the road? Wu Fang said, "We should contact the relevant authorities. Why didn't they put a cover with a lock on it?" I said, "Even with a lock, it won't help. If someone wants to steal from you, they'll still pry open a burglar-proof door, let alone a cover on the road." Wu Fang said, "The thieves these days are too brazen and despicable! Jingjie, don't you know any journalists? Get them to expose this and see if anyone takes responsibility?" I said, "Let's not bother them with this. I don't want everything to be a big deal and make a fuss."

I was still in pain, and the injured area was private, so I couldn't keep touching it. Wu Fang accompanied me to get an X-ray done, and after examining the results, the doctor said, "There's a slight fracture. It would be best to rest in bed for a month to recover. Do you want to be hospitalized?" I thought to myself: this injury is not life-threatening. Hospitalization would be expensive, and moving around would be inconvenient. There's no need to make a big deal out of it.

I was prescribed a lot of medicine and returned to my accommodation. Wu Fang had been well-behaved these past few days and didn't go out at night. She returned home after work to accompany me. She went grocery shopping in the morning, and I cooked for myself at noon and dinner. It wasn't a problem as I only had minor injuries. I told Wu Fang, "A woman should know the basic household chores, like doing laundry, cooking, and tidying up. If you're lazy or can't do anything, your home will become messy after marriage. Besides, a husband also needs you to take care of him. How can you manage if you can't even care for yourself?" Wu Fang laughed, "Why worry? We can hire a maid or part-time worker. As long as you have money, what problem can't be solved?" I didn't tell her that not all problems can be solved with money. There are laws, principles, and emotions. She is around my age, but her thinking is entirely different from mine. Is she too open-minded, or I'm too restrained?

I took a month-long sick leave, which impacted Hai Tang Chun's massage business. I have many loyal customers, and I'm considered a gem at Hai Tang Chun. When I didn't appear for several days, some customers began asking why they didn't see me around and felt something was missing. The staff knew I had an injury but didn't know where it was. Manager Xu and Big Brother Wang visited me with gifts and a consolation payment of 3,000 yuan. I knew they were trying to win me over, fearing that my sick leave might be fake and that I was considering jumping to another job. I reassured them by saying, "I won't leave Hai Tang Chun before completing three years here, even if someone offers me a higher salary, they won't be able to take me away!" Frequently job-hopping was not good; a stable job required perseverance, like the rooted water lily that could grow into something extraordinary.

The scar on my knee faded, and the swelling was gradually disappearing. I no longer felt pain when not touching it, but it still hurt when pressed. Wu Fang joked, "Isn't it ironic that you got hurt there, of all places? You wouldn't be a woman if it were a bit lower!" I glared at her, "Are you reveling in someone else's misfortune? Don't forget; I got hurt because of you too!" Wu Fang was taken aback, unwillingly saying, "How does my business relate to your injury? How am I responsible? Don't just make things up!" I laughed, "If you didn't go out with men but went home with me after work, and if you rode slower in front of me, then the one who fell would have been you, not me! So, I got hurt on your behalf, isn't that your responsibility?" Wu Fang laughed, "Why twist it around? Why is it suddenly my fault?"

Due to an unexpected injury, I remembered that I had to go to Yancheng for the Qingming Festival. We heard a knock on the door on the evening of April 4th, just after having dinner with Wu Fang. We were intrigued because we only had a few friends, and Wu Fang usually followed my advice not to bring guests home. Although I had known Mr. Fang before, we had cut off contact long ago. While Mr. Gao, the boss, knew where I lived, he wouldn't presume to come and see me. Besides, we had already paid the property management fee for the apartment. Who could it be? Wu Fang opened the door, and several people stood outside, making funny faces and laughing at us. With a loud "Wow," they rushed inside. They were Sister Xu and several sisters from Hai Tang Chun. Sister Wu and Xiao Hong didn't come because they didn't have a connection with Ah Lan, and their previous donation was out of sympathy. Seeing Sister Xu, I suddenly remembered that tomorrow was the Qingming Festival, and I couldn't believe I had forgotten about it. I didn't tell them about my injury. They had come as planned, ready to stay overnight at my place and head to Yancheng early in the morning.

I was embarrassed about the situation. On the one hand, my relationship with Ah Lan made it natural for me to go to Yancheng. On the other hand, my body hadn't fully recovered yet, and the doctor advised me to rest, making it unsuitable for a long trip. Sister Xu and the others had come, so how should I explain it to them? Besides Sister Xu, a few years older than me and whom I respected, Wu Fang, Ah Chun, A Ju, A Mei, and others, including the departed Ah Lan, were all like sisters to me. Afraid that I might not be suitable for the trip to Yancheng, Wu Fang explained the situation about my accidental injury. Hearing that I was hurt, they all became nervous and chuckled when they listened to the part about the injured area. Ah Chun said, "I haven't heard of anyone getting hurt there; you've set a Guinness record." Sister Xu said, "Fortunately, the situation isn't too serious; if it were a fracture, you might need surgery!" A Mei said, "Xiao Jing, you should have held them accountable. You can't let this go without consequences!" I laughed, "Whom should I go after? I can only consider myself unlucky."

At night, when it was time to sleep, Sister Xu said she would share the bed with me, and Ah Chun and Wu Fang could sleep together. The other two could sleep on the sofa, which could be opened up to become a bed. Sister Xu took care of me like taking care of a child. If I needed water, she poured it for me; if I needed to use the bathroom, she supported me. It made me feel embarrassed. I said, "Sister Xu, I'm not a patient. This minor injury is nothing to worry about. I can manage it myself." Sister Xu said, "You're still recovering; be careful. If you fall again, it will be difficult for your bones to heal properly, and you might suffer lingering effects for a lifetime." Hearing her words, I had nothing more to say.

Sister Xu instructed everyone to turn off the lights and rest well, as they would be heading to Yancheng the next day. Sister Xu decided they would go without me; I could go another time as there was plenty of time ahead. Although I felt a bit regretful, I had no other choice. Even with the lights off, no one seemed to be sleepy. Sister Xu and I slept on one side and kept chatting. I mentioned the incident of being abducted by the "Flowers in Their Youth" members and the fire they caused. Sister Xu said, "It's too dangerous. You are fortunate; every time, you manage to avoid danger! Xiao Jing, what are your plans?" I said, "I plan to continue for a few more years and open a training center like you." Sister Xu advised, "I suggest you don't open one. Firstly, it's not legitimate; without proper approval, you might be investigated by the authorities. If they find out it's an illegal training center, and you could be fined or shut down. Secondly, massage isn't a good profession. There are many competitors now, and making money is hard." I understood what Sister Xu meant. Although training massage therapists might be well-intentioned and help them survive, it could also lead them astray.

I said, "If I do proper massages, it could be a decent job." Sister Xu replied, "Your idea is right, but the reality is not simple. When men come for a massage, they are essentially seeking pleasure. If you conduct it too professionally, how much business will you get? People's hearts have changed; they are only after profits and pleasures." Sister Xu advised, "Xiao Jing, I suggest you leave this environment as soon as possible, find a good job, and marry a good man. That way, you will have a better future." I sighed and said, "I have thought about changing careers, but it's not easy. Massage is my strong point; what else can I do? As for marriage, it's still early; good men are rare. I have to look carefully. Men are afraid of choosing the wrong career, and women are afraid of marrying the wrong man. If I marry a bad guy, I might be more miserable than if I didn't get married! Moreover, even if I like someone, they may not like me back."

Sister Xu said we should stop talking and get some sleep as they had things to do the next day. She fell asleep in just a little while and began to snore evenly. I truly admired her; she was a woman who could let go of things. Although I had known Sister Wu before Sister Xu, in my heart, Sister Xu was my real sister! She guided me forward without losing my conscience and let me glimpse a glimmer of hope. Just like at this moment, the outside was pitch-black, the darkness before dawn. It wouldn't be long before the Morning Star would light up the night sky, and the morning sunlight would shine through the thin curtains and fill this room.

No matter where we live, time passes, taking away our youth but leaving behind life's experiences, allowing us to feel the preciousness and fragrance of life in our ordinary existence.

Chapter 54

Life Continues

Time doesn't slow down just because I got injured. Waiting makes time feel long, and daydreaming makes time feel expansive. Resting at home with nothing to do, I can only recall the past and daydream about the future to pass the time. Standing by the window, I see the beautiful park with tall buildings continuously rising, blocking my line of sight but not stopping my thoughts from soaring. During this period, I have been sorting through the past, reviewing my footsteps, and dissecting my soul with composure, hoping that those who are interested and destined can understand my story.

Sister Xu and Ah Fang went to Yancheng as scheduled on April 5th and didn't return until the evening of the 6th. I could see that they all looked desolate as if they had lost their souls. Ah Fang covered her face and wept, saying, "Ah Lan's family is so unfortunate! Her father went to sell vegetables on the fifth day of the Lunar New Year. While crossing the road on his tricycle, a car hit and killed him! Ah Lan's mother also fell ill..." When I heard the news, my mind went blank! A series of blows from fate followed one after another. In Ah Lan's impoverished family, only her mother was left. How could she survive this? Merciful God, why do you add insult to injury in her family's case?

Sister Xu went through a lot of trouble to find Ah Lan's family, and when she saw their plight, everyone felt deeply distressed! Ah Lan's mother was as thin as a stick, and the accidental deaths of her daughter and husband undoubtedly dealt a heavy blow to her frail and sickly state. When she saw Sister Xu rushing over from Suzhou, she couldn't help but burst into tears! She cried and said, "Ah Lan is so lucky to have such good sisters because of her accumulated virtues! But Ah Lan's life is so bitter; she left so early, and now you've come to see her, but she can't host you. I'm so sorry for all of you!" With Ah Lan's family in such a wretched state, even relatives no longer come to visit. Ah Lan's lonely and needy mother was left alone in the desolate old house, living in such a miserable state! Ah Lan's mother said she couldn't cry anymore; her tears had dried. The sisters went to pay their respects at Ah Lan's new grave and, before leaving, took out their money and hid it under her mother's pillow, leaving only enough for their travel expenses.

Although there were cracks in my coccyx, I could move around freely after about twenty days of recovery. Drinking pigeon soup and pork rib soup daily provided such good nutrition that, without exercise, I felt like I had gained some weight. The fat on my body was increasing, and wiping my skin with a tissue would leave behind oily smudges. However, I wasn't worried about getting fat. Massage is a physically demanding job, and once I resumed work normally, I would lose weight and maintain a slim figure. Have you ever seen a fat massage therapist who has been working at a legitimate massage parlor for several years?

If there were any, they were either newcomers or impostors. A genuine massage therapist is their best advertisement. Whether alluring, charming, exquisite, or handsome, they should be pleasing to the eye. If you're too overweight, the impression you give people won't be that of a legitimate massage therapist but more like a sumo wrestler.

Afterward, Mr. Zhang didn't contact me, and I didn't get him either. Occasionally, I would think of him, but the feeling was faint, like mist, and it would dissipate on its own after a while. Perhaps our fate had already ended, at least for now. Is he remarried? Does he think of me? I don't know, nor do I care to inquire. I must remember that I once met such a man, and that's enough. Whatever happens, he still lingers in my heart, and I genuinely wish him well! If we eventually became ordinary lovers, then these moments of beauty would also fade away.

Before I could return to work, Wu Fang relapsed into her old ways and began staying out all night again. I don't understand what she's thinking. What does she need? I can't figure it out. Despite making hundreds of yuan every day, why doesn't her bank account show any increase in savings? Where is her money going? Indeed, she wouldn't repeat the past and give her hard-earned cash to another man, right? They say that one learns from their mistakes, but I can't believe she would be so foolish. Perhaps she must think about something and take each day as it comes. She has the right to choose her way of life, and regardless of right or wrong, gain or loss, as long as she is willing, others have no right to criticize. Who can say clearly whether understanding or being clueless leads to true happiness?

As the saying goes, "Complain about the job but stick to it." After doing the same job for a long time, one may grow weary and even develop a reflexive aversion, feeling mentally disoriented upon arriving at work.

Wu Fang said she was experiencing this to some extent—feeling listless at work but spirited after work. I didn't feel that way. Although it's not exactly "love the job you do," I believe I should wholeheartedly do my best if I'm in a particular profession. My skills are nothing special compared to professional massage therapists, but perhaps being younger and engaging in opposite-sex massage draws attention. If I were working in the massage room of a traditional Chinese medicine hospital, my modest skills might only qualify me as an assistant. Nevertheless, I don't feel inferior. After all, over the past two or three years, I have earned some recognition and respect, which is enough to make me content.

The sisters from Nanxun invited me to hang out with them, but I declined. My massage career started there, and my innocence was shattered there. My first love also perished there, making it a place that brings back painful memories. Ah Fang called to inform me that the situation at Sea Paradise Sauna City was not great, as they couldn't openly engage in illicit massage services anymore. The relevant authorities were cracking down, but the sisters hadn't stopped taking private clients. In this line of work, they live off their youth. I could only respond with an indifferent "uh-huh." I can't persuade them; firstly, I have my impurity, and secondly, we despise false moral superiority. So, let everyone walk their path. There's a saying: "In this world, you reap what you sow." That's right, sow beans, harvest beans, and harvest melons. Good or bad, there are consequences, so let everything unfold naturally.

The episode with Mr. Fang left me feeling unhappy. He not only deceived my trust but also played with my feelings. I thought he was a good man, but he was adept at disguising himself. Because of him, I also lost some favorable feelings toward Mr. Gao. Since resigning from

Dongfang Bathhouse, I haven't visited anyone. On April 21st, the opening ceremony of the 9th International Tourism Festival was held by Jinji Lake in the park, and the entire venue was built on the lake, making it look like a fairyland. One afternoon, Wu Fang and I went there to take a look. Coincidentally, I saw Mr. Fang embracing a beautiful girl and walking intimately past me. He didn't even notice me, which showed his devotion to that girl. He had hugged me like that, swearing he liked me. The reality? He had ulterior motives, got me pregnant without asking for my opinion, and when I asked him for compensation, he seemed to have learned nothing from the experience. I wanted to kick him and expose his deceptive nature to prevent him from deceiving others. However, on second thought, it's not worth it. He's a scum, and my foot would get dirty from kicking him, my hand from slapping him, and even talking to him would make me feel dirty. Disregarding him is the best approach, and he will surely face the consequences sooner or later!

I still remember Mr. Gao's appearance and smile. Sometimes when I ride by the bathhouse entrance, I can't help but glance over. However, I don't want to enter his circle. I can understand his wife's actions, defending the "territorial integrity" of her family. If I were in her position, I would do the same. I am Mr. Gao's good assistant, and he trusts me completely. This atmosphere should have made me feel happy, and I wanted to attend training and become a true massage talent. However, the dream shattered, and reality prevented us from building a friendship. We couldn't be friends and could only be strangers. My relationship with the employees at Dongfang Bathhouse became more distant. Since I was no longer their colleague, I experienced a sense of detachment. It was such a contrast to the sisterhood I had in Nanxun.

The burned building across from Haitangchun was sold to a man from

Zhejiang by Boss Wu. I heard he plans to open a comprehensive entertainment complex there. Boss Wu lost quite a bit of money, but money is probably not that significant in their eyes. Whenever I think of the past at Haitangchun, I feel fortunate. Life is unpredictable, and the past's beautiful moments fade away in the blink of an eye. The employees at Haitangchun also experienced a scary event, nearly becoming unjustly dead spirits! Haitangchun's business is now profitable, with foot baths, massages, dining, and accommodations—making Manager Xu extremely busy. I'm still just an ordinary massage therapist and politely declined when asked to become a supervisor. I don't like being in a leadership position. Even as a class monitor, I refused the teacher's offer. Mr. Chen maintains a mysterious, elusive demeanor. Perhaps all big bosses are like that?

Unconsciously, I've been working for three years now, and it isn't easy to summarize the path I've walked. Whenever I recall past scenes, they seem as vivid as yesterday. People tend to be self-centered; perhaps I've described myself too favorably. I admit I am a good person with some flaws and a wrong person with some good traits. Regardless of condemnation or praise, I no longer care. I have my bottom line as a person. The past is in the past, and regrets are meaningless. What we should grasp is today and tomorrow. Please believe me; on each future day, I will live healthily and happily!

Dear friend, you can regard my words as an accurate diary or a fictional novel. No matter how you see it, I've shown you the reality of life. Life goes on; whether I'm a massage therapist tomorrow, I will still have dreams and love in my heart, a beautiful rainbow! If one day you meet me, remember that whether you are my client or my friend, I will be grateful to you for our chance encounter and the warmth of your handshake. I will join you in pursuing a better life!

Chapter 55

Silent Conclusion (Epilogue)

Memoirs of a Masseuse has ended, but my life continues just as before. When I left Chongqing, the mountain city, to work as a migrant worker, I, like all other working girls, carried beautiful dreams with me. The past is like smoke, and over three years in the massage industry, I went from being a clueless massage girl to a well-known masseuse. These thousand days and nights have been filled with sweat and tears. No matter how you perceive me, I remain without complaints or regrets.

Life is far more diverse and colorful than a novel. I have recorded a few ripples in life, not every footstep and emotion. My original intention was to record personal experiences and shed light on the inner workings of the life of a massage therapist. Therefore, I used a realistic approach but couldn't fully elevate the theme due to my limited ability. I hope everyone can understand and forgive me for this!

As massage therapists, we face discrimination and mistreatment from clients and endure insults. In order to survive, we bear humiliation, and to keep up appearances, we put on fake smiles. We do not expect the legitimacy of the massage industry; it's not a concern. All we desire is understanding and the respect we deserve. Profession and character are not distinguished by nobility or commonness; as the Buddha said, "All living beings are equal." However, in reality, equality has never existed. The only thing genuinely equal is that every person's life has only one chance.

Every massage therapist is like a book, with both black and white pages and colorful ones. The daily acts, bittersweet experiences, flirtations, exhaustion, and emptiness are not the content of our lives, but they are not the purpose. Sisters come from different places, have varying experiences, and the romances of massage therapists are diverse, but 99% involve moving from passion to indifference. We have grown accustomed to fake faces and have become numb.

Don't think our hearts have grown cold; deep down inside, we are still soft and gentle. We wash away the dirt we accumulate on the outside and remain beautiful. Regardless of how many stories I've experienced, how many men I've encountered, and how many storms I've weathered, love resides in my heart, not hate. I am like resilient bamboo, bending under the weight of reality and society, but I won't fall. We are ordinary women with emotions and desires, joys and sorrows. Just like everyone else, we are our parents' darlings. We leave our hometowns to make a living; we are insignificant grass seeking survival, not daring to have more extravagant expectations.

The first time I lost my innocence unknowingly, the first love withered heartlessly, and the silent departure of Ah Lan left me feeling lost and hurt. Jiangnan is beautiful, but my memories of it are not. Looking back on the past and writing these words is like peeling my heart layer by layer, exposing it to everyone. An indescribable sadness wells up in my heart. I've gained nothing more than money and lost so much! Although I haven't left that environment yet, I now have control over my life as a massage therapist. The simple work allows me to be self-reliant without selling my body or soul. I can sleep soundly and live openly, meeting the gaze of everyone without avoiding their scornful looks.

This work has been infused with much of my effort and emotions, but I don't need pity or sympathy nor wish to expose or condemn anything. It's merely a diary. Culture is something to be revered. There was a time when intellectuals commanded respect, but now, culture has fallen into a cheap façade that anyone can put on. They might not necessarily be cleaner than us massage therapists. For the sake of survival, we can understand and be tolerant. Still, I can't comprehend those female university students who don't study seriously and engage in massage work casually, wasting their education and squandering their youth. It's deplorable.

Perhaps many of you have read Maupassant's "Ball of Fat," Lao She's "Crescent Moon," or Yan Ge Ling's "Maple." They depict the tragic fate of prostitutes, revealing how they struggle through life carrying heavy burdens, showing the struggles of their frail yet strong souls. The work of a massage therapist also hovers on the edge of eroticism, somewhat similar to their life circumstances. In writing "Memoirs of a Masseuse," I intended to reveal the darkness and glimmers within human nature, portraying their real lives and inner worlds. You have your moral compass and will understand they are merely engaged in the massage profession, deserving dignity and respect.

Good and evil have nothing to do with the profession; we also have love and kindness. When we wanted to help Ah Lan, everyone did so spontaneously. Even in donating to disaster-stricken areas, we did not hesitate. We are not irredeemably fallen. We strive to save ourselves both in life and spirit. Some sisters have elderly and sick parents to support and siblings attending school. They carry the burden of the entire family, relying solely on their income from working outside. On the outside, they appear weak, but they are the pillars of their families. Their delicate bodies bear the weight that ordinary people cannot handle. They also experience pain, but they bite their lips and endure it. They also have tears, but they swallow them back.

Due to my limited ability and time constraints, I haven't been able to include many details, such as the intricacies of massages and foot baths, the heart-wrenching stories of my sisters, and their diverse experiences. I even forgot to mention that one sister almost got sold off by human traffickers. I focused very little on the intrigues between sisters or the dual faces of clients. There might be distinctions between good and evil in professions, but there is no differentiation between good and evil. Each person faces helplessness. As long as they don't lose their good nature, there is hope for a withered tree to blossom.

Experience is a wealth of life. Every step we take leaves footprints. Photos can only capture our images, while a diary can sketch our inner world. I will start anew for myself, my family, and all the friends who care about me. I don't despise the work of a massage therapist, nor can I say I love it, but I will treat it seriously. It is a way for me to be self-sufficient. Some sisters may fall into a dilemma, but it's not the profession's fault; it's a matter of the individual. Temptations are plentiful, and how many can genuinely remain pure and upright?

Many readers and friends have left comments and messages, and I sincerely appreciate them! Our hands are not cold; our hearts are still warm. We have love and feelings, looking forward to your closeness, joys, and sorrows, and looking forward to your readership. Many people have shown me understanding and concern, expressing their goodwill. One person even left a message saying he would wait for me, wanting to marry me as his bride. On countless nights, I gaze at the stars, looking into the distance, yearning for a broad heart to accept everything about me!

During the serialization of "Memoirs of a Masseuse" online, many people have helped and cared for me, and I express my sincere gratitude! There are also many more friends who silently follow me. I can sense their understanding and care, feel their warm gazes. We are equal, and we can be friends. Please believe me; I will cherish genuine friendships and have a beautiful life!

Let me extend my thanks and admiration to everyone once again! I appreciate your care! Thank you, and bless every single of you!

-- END --

www.ingramcontent.com/pod-product-compliance
Lightning Source LLC
Chambersburg PA
CBHW030250010526
44107CB00053B/1650